CHARACTEROLOGY

The Author and Master Characterologist Ann Koernig

CHARACTEROLOGY

The Art & Science
of Character Analysis

A Guide for Understanding Human Nature

Carl E. Wagner, Jr.

Illustrations by the author

Samuel Weiser, Inc.
York Beach, Maine

First published in 1986 by
Samuel Weiser, Inc.
Box 612
York Beach, Maine 03910

ISBN 0-87728-626-4

Library of Congress Cataloging-in-Publication Data

Wagner, Carl E.
    Characterology : the art and science of character
analysis.

    Bibliography: p.
    1. Physiognomy. 2. Phrenology. I. Title.
BF851.W25 1986   138   86-1553
ISBN 0-87728-626-4

Typeset in 10 point Andover
Printed in the United States of America

CONTENTS

This Book Is Dedicated

First, to Ann Koernig. Without her inspiration, hard work, and service, this science would be a faded dream of the past.

To Daphne Hogstrom, who persuaded me to take action and write it, for all of her advice and encouragement.

To my wife and children, who always put up with my various projects, for their understanding, love, and assistance.

To Barry Rosenberg and many other friends, students, and clients who have put their faith in me.

To Dolly for her meticulous typing and spelling corrections.

To all of the innovators of this science, and to the One Father whose divine plan and design is recorded, in part, in the features of man.

INTRODUCTION

Characterology, or character analysis, can be summed up rather simply as a study of human nature as it is reflected in the human form. From the observation of a person's face, body, hands, mannerisms, walk, or any other aspect that can be seen, we can determine that person's character, health, and vocational abilities.

Characterology is a somewhat inclusive term that covers many different techniques of character analysis based on observation. Phrenology, physiognomy, hand analysis, iridology, and other systems fall into the realm of characterology. These different expressions of characterology have had a fluctuating acceptance throughout their long history. Although these techniques have never been disproved, "respectable" science currently prefers to classify characterology improperly as "occult." In truth, characterology is a marriage between science and art. It is based on the observation of shapes, patterns, or forms that have repeatedly been shown to correspond to certain characteristics, quirks, health patterns, or types of behavior. The art comes in when we learn to blend and interpret the various combinations of features we see to arrive at our analysis of the subject.

Characterologists feel that human nature expresses itself in two ways: the inner self or inner states, and their outer form. Humans are physical, mental, and spiritual beings. These aspects are intimately entwined and integrated with each other. One's physical being, therefore, reflects his or her mental and spiritual state in a most observable manner.

Simple observation will convince you that the mannerisms and appearance of the miser differs from that of the humanitarian, the neurotic from the well-adjusted, the brave man from the coward, and so on.

Perhaps the most obvious reflection of the inner states on the outer form is that of the changes of expression prompted by different kinds of emotional stimulation. One cannot feel anger without a high adrenalin flow, flushed face, knitted brow, clenched teeth and fists. One does not experience deep sorrow without slumped shoulders, depressed psyche, and frequently tears. Any good actor will tell you that by assuming the characteristics of an emotion he or she can bring on the corresponding emotional state, in a kind of reverse process.

Characterologists believe that the intimate connection of spirit, mind, and body not only affects the expressions but also etches its story and patterns in a person's appearance. Just as scientists can classify things into their genera, then further classify them into species and subspecies, each with their own particular appearances and attributes, so also can characterologists divide the human species into types and further classify them, until a very accurate and specific description of the subject is the end result. The profile obtained from our observations will reveal the character strengths and weaknesses, the vocational endowments, the moral fiber, and the health patterns of our subjects.

We are frequently asked how heredity and nationality influence the features. We find that when family and nationality features are carried forward so too are the characteristics and traits they represent. The reasons some are born with a weaker constitution, less talent or genius, malformations, longevity, or whatever must be left to the realms of conjecture, philosophy, or metaphysics. Although my personal belief in karma and reincarnation supplies me with satisfactory answers to these questions, discussion on the issues must be left for another time. Characterology tells you what you are like, purely and simply. Let the philosophers and psychologists attempt to tell you why.

Many people with intelligent and scientific minds have devoted their lives to the study of human nature as it is reflected in its outer form. Those who claim to refute the validity of characterology have never tried to apply it. For me, that has always been the simplest test of the validity of anything. If it works and brings about the desired results time and time again, you have proof enough of its validity.

Plato and Aristotle were perhaps the first great thinkers to give credence to physiognomy and hand analysis in their writings; however, Lavatar (b. 1741) was the first important developer of the science of physiognomy. He was an artist, poet, teacher, and evangelical pastor. His system of physiognomy, or reading character from the features of the face, was evolved as he drew countless portraits of his friends and parishioners and noted their similarities of behavior.

One of our most recent physiognomists was Dr. Holmes Whittier Merton. Educated by his parents, who were both medical people, the precocious young Merton performed an anatomical dissection of a human corpse at the age of twelve and later became a specialist in brain anatomy. Even as a young man he developed an interest in studying men's character as it is revealed in their faces. He spent many years of his life visiting every imaginable place of business—factories, offices, workshops, retail stores—in order to determine the relationship between what men did well (or poorly) and the corresponding developments in their faces. Basing his findings on the principles of Dr. Sivartha* and other mentalists, he eventually formulated his own sophisticated system.

In 1918 the Merton Institute for Vocational Guidance was founded in New York City. Its advisory committee included some of the most prominent business and professional men of the day. The Institute, on Forty-fourth Street, was a great success, and Merton's techniques were widely accepted for their accuracy and dependability. He trained the personnel managers of such prestigious companies as the Budd Company of Philadelphia and AT&T. Dr. Merton was also an excellent portrait artist and illustrated his books and lectures with profuse examples of faces and their corresponding character. His system details ninety-nine divisions of the face and will be discussed later in this book.

In 1796 Dr. Franz Gall of Austria first discovered the mental faculties of the head, from which most forms of modern character-reading methods have started. Franz Joseph Gall was a physician and considered the greatest neuroanatomist of his day. He related the prominences on the head to various aspects of charater. This art/science is known as phrenology. He eventually isolated forty-two aspects based on the shape of the head. For example: Amativeness, or sexual love; Firmness, or stability of character; Benevolence, or the humanitarian instincts, and so forth. Because of religious disfavor with his findings, he and his student Spurzheim moved their practice to Paris where it found wide acceptance.

George Combe, a student of Gall and Spurzheim, brought phrenology to the United States. He made a long tour of the United States around 1838 and spent a good deal of the time inspecting hospitals, prisons, insane asylums, schools, and other institutions.

---

*I am told by Canadian phrenologist Jeffrey Wolfe that Alesha Sivartha was a pseudonym for Holme's father, Arthur Merton.

Among other notables, he examined the heads of President Martin Van Buren and Daniel Webster.

Phrenologists in general have been rather progressive thinkers. America's second woman doctor, Lydia Fowler, was one such avid phrenologist. She, her husband, and her brother-in-law were involved in women's rights, sex education, health reforms, modern architecture, indoor toilets, vegetarianism, and other like causes. They are also noted for publishing Walt Whitman's *Leaves of Grass* when other publishers were afraid to touch it. They formed a partnership with Samuel Wells in 1844 and established a profitable phrenological business in Manhattan known as Fowlers and Wells. From there they trained, lectured, and published as well as doing phrenological analysis.

The science thrived for many years and enjoyed the respect of numerous colleges and institutes of higher learning. With the advent of psychology—another human nature study—and its popularization, the places that should have gone to phrenologists went to psychologists. The basic difference between a psychologist and a characterologist is this: a psychologist attempts to tell you why you are what you are; a characterologist tells you what you are like.

Dr. Lloyd Spencer was perhaps the last great phrenologist. He helped to train my teacher, Ann Koernig, and corresponded with her on various aspects of character analysis. He also accurately predicted the year of his death.

Hand analysis is yet another aspect of characterology. It is perhaps the most accurate and in-depth method of all. The association of palmistry with any kind of reading from the hand makes its acceptance by the scientific community difficult. The development of this science can be credited to one man, Dr. William G. Benham.

As a young man Dr. Benham's interest in the validity of reading from the hand was stirred when a wandering gypsy read his hand. He spent the next sixty years developing his highly accurate system of hand analysis. Becoming a medical doctor to verify his findings of health weaknesses registered in the hand, he visited prisons, insane asylums, hospitals and morgues. He also studied groups of actors, lawyers, doctors, scientists, and the like to find out what they had in comon with their hand patterns. His resultant book, *Scientific Hand Reading*, is the bible on this work, and each detail was verified thousands of times before he included it in the text. His two prize students were Ann Koernig and her good friend Flori Mechter.

I cannot finish this brief summary of characterology without writing about Ann Koernig, who is the inspiration and basic source of material for this book.

Ann Koernig has devoted over sixty years of her life to the study of human nature as it is expressed in the physical form. In addition to being trained in metaphysics, she is also a Worthy Matron of the Eastern Star and has trained under some of the greatest character analysts of this age.

In 1919 Mr. Gordon Hargrave was teaching character analysis for salespeople. Ann took care of the administration part of the business while Mr. Hargrave did the teaching and publishing. The business started in Minneapolis and later moved to Chicago and then to New York. Mr. Hargrave had a noon class for executives and an evening class for the public in which he adapted his knowledge of character reading for the purpose of training salesmen to recognize the buying motives of their clients. Ann and Mr. Hargrave later sent out a monthly report containing concrete information about understanding human beings, entitled "Science of Selling" (SOS). They received thousands of letters of endorsement by people who were helped by it.

While working for Mr. Hargrave in the winter of 1922, Ann began to study with Dr. Elizabeth Young, who was teaching the work of Dr. Victor Rocine. Dr. Young was a nutritionist and well understood Dr. Rocine's work, which deals with nutrition as related to the twenty chemical types found in the human family. Dr. Rocine himself taught, counseled, and lectured until he was past ninety.

Ann started to study with Dr. Benham, founder of scientific hand analysis, about 1933. Since these were the Depression years, Dr. Benham taught her in exchange for her services as an assistant. She spent many years with Dr. Benham, helping with his classes and lectures. It was with Dr. Benham that she met and became close friends with Flori Mechter. These two women have carried on Dr. Benham's work in the highest standards possible.

Ann also studied and was proficient in the work of Dr. Merton, the physiognomist, and Dr. Spencer, the phrenologist. For many years she conducted the Parapsychology Forum in New York in which many enlightened and advanced minds in all realms spoke and lectured. In addition, and most important, she has devoted herself to the service of others through character analysis. She has helped many find career direction, solve personal problems, and isolate health weaknesses.

The work of the iridologists also should be included in this brief history of characterology. That of Dr. Bernard Jensen, naturopath, is especially notable because he modernized all previous work on iridology. Iridology is the science of locating health weaknesses in the body by the study of the patterns, colors, and texture in the iris of the eye. Jensen's work fully supports the health and well-being of the body and mind. In this day and age when so much junk food, devitalized food, and chemically preserved foods form a large part of our diet, Dr. Jensen's studies become of utmost importance.

The dedication, insight, tireless work, and inspiration of these and other characterologists through the ages have always been for the benefit of humanity. Like all great knowlege it will never die, regardless of its ups and downs of popularity and its detractors.

The uses, benefits, and value of being able to read people on sight seem obvious but should be enumerated here nonetheless.

Perhaps the single most important function of characterology is that it gives us an understanding of humanity and human nature. Most of us judge others and their actions through the tinted glasses of our own perspective. We know how we think and react, and we wonder about why another individual reacted in a manner that seems so wrong to us. How often have we thought, "If only he could spend one day in my shoes he would understand me so much better." Characterology gives us insight into the underlying motivations, methods, reasoning, health, quirks, impulses, priorities, desires, abilities, and actions of those around us. Therefore, it gives us a better understanding of our mates, children, relatives, friends, business associates, elected officials, neighbors—anyone and everyone we meet in this life cycle. It allows us to stand in another's shoes, so to speak.

Many of us experience self-doubt, career crises, confused relationships, and indecision about our direction in life. We are all seeking self-fulfillment, if only we knew who our "self" really is. In this context, the characterologist becomes a counselor. Counseling is really the traditional role of the character reader. A character reading can uncover unrealized potential, better self-understanding, and warn of potential health hazards.

A character analysis is strongly recommended for all children. Early recognition of inherent talents, vocational endowments, success potential, and mental or physical obstructions can prepare the youngster in many ways. Early training and education of innate abilities will give the child the proper background for success. When we are trained in areas of natural ability, we progress in life much more quickly, succeed more easily, and perform superior work; we are happier and more content with ourselves and our work. At present there are countless square pegs in round holes, performing inferior or mediocre work and feeling that there is something lacking in their lives but not exactly able to put their fingers on it. A characterologist can quickly identify these inconsistencies and direct us into areas suitable to our temperaments.

Even a basic understanding of Temperament would be of benefit to the parent and teacher. If educators wish to teach, they must first understand human nature. The Motive Temperament boy or girl is built for endurance and activity. They are not book students. They are like the winter apple, slow to ripen, but once they have learned something, they can put it to practical use for the rest of their lives. The teacher and parent may think such children are below average, but they are not. They learn, but slowly and steadily. If pushed the wrong way, they rebel and will never do well in school. When they are older, they may spend a lifetime studying some subject that interests them.

Mental Temperament children were born for books. They make excellent students but have a high absentee record.

Vital Temperament children are social. They learn how to get what they want without hard physical work. They are never profound but always fun.

In addition to the Temperaments, the individual mental faculties visible in the hands and face will determine in what area of study the child will excel and where he or she will do poorly. Music, math, literature, science, memory, art, and many other individual faculty developments will become obvious to the student of human nature.

The characterologist is a counselor and guide, but change and effort must come from oneself for growth to be possible. Our strong points must be utilized fully, and our weaknesses built up or overcome, whether they are poor diet, excess, lack of confidence, poor organizational ability, or lack of energy, motivation, or skill. Whatever the factors that make up the total you, a characterologist will uncover these factors in his or her analysis.

A basic knowledge of human nature is essential for parents, employers, and counselors of all types. Doctors, psychologists, social workers, and others who guide human lives should and must be grounded in the study of human analysis. So much more understanding, more accurate direction, and helpful guidance could be given if the counselor was knowledgeable in characterology.

Traditionally, characterology has served in other areas as well. It is a well-known fact that countless dollars are lost in industry due to the current unreliable methods of hiring employees. The money lost in hiring an employee, training him or her, establishing benefits, loss of time due to inferior ability, production of an inferior product, customer dissatisfaction, and finally terminating an employee is an amount that would stagger the imagination.

Recently, a study by the research firm of Yankelovich, Skelly and White determined that only one of four Americans find his or her work fulfilling. I believe this number to be even lower based on individual interviews with clients.

When characterology was at its peak in the 1920s and 1930s, many avant-garde companies used character analysis to hire employees and decreased their employee turnover to a very small percentage of what it had been. Such companies as Budd Company of Philadelphia, AT&T, Scott Paper Company, Packard Motor Car Company, Westinghouse Brake Company, Ford Motor Company, and others employed vocational counselors (characterologists) for employee management.

Résumé and prior training are certainly helpful in determining an employee's qualifications, but such methods do not take into account natural ability, leadership potential, health, ability to work with others, honesty, growth capacity, inherent quality, loyalty, and the like. Many of these factors are equally as important as, if not more important than, prior experience.

In business, in education, in seeking a mate, in increasing our understanding of ourselves, in all of our daily associations we can gain from our knowledge of human nature. This basic course in characterology has been consolidated from the work of the greatest characterologists of our time. With increased observation, study, and practice I know you will be rewarded and amazed by your work in human analysis. Properly applied, it can bring only health, happiness, and a better understanding of our fellow man and woman.

PART 1

THE BASICS

From the human face it can be seen what correspondence is. In a face that has not been taught to dissemble, all the affections of the mind present themselves to view in a natural form, as in their type. This is why the face is called the index of the mind; that is, it is man's spiritual world presented in his natural world.

—Emanuel Swedenborg

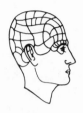

CHAPTER 1

THE PROFILE

We begin our adventure into character analysis with the profile. The profile is the most distinct view of the human face because we can see the outline of the features very clearly. The profile was employed almost exclusively in Egyptian art because of that fact, whereas the eye and torso were depicted in the frontal view.

As in all studies, we begin with the simplest and go to the more complex, but the basics of these first few chapters will prove useful throughout your study of human nature. Its very simplicity makes it of inestimable value to the characterologist. The principles are easy to grasp and easy to apply.

It must be stated from the beginning that no one should be judged entirely by one feature or one indication alone. You may find your reading does not fit the subject if you jump to conclusions based on a single feature or just a few. The art of blending and interpreting will be covered later, but for now, remember to use as much information about the face as you can before forming a judgment. A good characterologist may take several hours before coming to a final analysis of his or her subject, but it will be as accurate as possible, and the conclusions will be more helpful to the subject.

The basic divisions we will be considering with the profile are these:

1. The Upper Forehead: This is the seat of the intellectual faculties. Analysis, reason, reflection, and theory are shown here. This is the area of conception and theory.

2. The Brow Area: This is the location of the observational faculties, the area of perception.

3. The Eyes: These show our power of speech.

4. The Nose: This is our index of the intake of oxygen and the amount of energy we have.

5. The Mouth and Chin: This area shows what type of physical action we utilize and also the physical action of the heart.

In order to have a definite way of looking and measuring from the profile we must establish an imaginary line that we call the plane of the face. The plane is an imaginary line that is parallel to the profile and passes through the root of the nose and the septum. (The septum separates the nostrils.)

We all begin life with the Immature Profile, in Figure 1a. This does not mean that we all begin life on an equal basis, for there are

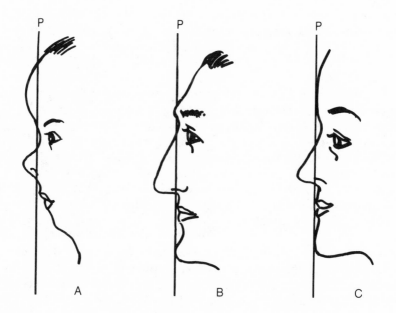

Figure 1. To give us a point of reference for measuring the profile, we use an imaginary line that marks the plane of the face. Indicated by the letter *P*, the plane of the face is a line parallel to the profile that passes through the root of the nose and the septum. Here we see a) the Immature Profile. This forehead shows thoughtfulness, philosophy, little observation or practicality. It is more abstract and metaphysical. There is a yielding chin. b) The Success Profile. This forehead shows factual, practical thinking, the ability to see and describe. This chin is assertive. c) The Plane Profile. This forehead shows memory of events, power to analyze and classify, ability to detect defects.

other factors we have yet to consider; however, at this stage we are as equal as we will ever be.

The Immature Profile shows negative mental and physical development, even failure characteristics. The Theory section of the profile (the upper forehead) protrudes past the plane of the face. In adults we call this the Theory forehead, or the concave profile. This means that the observational faculties are not yet developed. Visual understanding and coordination exist only as an unrealized potential in the infant. The nose is so insignificant it can barely be called a nose. It is in a very basic form and has no character yet. The chin recedes from the plane, which indicates impulsive action and a weak physical heart. This is the realm of the infant who knows only its basic needs and who still has a frail and delicate body. Keep this profile in mind, plus the meanings we have applied to it, because you will also find these indications in adults, and the connotations will be similar.

Let us contrast this with the Success Profile, shown in Figure 1b. When we call this the Success Profile, we do not mean that everyone with this profile will succeed in life and everyone with the protruding Theory forehead will be a failure. Both developments have their place in life, but both occupy different spheres. The forehead in the Success Profile falls back from the plane. This is frequently referred to as the convex profile. What this actually does is to bring the brow area forward. As we have mentioned, the brow is the seat of the observational faculties, and the Success Profile has those faculties strongly developed. The subject can make decisions quickly, based on *facts*. The observational faculties give the ability to judge weight, size, shape or form, color, order, distance, and motion. Any vocation or occupation that calls for quick and accurate decisions, sound judgment, and good observation will be best filled with subjects possessing this type of forehead. Many businesses require these qualities, and thus we consider this receding forehead one of the prerequisites of the Success Profile. The Theory forehead, which extends past the plane, is found on mental workers. Research, teaching, writing, science, philosophy, and similar areas are the forte of the Theory forehead.

In the Success Profile the nose is large, well developed, and well forward of the plane, showing that a good intake of oxygen is transmitted to the bloodstream, which in turn supplies the brain and allows for clear thinking as well as aiding in good health for the rest of the body. The large nose is always a favorite of the character analyst. We will be able to recognize some eighteen different character traits from the nose alone through the course of this book. We like large noses because they show initiative, industry, and energy. These are the producers in life. They will produce in their respective realm, whether physical, practical, mental, or spiritual. They always make hard workers, so you can see why the initiative, industry, and energy of the large nose is another aspect of the Success Profile. All of you readers with large noses should never again feel self-conscious about your noses. If there is intelligence and physical vitality to back it up, a large nose is always an asset. The small nose, on the other hand, gives us time wasters, putterers, or those who are just plain lazy. Some will rely on personality or good looks to get by.

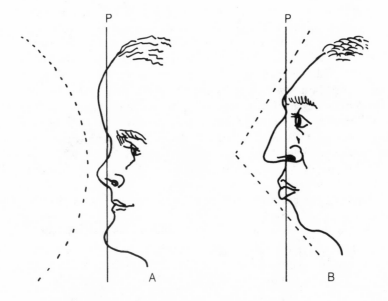

Figure 2. Here we see how facial features can combine relative to the plane of the face. A profile can tend toward two extremes. In a) we see the Concave Profile. The protruding forehead indicates an individual who is theoretical, meditative, a dreamer and fanciful; the deep set eyes indicate monosyllabic speech; the small nose represents deficient energy; the pronounced chin indicates someone who is slow to act and persistent. In b) we see the Convex Profile. The slanted forehead indicates an individual who is observant, practical, keen and alert; the buldging eyes indicate talkativeness; the high bridge nose, aggression and energy; and the receding chin indicates an individual who is impulsive and lacks mature deliberation and endurance.

The mouth in the Success Profile comes up to the plane, which shows controlled speech and good digestion. Why do these factors play a part in success? Tact, suavity and mannered or controlled speech are necessary when dealing with the public on any level. The ability to control one's speech is an asset; for example, an employer or foreman to an employee, a salesman to a client, a businessperson to a customer, and in almost all relationships, even those on a personal level. Good digestion is also important. The stomach and intestines feed or nourish the rest of the body. This is the first and primary source of good or poor health. A disordered stomach, indigestion, dyspepsia, or ulcers will cause a disordered mind. Moodiness, irritability, and lack of the capacity to think clearly can be the result.

The chin coming up to the plane points to controlled action. So the Success Profile can think quickly and decide quickly based on facts, has the energy and initiative to act on decisions, and will act in a controlled manner.

There is yet a third profile that we should consider briefly called the Plane Profile (see Figure 1c). In the Plane Profile the forehead, mouth, and chin touch the plane but do not extend over it. (Of course, the nose must extend over the plane to some degree in all profiles.) This profile gives us the people who make few mistakes. They are slow in making decisions, have controlled speech and determined action. When they come to a decision, they are usually right, which is fine except in situations where one must decide and act quickly. The Theory foreheads will often never come to a conclusion because they are forever weighing the pros and cons, considering the question from every angle and analyzing until the time for action is well past.

Before we conclude the chapter, let us examine the features separately. You must add these indications to the Fact, Theory, or Plane Profiles to draw your conclusions about the subject. Figure 2 shows how the features can combine relative to the plane of the face.

The Eyes: These are the focal point for the amount of words we use. Subjects with deep-set eyes are basically monosyllabic. Moderate or plane eyes use an adequate amount of words. Prominent eyes love to talk. When the eyes are very prominent (bug-eyes), the subject will be a regular chatterbox and can never seem to get to the point. Such people will strike up a conversation with almost anyone and then ramble on. With the proper education and a good mentality guiding them, prominent eyes can do well in voice occupations: i.e., sales promotion, writing, lecturing, singing, politics, and so forth. Television and radio abound with prominent-eyed individuals.

Large Nose: (Figure 1b, 2b) Initiative, industry, and energy are the key words that describe the large nose. They are the producers in any organization and have the ability to go quickly from one thing to another without a loss of time. A large nose will indicate good lungs and a good intake of oxygen, which is essential for body activity and clear thinking. A worker or manager in your organization with a large nose will know the value of the phrase "Time is money." Their efficiency and productivity will be of great value to themselves and their employer.

Small Nose: (Figure 1a, 2a) The small nose with a sway-back or concave appearance will be found on time-wasters and putterers. They will waste your time as well as their own and produce in a day's time only a fraction as much as the large-nose individuals. They are procrastinators and often just plain lazy unless the activity is a pleasurable one for them. Even then, their activity level is limited. Small-nose people should be taught to breathe properly in order to gain energy. We find that small-nose people also lack good attentive ability, concentration, and defensive qualities.

Mouth: (Figure 2b) The mouth is the external opening of the digestive system and as such it gives us an idea of the digestive apparatus. When the mouth protrudes past the plane, we read erratic digestion. In addition, it points to impulsiveness in speech and tactlessness as well. One who is blunt, runs off at the mouth, and may be vulgar—that is the trademark of protruding lips.

Chin: (Figure 1a, 2b) When the chin slants back from the plane, it shows impatience, impulsive action, excitability, and an excitable heart. This means that the physical heart itself is not strong, as well as the emotional connotations. If the chin comes up to the plane or slightly beyond, we read one whose actions are more controlled or one who acts more slowly. If the chin goes well beyond the plane, or when the distance from the ear opening to the end of the chin is long (a prominent chin), then we read the quality of "leg endurance" and a strong physical heart. Promient chins will be found on most athletes, runners, skaters, dancers, swimmers, and those whose occupations require leg endurance. Nurses, mailmen, and waiters, for example, also should have this feature.

The profile allows us a quick but very informative view of our subjects. The information we get from the profile can be used to give us an overall grasp of the nature of our subject and is especially useful when there is not enough time for more detailed observation. All of the areas we have covered in this chapter will give us additional information when we study them in detail in subsequent chapters of the book. Remember to practice and apply what you have learned with those who are close to you, historic or public figures whose characters are known, and pictures in newspapers, magazines, or elsewhere. Reading can give you only the principles, but observation is what this sciences is all about, and observation will increase your skill and accuracy.

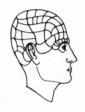

CHAPTER 2

THE FACE SECTIONS

The face sections provide us with some of the most fundamental facts of character reading expressed in such a way that they are easy to grasp yet perfectly accurate in their application. The face sections divide the face into the three basic aspects of human nature, *viz.*, the mental, practical, and physical realms. It is remarkable what a few bits of information will reveal when applied with a little intelligence and reasoning ability. My teacher, Ann Koernig, organized this information for her basic course "Sizing Up People on Sight" in such a way that the character student could easily identify and interpret the face sections.

One of the most beautiful and fascinating things about the divisions of the face considered in this chapter is that they can be applied to any face you will ever encounter regardless of race, nationality, sex, age, or position in life. The information applies universally, and the various combinations of the three areas will reveal much about our subjects. The simplicity, universality of application, and accuracy of interpretation are all tributes to Ann and the science of characterology.

The three divisions of the face sections shown in Figure 3 on page 12 are the following:

1. The Forehead Section: This we consider the mentality or planning section. You will remember that reasoning ability, memory, decisiveness, and other faculties used in planning and thinking are carried on here. This area is also called the Intellect. When large, it shows these qualities in abundance. When small, the qualities are lacking.

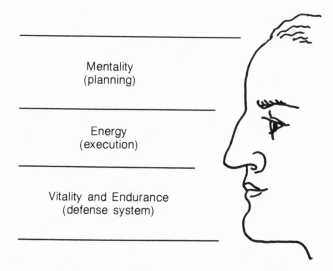

Mentality
(planning)

Energy
(execution)

Vitality and Endurance
(defense system)

Figure 3. The Face Sections. Mentality is measured from the hairline to the root of the nose; Energy is measured from the root of the nose to the septum; and Vitality and Endurance are measured from the septum to the bottom of the chin.

2. The Nose Section: This is the energy or execution section. Its development gives the ability to carry out and put into action that which is decided on by the Forehead and other influences.

3. The Mouth and Chin Section: This area shows the vitality and endurance possessed by our subject. Strength of constitution and life force are indicated here.

THE COMBINATIONS

We will consider all the possible combinations of the face sections, that is, intellect, execution, and basic strength. Everyone you meet will fall under one of these combinations and can be analyzed accordingly. The only possibility not depicted here is that rare individual who is totally balanced in all three sections. Of course, such people will partake of the best that all the sections have to offer provided their quality is good.

Quality is another aspect that should be briefly introduced here; we will consider it in more detail later. The human family runs in quality from very coarse to those of very fine temperament. Those of higher quality will accomplish much more than the medium and lower grades. In our consideration of the profile and face sections we assume the subject's accomplishments to be consistent with his or her quality. Sometimes the development of the face sections themselves will tell us something of the quality of the subject.

LARGE FOREHEAD, SMALL NOSE, SMALL MOUTH AND CHIN

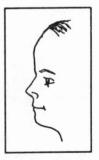

In this face the forehead is the largest portion of the face; indeed it is almost half the face. This produces a mental worker, those who are not paid for their labor as much as for their ideas. These are the idea people wherever we find them. They should have good educations to enable them to do the mental work for which they are fit. The lower portions of the face sections are lacking in this illustration. They will lack energy because of the small nose, and they will lack vitality and endurance because the mouth and chin areas are weak. Thus, such people must think of plans for people with larger noses to produce and for those with a heavy mouth and chin to endure until completed or accomplished. The small mouth and chin show that vitality and endurance are lacking in a marked degree. This section is frequently found small on subjects who burn themselves out early in life, at times barely reaching forty years of age. You need only follow the obituary columns in your local paper to verify this. Those individuals who are most long-lived will be found with large mouth and chin areas, whereas those who make their transition early will be found lacking in this section. Of course, there are many reasons for death. We are not talking about accident, suicide, violence, and the like but general vitality and susceptibility to disease, poor health, and lack of ability to hold onto life or endure privation. Subjects with the small mouth and chin will need long weekends of rest and relaxation and should even take daily rest periods to maintain their health. They have high absentee records and are never physical workers. They may hang onto their health, but must take the proper precautions and watch their diets and life-styles closely.

SMALL FOREHEAD, LARGE NOSE, SMALL MOUTH AND CHIN

One half of this face is made up of the nose section. This shows great energy and activity. As a matter of fact, twice as much physical activity as mental activity is indicated. Simply because a person is active does not mean that he or she is necessarily productive. Activity must be guided by intellect for the best results, and of course in these subjects the intellect is below par, so they may busy themselves with useless tasks or waste time on jobs that have little practical value. The small mouth and chin indicate a lack of the physical endurance to withstand their output of energy. Once again we have a subject who wears out easily and frequently approaches the brink of exhaustion. Their actions are not guided by intellect, and often the common sense to stop and rest is lacking too.

SMALL FOREHEAD, SMALL NOSE, LARGE MOUTH AND CHIN

The largest development in this head is in the mouth and chin section. This is the world of physical being, endurance, and vitality. The mental section is minus and so is the execution section. These subjects have no mental recreations. They never take an interest in a book and would never attend a lecture, visit a museum, or go to an opera or ballet. They can do hard physical work but are not very productive without a lot of supervision. They would much prefer to work off their excess physical energy through sports, recreation, or debauchery.

LARGE FOREHEAD, LARGE NOSE, SMALL MOUTH AND CHIN

In this face the world of ideas and mental work are present, as are productivity and the ability to put ideas into action. It is the vitality and endurance that is lacking here, so once again we are concerned with a type that may be burned out by 40 years of age if they are not careful. Rest periods are a must. These subjects should make themselves aware of the onset of fatigue and heed the warnings of their bodies. Since they are mental in makeup, their productivity is more likely to be in mental work, whether it be science, literature, accounting, education, or whatever.

LARGE FOREHEAD, SMALL NOSE, LARGE MOUTH AND CHIN

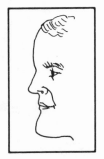

This is the development that we frequently find on the faces of executives. The mentality section and the mouth and chin section are more strongly developed than the middle section. These people have many others to do their bidding. They have the mental capacity and mental power to decide, reason, and understand; and they have the physical equipment to survive under pressure, to direct others, and to push projects to completion. Although the nose is the smallest portion of this face, it may still possess some strength and character. It is small compared with the other two sections but is seldom the concave nose that we studied in Chapter 1.

SMALL FOREHEAD, LARGE NOSE, LARGE MOUTH AND CHIN

Here we have productivity backed by powerful endurance. This creates a very hard worker who can go from dawn to dusk and then step out after the day is done. What these hard workers lack is mental guidance. They will be an asset as employees, productive but requiring supervision. Because of their strong vitality and energy, they will easily wear out lesser people and will continue long after others have tired.

If you want to develop your ability to analyze, you must begin to observe. There is no alternative; look, see, learn. When the Zen monk was asked by a devotee, "What are the [Buddhist] Scriptures?" the monk's reply was that they were "a hill of beans." What he meant was that reading without putting the words into action is worthless, only so many black smears on paper. Begin to observe all those around you, and as you apply the principles, you will increase your skill. Start with family, friends, and notable personalities in all walks of life and find the correlation between their occupations, character, and appearance. I may sound repetitious on this point and many others; I repeat them to stress their importance.

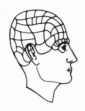

CHAPTER 3

THE TEMPERAMENTS

Modern science has a way of rediscovering ancient knowledge and making it acceptable by putting a label of scientific approval on it, as if it were not true until science has said so. The discovery of the temperaments is a good example of this. W. H. Sheldon, Ph.D., M.D., and S. S. Stevens, Ph.D., of Harvard found that people could be classified into types, each having its own identifiable psychological profile. They called these types, or temperaments, the ectomorph, the endomorph and the mesomorph, but the inherent temperaments were realized and utilized by character readers long ago. Aristotle called these types the "humours." They have also been called systems or temperaments by other writers on human nature. Jacque (an early writer on human nature) names the Temperaments "Sanguine, Bilious, Lymphatic and Nervous." Dr. Mary O. Stanton named her five systems "Vegetative, Thoracic, Muscular, Osseous and Brain, or Nervous." The classifications used by Dr. Gall and the phrenologists, as well as by Dr. Merton, the physiognomist, and Dr. Rocine, writing on the "Chemical Types," called the temperaments "Vital, Mental, Motive, and Muscular." All of the classifications, from Sheldon and Stevens back to Aristotle, have come to basically the same understanding of human nature and have simply used different terms to describe what they have found.

A temperament is a system of organs, functions, and faculties adapted to carry on the processes of life. Every man, woman, and child on earth possesses the four great body systems: bones, muscles, vital organs, and brain (which includes the nervous system). The reason that some people are large and others small is that larger people are built on the more bulky systems of the body—bones,

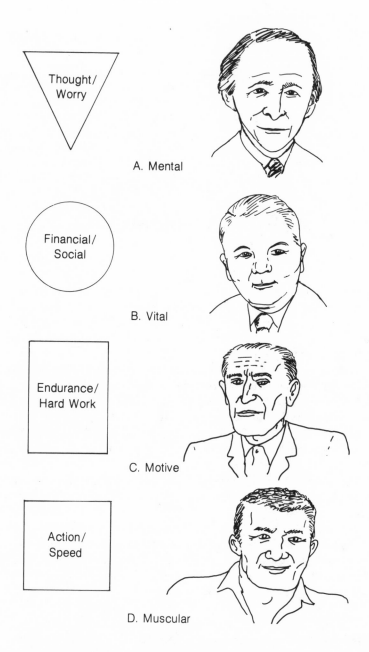

Figure 4. The Temperaments. a) The Mental Temperament, also knowns as the "brain" or "nervous" type; b) the Vital Temperament, also called the "nutritive" or "alimentive" type; c) the Motive Temperament, also called the "bony" temperament; and d) the Muscular Temperament, a subdivision of the Motive group. Manifestations of these four temperaments are shown in the geometric shapes on the left so the reader can become familiar with the basic head shapes.

muscles, and vital organs. Small people are constructed primarily around the brain and nervous system, which are the smallest parts of the body. It is absolutely ridiculous for people to attempt to make themselves the same size as another.

The Bible asks, "Which of you by taking thought, can add one cubit to your stature?" Each temperamental type may keep to a normal weight and size according to their height and type, no more and no less, and still remain healthy, normal, or beautiful. No amount of dieting can change one's temperamental preponderance.[1]

The temperaments discussed in this chapter portray people of a group. As a group, the people of a temperament will have the qualities mentioned under their classification, yet certain individuals of the group may vary; they may not have all of those characteristics mentioned, or they may have one aspect developed and others excluded. Individual characteristics are determined by phrenology and physiognomy and may vary the temperament to some degree, but the essential qualities of the temperament will remain. The temperaments themselves are produced by the predominating body function and by a certain group of phrenological organs being developed with others absent. This is what shapes the head and body accordingly and produces the temperament.

This chapter should be reviewed again prior to your study of phrenology or physiognomy because the information contained here is a necessary foundation to those sciences as well as part of our "basic" character analysis.

We follow the system of classifying the Temperaments as being four in number and known as the Mental, Vital, Motive, and Muscular (see Figure 4). These four are the most representative of humankind. They should be studied diligently and will reward you with judgments of character that will be quite perceptive. We do not mean to imply that there are only four types of people, for the Temperaments can combine in infinite percentages. Learn the basic four and, as you progress, the combinations will become more obvious.

---

[1]Recent research at Rockefeller University by Hirsch, Irving Faust and Rudolph Leibel seems to support these statements. Apparently the size of the fat cells in the body are closely self-regulated. In examining members of Overeaters Anonymous who are currently of what is considered normal weight but were formerly more than 200 pounds, the researchers found that although they looked normal, their body chemistries were deranged. Their fat cells resembled those of people with anorexia nervosa. The women did not menstruate, and their pulse rate was below normal. Their blood pressure was low, they were always cold, and they burned about 25 percent fewer calories than would be expected on the basis of their weights and heights. They looked biochemically like people who were starving.

MENTAL TEMPERAMENT

The Mental Temperament is also known as the Brain or Nervous type. In modern work it is known as the ectomorph (see Figure 4a).

Appearance: The shape of the head is roughly that of an inverted triangle, or pear-shaped, broadest at the top and thinning down or tapering toward the chin. The ears and the roof of the mouth frequently conform to the triangular pattern also. The head is relatively large in comparison to the body, which is slight, thin, or small. the skin is usually fine and delicate. The features tend to be sharp and the lips thin; the voice is high-keyed and flexible. The complexion is pale, and the overall structure is delicate. The hair is soft and silken.

Phrenological Organs: Causality, Comparison, Ideality, Spirituality, and Veneration are generally prominent, whereas the backhead is usually weak. Most of the neural functions—such as intellection, emotion, hearing, seeing, tasting, smelling, reasoning, memorizing, attention, analysis—are carried on by the Mental Temperament.

Keynotes: This is the thinker with a curious and investigative nature. Romance, beauty, ideals, history, literature, philosophy, and the scholarly and contemplative life all belong to the Mental Temperament. Mental Temperament people associate themselves with cultured people, books, art, music, metaphysics, literature, and intellectual progress. Scientific construction, scientific developments, idealism, and hero worship also apply. Because of their idealism and hero worship they can become extremists or faddists, and they frequently become diet faddists. Generally they are more introverted, shy, and inept in the social graces. They tend to be self-conscious, secretive, and sensitive.

Health: This temperament consists of the brain, nerves, ganglia, nerve plexuses, and skin. The nerves and nervous system are the most prominent factor in the makeup of the Mental Temperament. They tend toward peculiarities of character, changeable moods, and worry. They may use tranquilizers to calm their nerves but should never use as large a dose of any kind of medication as the other temperaments do. If possible, they should avoid drugs, coffee, alcohol, and tobacco because of their very negative effect. They are active in body but lack stamina and vitality. They are nervous and restless rather than physically active in the sense of motor energy.

VITAL TEMPERAMENT

This temperament is also called the Nutritive or Alimentive type, the endomorph of Sheldon and Stephens (show in Figure 4b).

Appearance: This temperament is distinguished by breadth and thickness of body, rounded head, ears, and roof of mouth. These individuals have a large or full base to the head and hands; full figures, curvacious with smooth skin; full lips and large ear lobes. The expression of the countenance is pleasing and often cheerful. They appear soft and voluptuous. Their hands are broad and plump but not made for hard work. The complexion is usually florid, rosy, or sanguine in the lighter races.

Phrenological Organs: Noted for large animal propensities, especially Amativeness, Alimentiveness, and Acquisitiveness. Benevolence, Hope, and Mirthfulness also are usually developed.

Keynotes: This is the financial, executive type, a natural manager of people and money. Buying, selling and financial administrative responsibilities are their forte. They think big when thinking in terms of money—or anything else, for that matter. They want to buy by the carload and rake in money by the truckload, especially if it is an easy buck. They like comfort and ease in life, delicious foods, and the society of others. This fits the Vital Temperament for work in food careers, as chef, salesmen, host or hostess, hotel work, and the like. They love social life, banquets, and plenty of lavish ritual. They are sometimes brilliant but not inclined to close study or hard work. They are ardent, impulsive, versatile, cheerful, amiable, and genial. This Temperament experiences few divorces.

Health: The Vital Temperament consists of the vital organs and vital fluids: the lymphatic system, the circulatory system, and the sexual system. Also included are the digestive system and the funtions of secretion, absorption, nutrition, respiration, and elimination.

They can easily become victims of overeating, and although they have the longest digestive tract of the temperaments, are the best nourished, and have better assimilation, still they may ruin their health by overindulgence. High blood pressure and heart ailments also can be the result of too many rich foods.

MOTIVE TEMPERAMENT

This is the locomotive, or mesomorphic, type, also called the Bony or Osseous Temperament (shown in Figure 4c).

Appearance: The Motive Temperament is easily identified by the rough, long, square contours of the head; relatively low forehead; square shoulders; long arms and legs; and a generally rugged, angular appearance. The features are strongly marked, with large cheekbones and Roman nose, long square teeth, large joints and bones, and often coarse skin and hair. The lips are set and the eyes are sharp and searching. A harsh or stern expression of countenance is typical. Deep lines and furrows frequently mark the face.

Phrenological Organs: Full or large Firmness, Combativeness, and Destructiveness are present, and there is also a strongly developed Perception region. The backhead is frequently small.

Keynotes: This is the *bony* Temperament. The framework of the body lends to action, protection, locomotion, executiveness, strength, endurance, and great power, making these individuals good in careers where physical strength, ation, hard labor, and power are required. We find Motive people among mechanical and construction engineers, superintendents, foremen, production men, farmers, pioneers, truck drivers, trainmen, sailors, or in any form of transportation—air, land, and sea—sports, and the military.

This Temperament is strong and firm in tissue and set in their characteristics. They are independent, love freedom, and are practical, durable, and powerful in physical strength or speech. They can be too direct or blunt at times. They need to expend a lot of energy outdoors: camping, hiking, hunting, exploring, or on adventure on land or sea, in air or in space. They are the doers in life, and action is their middle name. It is the Temperament of work—they make work out of play.

Health: This is the system of locomotion, consisting of the bones, skeleton, nails, teeth, and motor centers of the brain and spinal column. The Motive Temperament consists of the framework of the body. The type tends to excess, overdoing, drinking, and smoking. Problems in the lungs and liver, hardening of bones and joints, hardening of the arteries, and problems stemming from excess occur.

MUSCULAR TEMPERAMENT

This is a subdivision of the motive group and is represented by the short square (see Figure 4d). It is also sometimes referred to as the Ligamentous or Fibrinous Temperament.

Appearance: The face takes on a squarish, or oval-square, appearance. The teeth are small and somewhat square. The neck is thick and muscular, the body agile and muscular in appearance. The back, chest, arms, and legs appear well padded and firm, but not necessarily muscular in the sense of a body builder.

Phrenological Organs: Strong in the backhead and propensities. Combativeness, Vitativeness, Destructiveness, Mobility (in the chin area), Form (especially Motion Form) are typical.

Keynotes: This system provides for speed and strength combined and allows for quick movement, grace, and love of action. Of all the Temperaments, this is the most versatile. The Muscular Temperament is mentally alert, practical, and has balance in judgment. They can sum up things at a glance, and this ability, together with their other traits, including adaptability and grace, suits them for certain vocations. They are the personification of balance and grace as they walk, dance, skate, or perform and are found frequently as athletes, daredevils, dancers, and performers. They make the best salespeople in the world and are frequently self-employed. (The long-square or Motive is generally a moneymaker for others, whereas the short-square or Muscular makes money for himself.)

Health: This system is predominated by the muscles, tendons, ligaments, and hair. Health problems stem from excess. The blood, blood pressure, and respiratory system seem to be the weakest areas when health problems appear; however, this group is basically thick-skinned and they have strong constitutions.

Before closing the chapter on the Temperaments we should consider the old classification known as the Lymphatic Temperament for the simple reason that students tend to confuse it with the Vital because both have a heavy body structure. In character, health, and appearance the Lymphatic and the Vital are worlds apart. The flesh of the full-bodied Vital type is alive, healthy, and pleasingly voluptuous, whereas the heaviness of the Lymphatic is spongy, lacks tone, and is offensive. The Lymphatic is characterized by an abnormal preponderence of the absorbent system and a sluggish action of the circulatory system and organs of elimination. They exhibit rather bloated bodies, poor skin color, and poor hair quality, in addition to other signs of an unhealthy condition. The keynotes are an insurmountable mental and bodily languor, sloth, apathy, laziness, and procrastination. They are sad, timid, and feeble, slow in body movement, inefficient and dull in brain function. There is too much water in their systems. Frequently they are very imaginative, but unless there is a mixture of more vigorous elements in the constitution, the imagination is not productive of tangible results.

As you can see, each of these Temperaments is determined by the predominance of the class of organs from which it takes its name. In the first case it was the brain and nervous system that exerted control and power, next the vital organs located in the trunk of the body, then the osseous and muscular systems. Each of us tends to perpetuate our own Temperamental constitution. Our faculties cause us to select foods, climate, habits, work, thoughts and associations that reflect our own systems.

The intimate interconnection of mind and body is illustrated here as elsewhere in characterology. The nerves that extend to countless points in the body and have their focus in the brain rely on good health for their best manifestation. Ill health, weakness, and exhaustion have a strong effect on the mental and nervous condition. Hope, joy, and happiness quicken the circulation, brace the nerves and give tone to the muscles. Grief and despondency derange all functions of the body and mind, especially those of digestion and secretion. In the same way, all conditions of body and mind act and react with one another. Those who propose to read character must acquaint themselves with the various states of health and the mentality as well as developing their observational abilities.

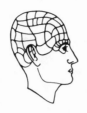

CHAPTER 4

THE FACE AT A GLANCE

Reading the features of the face is properly called physiognomy. The science was organized by Lavatar in the late 1700s and brought to perfection by Dr. Holmes Whittier Merton in the early and mid-1900s. We will investigate Dr. Merton's system a bit later. In this chapter we hope to familiarize you with face reading, especially the aspects that are most common, and will provide information that does not require the refined comparison, close scrutiny, and evaluation of Merton's system. These are the fundamentals. We only wish to remind you that one feature alone does not make a personality. You must begin to blend what you know—gauging the amount of intelligence guiding the other aspects of character, the amount of vitality sustaining the individual, the individual's inherent quality, and so forth. Of course we must teach the aspects individually and cannot give every possible combination found in Nature. That is where the art of character reading must be employed.

Some features will blend, go together, and point the character strongly in one direction. Other features will add balance, refinement, contrast, and so forth. Common sense, practice, and observation will guide you to the right conclusions.

Those who feel they can hide their character by putting on a few clothes or controlling their expressions or by speaking lies to mask their real feelings fool only themselves. The face "speaks" and cannot lie. It is the expression of our inner state. The mannerisms, body posture, head, face, hands, and walk are all very visible to the trained observer. They cannot be masked or disguised very easily.

We will commence our study of the face from the top of the head and work our way down, taking the signs as we go.

THE HAIR

The hair in general is a good indicator of the amount of vitality and energy we have. Abundant, full, thick, wavy, and dark hair is found on people with ardent and vigorous vitality; whereas thin, ashen, pale, lifeless hair shows a weak constitution, indolence, and a dreamy temperament. Dark hair in general shows a more sentimental nature. Dark brown, black, or red hair that is wavy or curling and very thick will suggest strong affections, ardor, energy, and force of character. Black hair that lies in a lank and lifeless manner suggests a melancholic disposition. Thick, bright golden hair that is wavy and lustrous, with deep color, is often found on active, poetic, and artistic personalities; whereas pale yellow hair without undulation or luster indicates no real force of character, a poorly nourished constitution, and lack of energy. Men with this hair color are sometimes effeminate in tastes and lack decisiveness. Both sexes tend to be fickle and inconstant.

Fine hair is an indication of an idealistic, sensitive, refined, aesthetic, and cultured individual, whereas coarse unruly hair points to a coarse, rude, and unrefined type.

The hairline itself is indicative of character traits. There are three basic hairlines that give distinct meanings—these are shown in Figure 5.

The *straight* hairline shows that the person is too direct in speech, does not know how to use tact, or does not care to. This is not an asset vocationally or socially and is a difficult trait to overcome. Remember from the Profile that tactful speech is read when the mouth is behind the plane of the face, and tactlessness is shown when the lips protrude beyond the plane. Protruding lips and a straight hairline would be enough evidence to read a lack of tact. The *receding* hairline that gives the appearance of a *V* in the center and exposes the phrenological faculty of Agreeableness on either side of the peak shows us suavity, tactfulness, and well-mannered speech. Courtesy, humor, hospitality, and agreeableness are all necessary to the executive, and it is rare to find a higher-caliber executive without

Figure 5. Three hairline types. a) straight; b) receding; and c) oval.

this hairline. Of course, this same executive could be so cordial and smooth that you may be out the door before you realize that you did not get what you came for. The *oval* hairline is indicative of musical ability. With the long chin line, dance is also a possibility.

FACIAL LINES

You will find many more lines on the face than will be described in this section. It would be impossible to enumerate all of the lines that can be seen, nor would it be necessary. Deep lines always come from strong characters. A thoughtless, idle mind never produces wrinkles, nor does a more happy-go-lucky personality.

Horizontal lines on the forehead are lines of Concentration or Reform. (See Figure 6 on page 28.) They can often be seen in the faces of reformers, ministers, and humanitarians, kind and progressive people.

The single vertical line over the nose is the line of Intensity or Penetration. It points to self-examination, precision, accuracy, strong character, dutifulness, truthfulness, deep investigation. People with such lines are frequently moralists and disciplinarians.

Two creases in the same location are called lines of Judgment. People with these lines demand honesty and justice of others.They watch the conduct of others closely but do not necessarily watch their own conduct so closely.

In generals, rulers, commanders, and people of authority, a deep horizontal line appears at the upper part of the nose almost on a level with the eyes. This shows an active will used in an authoritative way.

Lines that appear at the corners of the eyes are called lines of Mirth or Wit. They almost always appear in a laughing face, but in some individuals (as with all of the above lines) they will be present even when the face is quiescent.

Truth will produce folds and wrinkles above and below the eye. Hospitality will give upright wrinkles just in back of the corners of the mouth. Friendship will cause slightly converging wrinkles in the red part of the lips.

Not only will habit and continuous character traits etch lines, they will affect our entire appearance. For example, secrecy will make small wrinkles under the lower red lip in the white part of the underlip. Such people tend to have longer, more pointed ears. They draw the head down to the shoulders, which makes them appear to have a short neck. They button up all of their clothes. The entire face is foxy and sly-looking. They never say anything about themselves or

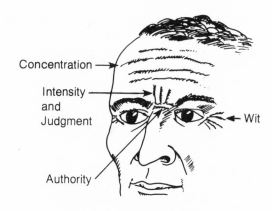

Figure 6. The lines of the face. Three basic areas for lines are the forehead, between the eyes, and at the corners of the eyes, although lines may also appear on the nose, cheeks, corners of the mouth, and elsewhere on the face.

their own affairs, but they pay close attention to what is being said that may be important to them. They are strategic, and make good use of this information.

Parsimony lines appear on the nose or all over the face in people who are misers by nature or habit. These lines are short, shallow, and numerous and make the skin appear shriveled and wrinkled. The stooped walk, clutching hands, forward-bent head, and miserly lines make them appear aged, sad, miserable, and quite eccentric. As Dr. Rocine states on the subject, our disposition is our face writer and historian. Our histories are written in our faces.

THE EYEBROWS

The eyebrows add much expression to the face and are a good source of information about the subject. They must be used in combination with other patterns; however, they should suggest the impressions that follow.

In scrutiny and discernment we draw down the eyebrow in order to eliminate and exclude all except the focus of our attention. In expressions of anger the eyebrow is also depressed because the object that caused the anger is being keenly inspected.

Eyebrows that run straight across are considered more matter-of-fact, practical, and scientific; whereas eyebrows that are slightly arched show sensitiveness, tenderness, sympathy, and expressiveness. They can show dramatic talent, storytelling and selling ability, and they are found in artistic, dramatic, religious, and social people.

Eyebrows that are so arched as to give the appearance of being raised in astonishment will show a weak and silly nature and the absence of any serious thought.

Eyebrows that are straight at their commencement but gently arched as they reach the temples show a pleasant combination of firmness of purpose and tenderness of heart.

Eyebrows that lie very close to the eyes, forming a direct, clear line on strongly defined browbones (the supraorbital bone), indicate strong will and extreme determination. This could be for good or evil depending on the rest of the face. People who show this characteristic can be passionate, jealous, harsh, and rude. By contrast, weakly marked eyebrows or those placed very high on the head will never show a deep or profound person.

Eyebrows starting close to the eyes that raise high and suddenly at their termination, to form a peak and leave much space between the eyebrow and outer corner of the eye, show an aptitude for figures, engineering, and scientific direction.

Eyebrows drooping downward at the termination denote tenderness and melancholy.

Thin, weak, or deficient eyebrows indicate a lack of mental and physical force and a weak constitution, whereas thick eyebrows are indicative of a strong vitality.

THE EYES AND EYELIDS

We have all heard the expression many times that the eyes are the mirror of the soul. It may be because the eyes are so closely connected with the brain and are so highly sensitive that they register so much. The eyes are particularly indicative of the health patterns. The only organ that can reveal as much or more about the health are the hands, and they require an entire study in themselves.

A well-balanced pair of eyes are those that are set in the head with the distance of an eye separating them. Eyes that are closer together than this tend to see things in detail and are small and petty in their outlook. They are quick to criticize and condemn. If the character runs to deceit, it will be in trivial matters.

When the eyes are separated with the space of an eye or wider, the subject has a larger concept of things, is more open-minded and more tolerant of others. Such people are considered more highly evolved, and the phrenological organ of Form is generally large. Eyes that are too far apart may denote stupidity.

We already know from our earlier instruction that prominent or pop eyes denote talkativeness, an easy flow of words, and the possibility of voice vocations, and that receding or deep-set eyes show a lack or want of words and a person slow in speech. In the same way large eyes can be described as more outgoing. They indicate a tendency to trust others more readily and make friends more easily than do small eyes. Large-eyed people are more talkative and expressive, more inclined to give help when requested. A person with small, inconspicuous eyes tends to be more isolated, suspicious, and matter-of-fact.

Large eyes indicate lively emotions and activity of mind and body. They are more quickly impressed, but deep-set eyes have deeper and more accurate impressions.

How much people open or close their eyes while talking to you is an indication of how much they are revealing of what is on their mind. Wide-open eyes tell everything; those with extremely wide-open eyes demand expression and cannot keep anything back. They cannot hold a secret.

Wide-open eyes are recognized by an arched upper eyelid. This high arch shows sympathy and the desire to tell everything they know.

Children start life with these arched eyelids. When the lid comes down and starts to cover the iris, that is when we start to hold our own council, to shield our thoughts. The more we develop secretiveness, the further down the lid comes. When someone closes his or her eyes while talking to you, so that only a narrow slit is open, that person is guarding every word, and you are getting very little actual information.

The slant of the eyes is also expressive of character. Deceit is indicated by eyes that slant downward to the nose like a cat's or a fox's. Always be on guard for deceitful actions. When the eyes slant upward to the root of the nose, then you have met a straightforward and honest individual. In a marriage the cat-eyed partner probably will be the double-dealer.

Straight-across eyelids are an indication of cruelty. The eye seems to look out of a crack, and the lid is straight and down in extreme cases. Because of their deep-set quality such eyes indicate people who are unexpressive and uncommunicative. Take note of the eyes of Bokassa, the tyrant who cannibalized his enemies, and the eyes of John Dillinger.

If you want to develop a powerful stare that cannot be broken, all you have to do is stare at the root of someone's nose—you will not be stared down.

The color of the eyes has some significance. Light- or dark-colored eyes are one aspect used to help determine whether a person should be considered a blond or brunette, an important classification to be discussed later. Light-colored eyes seem to have more eye problems and are weaker than dark eyes. Dark irises seem to indicate more exact inspection of objects and firmer character.

Green eyes are associated with deceit, and yellow eyes with cruelty. Gold or glints of gold in the eyes are said to be helpful in healing, as are green in certain cases.

Blue eyes denote a cheerful disposition and are more yielding than dark eyes. Pale blue, steel-colored eyes that have ever shifting eyelids and pupils suggest a deceitful and selfish nature.

Gray eyes with varying tints denote intellectuality, impressionability, and poetic and artistic impulses.

People of the Mars type are said to show a sudden red light or red tint when under the emotion of anger.

Black or brown eyes indicate a passionate and affectionate nature.

There are eyes that have no color or are very feebly colored. The black of the pupil stands out by contrast to the lack of color around it. These eyes are expressionless, with a dead, fixed look. They are the eyes of the lymphatic Lunarian type and indicate a listless, feeble disposition incapable of enterprise and a cold, indolent, selfish nature.

Eyes that show the white surrounding all four sides of the iris denote a restless, uncertain nature, incapable of repose or concentrated thought.

A similar condition, known as *Sampaku* (from the Japanese word "three-whites"), which shows the white of the eye on both sides and bottom of the iris when seen from eye level, denotes problems in the nervous system and physical or mental imbalance; it also has been associated with sudden and tragic deaths. John F. Kennedy and Martin Luther King, Jr. are reputed to have had this condition. The death connotation probably comes from the way the eyeballs seem to gaze up into the head in dead people showing the white beneath the iris. At any rate, it is never a positive health indication.

A variation of this condition called wolves' eyes shows the white on both sides and on top of the iris and is frequently found in people of a violent nature. Charles Manson, the cult murderer, has such eyes.

The iris of the eye is also an accurate indicator of the health of the body. Clear blue or light brown eyes with no spots, spokes, rims, or clouds indicate the best possible health and disposition. As far as color goes, the iridologist would consider any color other than blue or

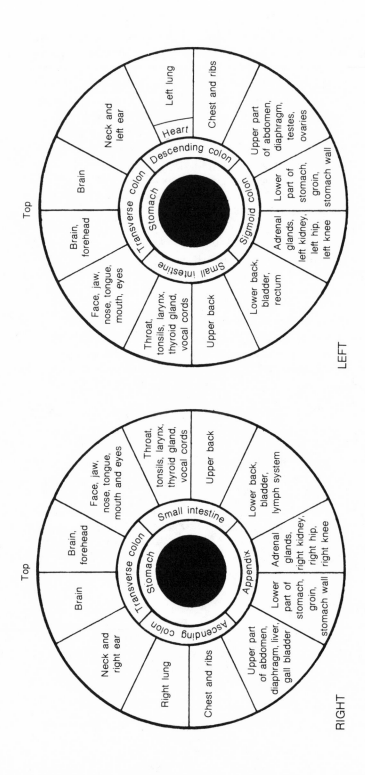

Figure 7. The iris is divided to correspond to various body areas. Students should note that the chart is set up as if you were looking at another person—the right eye is on the onlooker's left. For self-analysis, this must be reversed.

brown to indicate a health defect. The science of iridology requires a separate and involved study, so we do not wish to attempt to make it appear too simple in this book but only suggest how it is applied. The interested student should seek out Dr. Bernard Jensen's textbook on this subject, *The Science and Practice of Iridology.*

Utilizing the oversimplified chart in Figure 7, we see how the iris is divided into the various body areas. Any spots, discolorations, spikes, or clouds located in these areas will indicate toxic material, tissue degeneration, and other health hazards. Black or very dark spots are more serious; white shows the developing symptoms or the healing of problems that have already occurred.

In many cases you will find red, orange, or yellow star-like patterns surrounding the pupil. This is the stomach and intestinal area and reveals a highly acid or toxic condition existing in these organs. The fact that all other organs and functions of the body radiate from the stomach area points out the importance of diet to the health of our bodies. Diet is one of the single most important aspects of good health and longevity. All the medicine, drugs and surgery in the world cannot restore health to the body. Doctors can mask, cover, or remove what they perceive as the problem, but the healing comes from within. The body is its own best doctor if we feed it properly with natural, unrefined, and well-balanced foods.

THE EARS

Large ears, like large noses and large thumbs, are generally a good indication. In the case of the ears, it suggests one more highly evolved in terms of his or her spiritual and moral state. Although even this fine indication can be perverted, we frequently find large ears on the heads of judges, humanitarians, and spiritual leaders. Large-eared people are generally more independent and at times can even be stubborn. Those with small ears have a long way to go to catch up with their large-eared brethren. They tend to be slower thinking and more selfish; they lack the giving, sharing, and unselfish tendencies of large-eared people.

You will recall from our chapter on the Temperaments that the Mental subject has triangular-shape ears, the Vital has large lobes like the Buddha, and the Motive seldom, if ever, has lobes.

Sedentary individuals have ears that lie close to the head. Ears close to the head show great caution, prudence, accuracy, and punctuality. Ears that stick out away from the head show a physically active person such as those involved in sports, hiking, and bicycling; they also denote a disposition to rove.

Hair in the ears act as antennae, making us more alert to sounds. Cupped ears catch the tones of music or machinery and are found on good musicians, mechanics, and doctors who have to listen to the sounds of the body. Delicate ears suggest refinement, as do other delicate features.

It seems that what we call degenerate ears—those that are ill-formed, irregular, and discolored—are peculiar to crime, degeneracy, evil, and sin. A deformed ear is a sign of a deformed soul.

Dr. Rocine states the following in his work: "Pointed ears show cunning, like those of a cat or fox. A sly step, a foxy appearance, a tendency to use the 's' sound in conversation, a pigeon-toed stance and walk, speaking in an aspirate tone of voice, a tendency to look here, there and everywhere when speaking, a soft whispering utterance, closed lips, a mysterious smile, condescending manner, looking at people and saying nothing, buttons closed, closed hands... these are all indications of cunning."[2]

THE NOSE

You already know some basic facts about the nose from the profile and face sections, discussed in Chapters 1 and 2.

We all start life with that little bump that we honor by calling it a nose. Actually it is the external opening of the respiratory system, the breathing system. As long as the nose is babylike, it is susceptible to respiratory problems and must be protected. As the baby learns to breathe and character develops, the nose becomes larger and takes on a more specific shape. Throughout life, our character changes and so do our features. We are not the same in youth as in old age.

You will remember that the large nose shows Industry, Energy, and Initiative and the ability to go quickly from one thing to another, whereas the small nose shows lack of energy, laziness, and procrastination. A large nose always shows strength of some kind, though it does not necessarily denote a high order of intelligence. The small, saddleback, up-turned nose is also indicative of liveliness of disposition, sociability, quick impressions, feminity, conversational talent, sentiment, and emotionality. Remember, the entire face, temperament, quality, and other factors must also be considered.

There are noses that are broad in the trunk and those that are narrow in the trunk. (See Figures 8a and 8b.) These indicate two

---

[2]Victor G. Rocine, *A Correspondence Course in Character Reading at Sight, or A Key to Human Hearts and Human Dispositions*, Rocine's Publishing Efficiency Service, Portland, Oregon, 1934, p. 56.

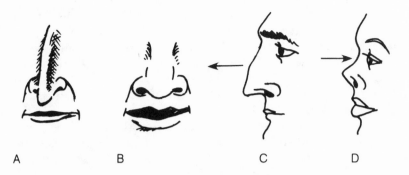

A   B   C   D

Figure 8. The nose. a) The Aristocratic nose indicates a person who keeps his distance and has poor mixing ability. b) The Common nose indicates an individual who has good ability to contact others, and who is easy to meet. c) The High Bridge indicates a person with force and aggression. d) The Low Bridge indicates a person who is emotional and lacks fight.

vastly different types of people. If we look at the dog family, we find that those dogs with long pointed snouts are the least friendly (Dobermans, for example), whereas those with blunt snouts are good-natured and make friends with almost anyone (hounds and hunting dogs). As with the dog family so it is with the human family. Noses that are sharp and generally long and thin in the trunk (see Figure 8a) are found on people with poor mixing ability. This we call the aristocratic nose, or the English nose. (Observe the nose of Prince Charles of England, a nose both aristocratic and English!) These individuals do not offer their hands readily for a hand shake; nor is their grasp warm once given. They prefer to be called by their proper name or title until you get to know them very well. They do not become overly familiar and tend to be high-hat and slow to make new friends.

Broad-nosed people are just the opposite; like broad-nosed dogs, they are more friendly. (See Figure 8b.) They are people you can get to know easily. They call you by your first name immediately. They tend to become too intimate too quickly. They will put a hand on your shoulder, act too familiar, request favors, and so forth. The broad nose (or more properly, the broad-trunk nose) reaches its extreme in certain Polynesian and Negroid peoples, although it is found in any nationality.

You should always remember to take racial characteristics into consideration when making your estimates. What is average for one race may be extreme for another. Extremes in any race are read using the principles you are learning. Certain character traits may be racially dominant also. In the case of the Negroid nose and the

German or Scandinavian nose we can easily see that Divine Intelligence was at work in creating these nose shapes. The cold northern air requires a long nasal passage and slower volumes of air, so that it may be warmed before entering the lungs. The humid tropical climates do not require nasal length to protect the lungs.

A high bridge to the nose is sometimes referred to as the Roman nose (shown in Figure 8c) and points to the solo player in life—those who work best alone, are poor in partnerships, and tend to want to do things their own way. A moderately high bridge is helpful in fighting the battle of life, but too much height may lead to argumentativeness and too critical a disposition.

The high-bridge or Roman nose is a moral battering ram. It pushes its way despite personal suffering and has been responsible for much of humanity's advancement. It carried Washington to triumph and was an aspect of Lincoln's unyielding strength. It has been found high on the founders of religions or sects where great aggression was required. It stands out boldly on the faces of Calvin and Martin Luther among others. As Alesha Sivartha said: "Nature never puts a great cause upon a saddle-backed nose and expects that it will ride into power."

The low bridge, shown in Figure 8d, lacks the defensive qualities with which to fight life's hard knocks. These subjects must use personality, charm, imagination, or other assets to deal with life. They cannot maintain a sustained battle for any length of time and would rather take the easy way out. Of course, the intake of oxygen is limited. Oxygen is directly related to heat production and the energy level in the body.

The short or upturned nose is calculated to receive rapid impressions and thus induce rapid emotions. The long, drooping nose indicates scrutiny, cautiousness, and even a meddlesome disposition, as it receives impressions more slowly but retains them much longer.

A drooping tip suggests pessimism, acquisitive tendencies, shrewdness, sagacity, commercialism, and clannishness.

The indications found in the nose are numerous and will be covered in detail in our study of Dr. Merton's work.

THE MOUTH BRACKET

The mouth bracket encompasses the area that is bordered on top by the bottom of the nose, on the sides by the parenthesis of the mouth, and on the bottom by the edge of the upper red lip. (See Figure 9a.)

A   B

Figure 9. The mouth bracket. a) A full and wide area (indicated by arrows) is called the Humanitarian mouth bracket. b) When this area is not full and wide, the humanitarian pattern is weak in influence.

When this area is full and wide it adds to the humanitarian pattern (like large ears and a high moral area in the anterior tophead) and we call it the Humanitarian mouth bracket. It suggests higher ideals, service to others, an idea of the larger self. Similar to the qualities found in the anterior region of the tophead, it pushes the subject toward self-sacrifice, benevolent feelings, service to mankind, and good hopes for the future and future generations. More self-concern and less faith in humanity are suggested when the bracket is small, as in Figure 9b. The short upper lip (see Figure 10a on page 38) shows a person who needs flattery, praise, and congratulations. Unlike those with a large bracket, people with short upper lips cannot stand criticism, ridicule, or condemnation. It literally tears them apart and turns them off. You can get almost anything out of them with praise. The old saying, "You can catch more flies with honey than with vinegar," certainly applies here. When the upper lip is so short that it appears that the upper red lip will touch the nose when these people smile, an extreme need for flattery is indicated. Many of the types attracted to the theater and entertainment world have short upper lips; they thrive on applause and public approval.

THE MOUTH AND RED LIPS

Facial beauty is largely dependent on the lips. The lips provide us with an understanding of the emotional faculties in a person and also provide us with an understanding of the will of that subject.

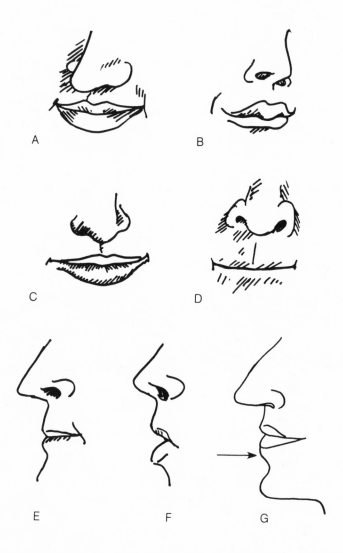

Figure 10. The lips. a) The short upper lip indicates someone who needs flattery. b) The feminine lip indicates receptivity, friendliness, and agreeableness. c) The masculine lip indicates a developed sex impulse. d) No red lip indicates control, dryness, friendlessness. e) Compressed lips indicate self-control, whereas lips that are slightly opened (f) indicate no self-mastery. g) A fullness below the lower lip shows an affinity for raising and breeding animals, as well as children. It is the parental instinct.

No artificial method can ultimately shape the lips nor improve them to any extent. Dermatologists, cosmeticians, and plastic surgeons cannot truly reconstruct the lips because they are under control of the emotions.

The individual who is ruled by such mental qualities as vanity, sensuality, appetite, bitterness, and cynicism cannot have beautiful lips. The formation of beauty in the lips—or in any part of the physiognomy for that matter—is the result of soul qualities. If one hopes to attain beauty, one should develop sympathy, honesty, hope, love, self-respect, parental love, and other noble sentiments.

A vain person will almost always lift his or her upper lip so that the teeth show. In a cynical person, the upper lip is pulled down at the corners in a permanent frown when the face is quiescent. Strong appetites make the lips large, protruding, and sensual in appearance. Other negative qualities will also affect the appearance of the lips.

The red lips are the emotional part of the face and are equivalent to the backhead (which will be discussed in Chapter 5). We prefer lips that rest lightly on one another and are not pulled tightly nor hang open and loose. The former condition points to excessive intensity whereas the latter indicates lack of will and energy. There is not even enough will to keep the mouth closed.

The upper red lip is considered the feminine lip. When it is full, we find a more receptive, friendly, and agreeable personality—individuals who mix well with others, make warm friendships, and try to make life better for those around them. The upper red lip is expanded to receive agreeable impressions and shows passive gratification; therefore, it is considered feminine. The feminine lip is shown in Figure 10b.

The bottom red lip is the masculine lip (see Figure 10c), the sexual aspect of the emotions. When this lip dominates, the subject will be aggressive sexually, have sexual magnetism, and be drawn to the opposite sex.

When both lips are developed, the character is both actively and passively voluptuous.

Lips that are too full, especially with eyes that move slowly under heavy lids, indicate extreme sensuousness and a character too voluptuous, too emotional, too sexy. Thick, full lips, a full backhead, and sensuous eyes with heavy lids can be a combination that will show gross sensuality and will need strong balancing factors in other areas of the face and head.

Thin lips tend to selfishness and are more in control of their emotions. Thin lips show sobriety. Very thin lips show people with little feeling of fellowship, emotions too controlled or nonexistent, and even selfishness, miserliness and definite dryness of character. In certain faces thin lips may simply show sobriety and lack of voluptuousness but still have fraternity and kindness present. A lipless mouth, showing a thin, straight line without curves, indicates industry and precision. It also denotes a mercenary, cold, and critical mentality. Figure 10d shows the lipless mouth.

Large mouths give flexibility, volume, and whatever is needed for use in voice vocations such as public speaking , singing, sales, and teaching. A career in those areas is advisable for people with large mouths. Television provides us with many examples of the large mouth and its applications to the voice vocations of singing, broadcasting, acting, and the like. You will also frequently note prominent eyes to go along with the large mouths.

When the corners of the mouth are sucked in, it shows love of approbation or praise.

In criminals the mouth is frequently twisted because the emotions are twisted. The lips themselves tend to be too full or too thin, or in some other way are out of balance.

When the mouth droops, it shows disappointment and cynicism or contempt. Oblique mouths suggest cynics and chronic complainers.

Bowed lips, or lips in the shape of cupid's bow, are a strong indication of the Venus or Love type for whom love, passion, and compassion are their natural expression.

In addition to the emotions, some aspects of the will are revealed by the mouth. Self-esteem, firmness, energy, secrecy, resolution, and honesty all have a tendency to close the lips. Subjects who have the power to compress their lips have the power of self-control to a large degree (see Figure 10e). Protruding lips, hanging lips, and a mouth that cannot be held closed indicate an individual who cannot control his or her emotions or appetites. No one can have a strong, noble, and controlled character if they are unable to control their own lips. A person with a feeble will will have lips that droop. When people let down their moral will, their lips also are let down. When the mouth is open, lips hanging, there is no restraint or self-mastery in that individual. Laziness is another aspect of lips that cannot be held closed. These lips are illustrated in Figure 10f.

Children who lack self-mastery will have open lips. They breathe through the mouth. This is not a good habit for them to form. Among other things, it exposes them to respiratory infections, colds, phlegm, and so on. There is only one remedy. Children must be taught self-mastery and control of will power. When children learn to shut their mouths, they will breathe through their noses. This will have its effect on nose development. The nose will grow larger and the nostrils will become more expanded. Proper growth and development of this important feature also will improve a child's character.

When there is a fullness below the red of the lower lip, as shown in Figure 10g, we have what we call the breeding instinct. This shows an affinity for raising and breeding animals as well as children. Even if these people have no children of their own, they will reach out to others' children. They are found as breeders of dogs, cats, horses, etc. They often adopt children or become guardians of children.

THE JAW AND CHIN

The jaw/chin area encompasses the entire area below the bottom of the nose, the entire lower third of the face. From our previous study we know that a strong jaw and chin show vitality and endurance. This area should be in proportion to the rest of the head. Strong jaw/chin people excel in sports and as explorers, fishermen, sailors, and the like. They are frequently long-lived individuals.

The Mental Temperament has the weakest chin area. Visualize the inverted triangle. The Motive Temperament has the strongest chin area and is stirred on by competition.

The chin line, or "leg" line, is an imaginary line that runs from the external opening of the ear to the end of the chin (see Figure 11). When this line is long, it adds the motivation and frequently the strength and endurance for leg activity. Dancers almost invariably have a long chin line and what we call masculine bodies. Also observe the chins of baseball players, track stars, mountain climbers, and the like. Football players and boxers tend to have full and wide jaws but not necessarily the long leg line.

Wads or lump-like developments below the cheek on the jaw area add the ability to deal with the rough side of life. We sometimes

Figure 11. The chin line. This is a line that runs from the external opening of the ear to the end of the chin. This figure represents a long chin line, which indicates mobility, strength, and endurance in the legs.

refer to this as the Mars equipment. These wads may be found on executives and foremen, labor leaders, and the like, or they may be found on criminals, especially murderers. They encompass the various aspects of the will that deal with aversion, destruction, and stability. The ability to tear down the old and replace with the new and the ability to destroy come from this same area. It is only the quality of the intellect behind these propensities that will direct them for good or ill.

The smooth face cannot cope with the rough edges of life so easily. The large jaw/chin that is also smooth will show physical endurance, mobility, or leg activity but will be found more in the realm of performers, skaters, skiers, and so forth, and not in crime, in politics, or in executive positions that require contact with the rougher elements of life.

In this chapter we have given you enough information to analyze almost any face you come in contact with. You are becoming acquainted with the various ways in which combinations of features affect the personality, yet we have only scratched the surface of this great science and art. By now the serious character student should be able to identify subjects as to their proper realm and sphere of life and should begin to detail how the character is expressed in that sphere.

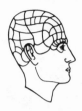

CHAPTER 5

THE HEAD DIVISIONS AND SECTIONS

Along with the Temperaments, this chapter is based on the fundamentals of phrenology. It is, in fact, phrenology in its most basic form. Here we will establish the divisons or groups rather than study the individual organs of the head.

The association of the organs or faculties is such that they form in groups that are either similar in the nature of their work or dependent on each other for their expression. It is because the faculties tend to group that we can do a fairly accurate reading without the knowledge of each separate faculty. The groupings give us the main thrust of the character; the individual organs give us the shades or nuances of character in more detail. I would suggest a review of this chapter prior to your study of phrenology.

THE HEAD DIVISIONS

The head divisions reflect the three basic propensities of mankind: the animal or material drives, the intellectual or commercial faculties, and the spiritual thrust. A perfect balance of these three divisions would make a person total and harmonious; however, the perfectly balanced person is a rarity. It is because of this fact that we are able to read character at all. An individual personality must have distinct and individual physical characteristics.

The three basic head divisions are shown in Figure 12 on page 44: the region of Spiritual Endeavor, the region of the Intellect, and the region of the Propensities. The predominant development of one or more of these three areas will indicate to us the motivating forces that guide our subject.

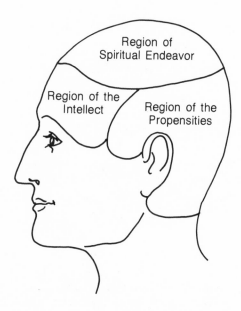

Figure 12. The head divisions. The three basic divisions demonstrate phrenology in a nutshell and allow us to make a rapid assessment of character. The divisions are the region of the propensities (base of skull), the region of the intellect (the forehead), and the region of spiritual endeavors (the top of the head).

THE BASE

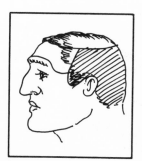

The base of the head includes the faculties of sexual love, marital love, love of children and pets, love of friends, and love of home and country. The physical recuperative powers also are located in this division. When the area is full and developed, there is a strong hold on life, great physical endurance, and the ability to withstand privation and hardships. With large development there is strong physical heat, strong acquisitive tendencies, and the fighting instinct, especially for self-preservation. A heavy base of the head is the outstanding physical characteristic of the region of the Propensities. A heavy base of the head always goes with a heavy body. We never find the region of the Propensities strong without the body structure to carry out those propensities. This is the world of instinct. Instinct relates humans to the animal world. All animal heads are developed at the base.

THE FOREHEAD

This is the intellectual region (or middle division) and includes the entire forehead and sides of the forehead. This is the world of practical affairs, business life, writing, communications, industry, commerce, construction, and finance. Just as the instincts relate humans to animals, the Intellectual Division relates humans to each other. The faculties of reason, memory, music, perception, friendliness, language, and money sense are all found in this area.

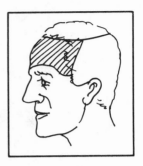

THE TOP-HEAD

The Spiritual Division is from the hairline up. The top division is the last area to be developed in the evolution of humans. This area represents the professional and spiritual endowments. When the top-head predominates, the individual tends to the professions, spiritual life, or a life of service to others. The higher the head, the higher the ideals will be and the higher the state of spiritual evolution. Qualities of imagination, venera-

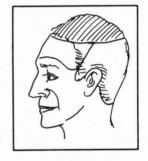

tion, and appreciation of the subtle, sublime, and magnificent are present in this division. This area of intuition introduces humans to the world of spiritual values.

THE HEAD SECTIONS

With our study of the Head Sections we begin to localize the areas of the head a bit more (see Figure 13 on page 46). All measurements of the Head Sections are made from the center of the opening of the ear to the extremity of the section under consideration. The distance of these areas from the center of the opening of the ear will determine their relative strength.

We will not consider the Frontal Section in this chapter. The reason for this is simply that we have covered its meaning in the Face Sections and again in the Head Divisions. In short, it is the seat of the intellectual faculties, and no more need be said at this time. The

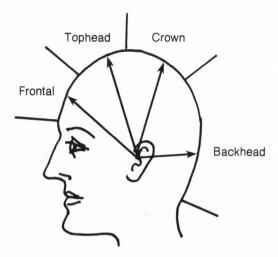

Figure 13. The head sections. All measurements of the head sections are made from the center of the opening of the ear to the extremity of the section. The distance will determine their relative strength.

specifics of this area will be covered in our study of phrenology and again in the work of Dr. Merton. When very highly developed, the Mental Temperament will usually be in the lead; however, the presence of one section does not necessarily eliminate the possibility of having other sections developed as well. Here as elsewhere, a good balance will give the best possible reading.

THE BACKHEAD

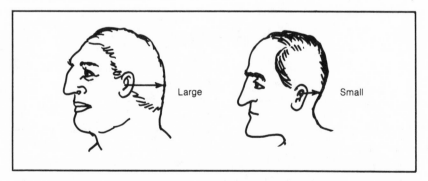

The backhead is noted for the sexual faculties, which are situated at the point where the neck ends and the head begins. A good relationship of the backhead to the rest of the head is to have one third of the head behind the ears and two thirds of the head in front of the ears. The intellect should rule, but we need good emotions also. When a large portion of the head is behind the ears, then the entire backhead is strong, showing strong emotional development. Sexual energy produces heat. A warm personality, strong sexual attraction, and the ability to work with people come with a developed backhead. People with small or deficient backheads have no ability to work with people. It is doubtful whether they should be given work with animals. People with no backhead usually have poor color and skinny bodies. People with no backhead could be killers in cold blood. One with a strong backhead may kill in the heat of passion or jealousy, or to protect loved ones, home, or country; but those with no backhead can kill without mercy and in the most cruel, cold-blooded, and inhumane manner possible.

A large backhead shows physical heat, good color (blood supply, nourishment), compassion, sympathy, heavy body, ardor, and the ability to hold onto life. It shows reserve power, force, vitality, vitativeness, gut strength, resiliency, warmth, and all those magnetic, forceful, life-giving qualities. No wonder the strong backhead makes a heavier-set person with the ability to recuperate, enjoy life, and attract others.

THE CROWN

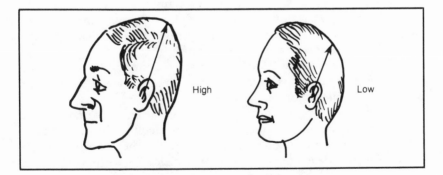

High   Low

The crown is the symbol of authority. Self-confidence, a strong ego, self-esteem, and an authoritative attitude (rulership and command) come with or from the high crown. Persons with a high crown stand more erect and come down heavily on their heels when they walk. They have command of themselves and can therefore command others. Ambition is another keynote. If one has an ample backhead, he or she functions well with the public and is a respected leader. The high crown means dignity, self-confidence, self-importance, the knowledge of one's inherent strengths, abilities and powers.

When the crown is lacking, subjects lack self-confidence and need the support of others. They will not push themselves forward, and although they may be extremely talented, they do not have the ambition and self-motivation to push through to success. A person with a low crown needs a mate with a high crown.

THE ANTERIOR TOP-HEAD

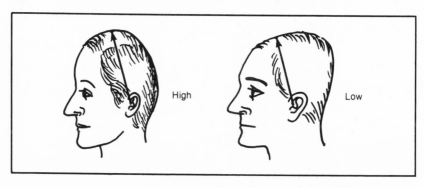

The anterior parietal section of the head is dominated by benevolence. It represents all that is good in human nature: self-sacrifice, self-effacement, service to mankind, hope, and love of the divine. The anterior top-head section starts where the forehead curves to become the top-head, and extends back to a point that would intersect a line drawn straight upward from slightly in front of the ear.

As the crown shows faith in ourselves, the anterior top-head shows faith in others. People with this area high will serve their brothers and sisters of humankind.

A person with an undeveloped anterior parietal section will have very little imagination. Ideality is one of the faculties that adds size to this area and fosters imagination, creativity, and the use of adjectives. This is where ideas come from. In any field, the anterior parietal section is necessary for creativity. People lacking it have no faith in others, and everything must be proved to them. This section is found large on founders of businesses and other enterprises. It has given them the vision to project ahead and has added business foresight.

Those interested in the psychic, occult, and religion also are developed in this area, as are poets, artists, writers of fiction, and inventors.

Whe⟋ ⟍s the selfish tendencies, or the
physic⟍ ⟍d represents the spiritual
qual⟍

⟍ AND LENGTH

⟍ wide head versus the narrow head. This
⟍of characters will be one of the most useful
⟍ver learn in characterology. It is especially
⟍ning the relationship of partners, in business,
⟍riage.

⟍nsidered the frontal, top-head, crown, and backhead;
no⟍ ⟍nsidering the sidehead. The wide or narrow sidehead is
meas⟍ ⟍y the distance or width of the head directly above the
ears, as shown in Figure 14. It is noticeable also when considered as
the distance outward from the corner of the eyes to the area above
the ears.

Figure 14. The sidehead. The wide head indicates a dominant individual; the narrow head indicates a passive individual.

People with wide heads are carnivorous and should never be total vegetarians. Note wide-headed animals such as lions, bears, wolves, dogs, and cats. Wide-headed people are *aggressive*, positive, forceful. They dominate situations and do not give in. They are the victors in life and the *masters* of any situation. They do battle with life's hardships and problems and never give up fighting.

People with narrow heads are herbivorous by nature. (However, we do not recommend pure vegetarianism.) Take note, once again, of the narrow heads in the animal world. Giraffes, horses, antelope, deer, and the like are all narrow in the head. Narrow-headed people are passive, docile, dominated by the wide heads of the world. They are the victims of life and take defeat without much fight. They are the ones who are mastered in any situation.

The countries that are wide-headed tend to dominate. Russia and the United States are basically wide-headed countries. The narrow-headed countries will be dominated. We have seen many narrow-headed rulers who have later been found to be merely puppet leaders. Examine the heads of our presidents: Woodrow Wilson was a pacifist; compare his head with that of the aggressive Teddy Roosevelt.

A few years ago the abduction of Patti Hearst made all the headlines. It was believed that she joined her abductors as a willing accomplice in crimes against society. Yet as character analysts we know at a glance that she is narrow-headed. She was frightened,

Figure 15. Head length. Long-headed individuals tend to prepare for the future; short-headed individuals tend to "live for today."

brainwashed, controlled, mastered—she could not withstand the will of her captors.

When examining marital partners, business partners, friends, or even enemies, we know that the widest head will dominate. Two wide heads will conflict and battle each other. (Consider again the United States and Russia.) Generally, they will eventually separate. Two narrow heads will blame each other for their lack of progress, lack of initiative, for being too passive, or whatever.

Wide heads will battle sickness and make better recoveries. Narrow heads will give in to sickness.

Surgeons and butchers will have wide heads because they must cut. (The faculty of Destructiveness is located in the sidehead.) The wide head denotes strong self-preservation instincts. It imparts energy and the executive ability necessary for us to overcome obstacles and remove whatever is contrary to our welfare. It allows us to destroy, defend, endure, inflict pain (as in a surgical operation), or kill for survival.

Narrow-headed subjects are not forceful; although if the crown, including Firmness, is high, we have found them to be persistent and immovable, even stubborn. Narrow-headed people are not executive or severe. They tend to shrink away from pain of any kind and are more easily discouraged.

The wide, short head is usually a generalist; the high, narrow head tends to be the specialist.

The head length is measured from the profile view and is the length from the most frontal point of the forehead to the back of the head (see Figure 15). Short-headed people are "today-minded" and want everything now; they are impatient and are poor savers. They do not consider the future, either their own or their posterity's. Long-headed people will sacrifice for the future and are concerned about tomorrow.

The relative head lengths are another important aspect to consider in compatability for marriage or business. Don't be surprised if you find yourself voting for our next president based on the shape of his or her head; it would be much better than listening to campaign promises, after all.

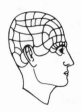

CHAPTER 6

BODILY EXPRESSIONS OF CHARACTER

The body speaks to us with clear and precise signs in a language all its own. There are a great many books that are devoted entirely to this facet of character reading. Our observations will be different in some ways but will supply us with valuable information on human nature that cannot be obtained in any other way. Many people are natural readers of character and intuitively interpret the mannerisms, appearance, and attitudes of others. People are the proverbial open book to those trained to observe. We cannot disguise our inner nature. Neither the master magician nor the Hollywood makeup artist can do more than add a superficial disguise. We must constantly train ourselves to notice the way people conduct themselves: how they stand; the shape of their bodies; the coloring of their skin, hair, and eyes; their voice; their posture; and everything about them.

THE HANDS

We say that the hands are an organ of the brain. What we mean is that the hands perform no motion without direct orders from the brain. Clutching, waving, holding, picking up, pointing, or whatever the act of the hands, they are directed by the brain. The link between the brain and the hands is responsible for the way the hands react unconsciously to mental states.

The thumb is the digit that reflects willpower, and the shape of it tells us of the degree of will and the way in which that will is expressed. When a person's willpower is in abeyance, when he or she is dominated by someone else or by circumstances, the thumb is automatically held inside the fingers. When we see a person with the thumb hidden by the fingers, we know that person is not in complete control of his or her will at that particular time but is being controlled either in the external world or in themselves.

Gestures of the hands offer plenty of easily seen tipoffs to inner states. Open arms are and always have been an expression of welcoming, love, warmth, and acceptance. People who keep their hands in their pockets (unless they are trying to keep them warm) are hiding something. Watch their eyes. Half-closed eyes and hands in the pockets indicate that motives and statements are half-hidden. Subjects who keep their hands behind their backs are being cautious. They don't want to fall into any traps. It shows hidden motives, repulsion, avoidance. Fidgety hands, hands that finger this and that and can't be still, usually indicate a person lacking direction but full of energy—even if it is only nervous energy. If we give such persons something to do, some direction, they may be off immediately and put their nervous hands to some task. Once a decision has been made, once the mind is made up and the time for action has arrived, the hands take on a different appearance. The fist is clenched. The clenched fist shows determination; the moment of action has come.

When you are talking to people, watch their hands. If their hands are open, their mind is open, and your ideas are being accepted; your sale is made. If the arms are crossed over the chest or the hands folded, it shows a barrier is up. The Great Wall of China itself would not keep you apart any better. The mind is closed. You might as well talk to that Great Wall; your words are bouncing off a dense, closed mind.

The handshake is the tipoff as to the amount of energy your subject possesses. A firm handshake with a good grip shows abundant vitality and energy. The subject is a hard worker with a vigorous constitution. Hands that are too hard, with an iron grip, denote a rigid mind and an excess of vitality. Those persons will work from dawn till dusk and have energy to spare, but the mind directing the energy is as rigid as the hands. It is practically impossible to change their minds. The only way you could get them to agree with you is to make it seem to be their idea. Hard-handed: hard-headed.

The elastic, resilient, springy, and warm handshake is the best. The mind is alert, progressive, and intelligent. The warmth of the hand points to a warm personality and a good blood supply. Cold hands point to poor circulation and frequently a cold personality. The statement that cold hands mean a warm heart is not necessarily true.

The soft, flabby handshake belongs to the lazy daydreamer. They may do some mental work, but physical work is avoided if possible. Soft hands also denote idealism and are found frequently on musicians. The flabby hand points to an unreliable and lethargic personality.

The handshake in which only the tips of the fingers are offered in a brief touch belongs to a person who does not really want to know you. He may feel superior and beyond your station in life. This is a condescending handshake.

THE FEET AND WALK

Many people have difficulty in walking properly because their feet hurt. If shoes are correctly fitted, then we must look to another source for the discomfort. Some other organ or organs are sick, and that makes our feet sore. Foot zone therapy or reflexology is a study of this condition of referred pain. (See Figure 16 on page 56.) All health-conscious adults should be aware of this method of promoting health and relieving blockages in the body by massaging or applying pressure to the corresponding area of the hand or foot. We would refer the interested student to the books of Mildred Carter for an in-depth study of this subject. Your feet are not just the ends of your legs," as my teacher would say. They are a distinct part of the whole you and reflect your nature just as your head, face, and hands do. The walk reflects the mind directing it; hence it is a key to understanding people.

An organized walk and the placing of the feet in a graceful yet firm manner reflects a mind that knows what it wants and is going after that objective. Feet that are placed down in a clumsy, floppy manner show a lack of refinement and mental direction. A walk that takes one all over the sidewalk shows the same thing, a lack of mental direction.

Those living in big cities can ascertain a great deal by listening to footsteps, without even seeing the person they belong to. Be aware first whether the tempo is regular, energetic, and positive—that individual knows where he is going. Observe how the steps are taken. If the walk is shuffling, uncertain, stop and go, or side to side, or deviates in any way then you should become suspicious and cross the street or wait at a lighted corner for the individual to pass. Derelicts shuffle around, uncertain whether to cross the street or go to the curb to pick up a cigarette butt. They have no set goal.

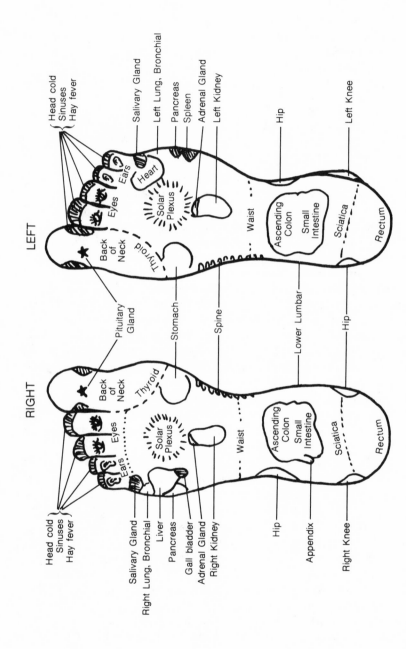

Figure 16. The zones of the feet show reflex conditions found elsewhere in the body.

Executives have a firm tread; direction is given to their feet, and they have good shoes that are not run down at the heels.

Nurses walk with a firm, unusually long stride. They know where they want to put their feet and are used to handling them efficiently. Their good swing of body, firm tread, and long stride can be easily recognized. Waiters and waitresses also have to acquire a certain efficiency and purposefulness in their stride.

Dragging the heels shows that emotional or physical problems are present. People who come down hard on their heels are more apt to be decisive, assertive, and executive in mentality. They can be determined, combative, and even dogmatic.

If we watch people closely and study their walk, we can learn important lessons. People act the way they feel. When a person is timid, the walk is timid. When a person is proud, the walk will be erect, lordly, and more dignified. If the mind is active, it will quicken the step. A daring person has a long, positive stride. Despondent people walk slowly and drag a bit. The walk of a lazy person is lacking in energy—it looks as slothful as the person. A foxy or catlike walk shows cunning, trickery, or deceit. An aimless walk shows an aimless mind; a controlled walk shows a controlled mind.

The character of people is written in all their actions, movements, and appearances. Pay attention to walks and you can sum up your subject from the encyclopedia of nature.

Dr. Benham's wonderful system of hand analysis points out the different walks associated with the seven types of people. We will consider these types and their walks later.

THE STANCE

One should stand tall and erect, head held high, buttocks together, abdomen pulled in; a straight line should run from the crown down the spine to the legs. This means that the solar plexus (the nerve center of the body) is expanded and functioning normally so that the blood can reach the brain with fresh oxygen, giving a positive frame of mind, confidence, poise, courage. The feet should be firmly placed, weight on the balls of the feet, with the toes pointing almost straight ahead. One foot should be slightly ahead of the other for better balance and for the psychological effect of being able to go forward, ahead—capable of solving life's problems. Observe the stance of the championship dog, how erect, alert, vigorous he looks; contrast it with the mongrel whose posture shows him to be abused, dejected, and frightened. As with dogs, so it is with people.

Think vertically!!!

Sit tall, stand tall, walk tall, and think tall to raise your consciousness. When you fold your arms, you have closed your mind. When you fold your legs, you have closed your mind. Do not cross arms or legs. If you want to close your aura to protect yourself against someone's power or influence, then cross your right foot over your left at the ankle. Keep your fingers and thumbs together, fold your arms, or fold your hands, interlacing the fingers.

Happiness and joy expand; sadness negates and contracts. Much has been said about Rodin's famous statue, *The Thinker*, but now you will hear something new for the first time. This is not a thinker as much as a man looking backward on the failures of his life. He is not looking forward; his back is prominent. This is a negative posture. His head is bowed; he is not up on his toes ready to go forward and battle life. This is the posture of defeat, not of contemplation.

Old age spreads the position of the legs and feet to balance the body. Those with youthful stance are still young regardless of calendar age. Refinement is indicated by good posture, legs and feet close together. A pigeon-toed walk shows deceit, the same as when the eyes slant down toward the nose.

THE VOICE

Your voice has a powerful influence on those around you, and it reflects the state of the mentality behind it. Human emotions are revealed by the voice. A person with a low, controlled, full, round voice shows self-mastery, sureness, and control. In the words of phrenologist O. S. Fowler, "Whatever makes a noise, from the deafening roar of the sea...to the sweet and gentle voice of a woman, makes a sound which agrees perfectly with the maker's character. Thus the terrific roar of the lion, and the soft cooing of the dove, correspond exactly with their respective dispositions."

The tone of the voice can induce a quarrel even when there is no real provocation. Talk to another in a high, excitable way and you will find the voice of your listener taking on the same inflection. In a few minutes he or she is ready to jump down your throat. "A soft answer turneth away wrath; but grievous words stir up anger" [Proverbs 15:1]

On the other hand, a steady mellow voice under control can calm an irritable individual. Being the master of your voice you can be master of another.

A metallic ring to the voice shows a cold, unsympathetic person. The loud, burly voice indicates a loud, uncouth, and coarse braggart. A weak voice denotes a weak individual lacking in mental and physical strength without the courage of his or her convictions. The high, shrill voice denotes nervousness and an irritable disposition.

Try to develop a pleasing, rich voice that will stamp you as a person of refinement and culture, a person who has self-control and is master of every situation. Develop the good erect posture we have discussed and practice developing a pleasing voice. Remember, the person who wants to quarrel or argue, or a nervous, irritable-voiced person, is quickly soothed by the modulated tones of a controlled voice.

Pay close attention to the voices of others and to your own voice. Observe the nuances, resonances, harmonies, and discords. Voices are as individual as fingerprints, and the truth or meaning of the sound is always there to be recognized despite the actual words used. Your voice is your soul essence in a form that can be perceived by others. Remember the power of words—they are subtle yet powerful vibrations. Truth always carries power. An old southern man once said,"The truth gotta stand, and a lie gotta fade away." When you lie, that sound is transposed over your soul essence.

Also consider silence. Excessive talkativeness indicates a lack of concentration—talkative people derive little information from outside sources because their minds are cluttered with continual chatter. They affect their own minds and compel the attention of those around them. Some reasons for excessive talkativeness could be a desire to be agreeable, nervousness, conceit, lack of self-control, a shallow but active mind, or an exuberant nature.

Reasoners and imaginative types think more and speak little. Many silent people are clever, wise, and economical with money as well as with words. The judgment of silent reasoners can often be relied on. Just remember that there are those who learn young that silence is more impressive than speech. Silence may be caused by timidity, a serious disposition, daydreaming, a scheming mentality, a reasoning mind, or an inactive mind. It also may be dangerous to talk too freely with silent people, for what you reveal will be remembered. Excessive silence can be as objectionable as excessive talkativeness. It can be a form of aggression.

BODY/HEAD PROPORTIONS (SEX TYPE)

We speak of the body/head proportions as being either andromorphic (masculine), gynomorphic (feminine), or homomorphic (also called harmonious). Insight into these body/head proportions must be preceded by a basic understanding of the Universal Law of Opposites, or the yin/yang principle represented in Figure 17. In essense this law points out the balance of all the positive and negative forces of Nature and their interdependence.[3]

Man as a positive masculine unit seems to be balanced only by the negative feminine polarity. So far, this is the only way in which humanity can re-create and perpetuate itself. The yin/yang mandalas are all bisexual, a balance of opposites. We also see in the yin/yang symbol that there is a little bit of yin in the yang and vice versa. Nothing is usually totally positive or totally negative.

Men and women are mental and physical complements of each other; the mental faculties are also harmonious in this way. The physical differences of sex produce mental differences because the brain and body are related in action and sympathy with each other. So long as women are the sex that bears children, their nutritive system and organs must predominate over the nervous and muscular. This affects their temperament and brain faculties. Neither man nor

---

[3]The Law of Opposites, or yin/yang, and the terms positive/negative or masculine/feminine should not have values attached to them. They are opposite polarities that can be equally beneficial or equally destructure. They are two sides of the same coin; they are the front door and the back door of the same house; the opposite poles of a magnet; positive and negative electrical charges. In the yin/yang mandala, the positive and negative aspects are illustrated as being equal, yet dependent on each other—interlocked, balanced.

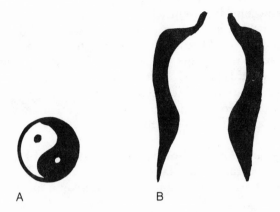

A   B

Figure 17. The Universal Law of Opposites gives us insight into studying body/head proportions: a) illustrates the yin/yang principle; b) shows how the principle is applied in comparing body types. Here we see the masculine and feminine forms contrasted.

woman is the superior sex. They possess equal quantities of power, but it differs in kind.

The masculine faculties are vigorous, muscular, hardy, bold, cool, and scientific. The feminine faculties are sensitive, yielding, gentle, loving, ardent, and intuitive. The masculine/feminine proportions have absolutely nothing to do with the sex of an individual, in the sense that the masculine body/head will be found on women, and feminine proportions can be found on men. It may be true that these masculine or feminine proportions are carried through from past lives that were experienced in the body of the opposite sex. A woman may possess a masculine body or head; a man may possess a feminine body or head; or both may be harmonious or any combination of body and head. (See Figure 18 on page 62.)

The typically masculine body structure is identified by square, flat shoulders, high waistline and relatively short torso, long legs, long arms, and flat chest—a body designed for activity, leg endurance, and strength. This is the body structure that is almost invariably found on dancers. Even the petite ballet dancer will have the square shoulders and comparatively long arms and legs of the masculine body, not to mention the long chin line. In a widely known current commercial avertisement, a ballet dancer is paired with a ball player; both have the masculine body proportions, and both are built for activity, endurance, and achievement.

The typically feminine structure has sloping shoulders, long torso, short arms and legs, and a full bosom. Intuition, persuasion, passiveness are the way it displays itself. The emotions are strong in this type. The comedian Benny Hill has the feminine body structure. It is no wonder that his hilarious antics center around women. A man with a feminine build and a large backhead and top-head has powerful sex instincts and is usually a favorite with women. He gravitates toward them and understands their nature, tastes, work, inclinations, and motives; he devotes himself more to them. A man with weaker amatory inclinations and a masculine build usually favors men, succeeds better with them, and takes more interest in their work.

The masculine head, shown in Figure 19a, is most developed in the crown or posterior parietal section. This area is found high and slopes down toward the forehead. There is only medium or slight development behind the ears. The masculine head is strong in Rulership, Firmness, Self-esteem, Dignity, and generally in Conscientiousness and Combativeness. This is the military type of head. Such people accept responsibility more readily and are by nature authoritative. They are frequently disciplinarians and dogmatic in views.

A   B   C

Figure 18. Body proportions. a) The feminine body structure. b) The masculine body structure. c) The harmonious body structure—a combination of both feminine and masculine traits.

The feminine head, Figure 19b, is dominant in the backhead and anterior parietal as seen in the above figure. The qualities displayed by this head development are Benevolence, Self-sacrifice for others, Spirituality, Faith, Hope, and the Love faculties exhibited in the backhead—Sexual Love, Love of mate, Love of home, children, pets— all of which generate magnetism and warmth. Such people are best placed in careers dealing directly with people, especially children. Those with the feminine head and body have softer thought patterns a warmer facial expressions; they are a friend to all in need.

In addition to the masculine and feminine body/head proportions we have the neutral or harmonious type. Those folks are, of course, balanced—neither too positive nor too negative. Many public figures possess the harmonious body and the masculine head. This is a great power combination. You should know what your body/head proportions are; they will tell a great deal about the way you project your personality. Table 1 on page 64 lists some examples.

Just as the body/head proportions have nothing to do with the gender of a person, neither have they to do with physical strength per se. I have worked side by side with a man having a feminine head and feminine body, yet he weighed more than 250 pounds and was over 6 feet 4 inches tall. He could lift weights that other men could

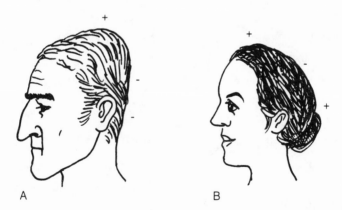

A   B

Figure 19. Head proportions. a) The masculine head. b) The feminine head. Note the areas of development: the plus and minus signs over the head sections will show you which of the sections are more developed, which are less developed. Refer to figures 12 and 13 to refresh your understanding of the sections and what they represent. A masculine head tends to be weak in social and altruistic faculties and indicative of coldness; a feminine head has a fuller development of Love faculties and is more indicative of warmth.

not get off the floor. The proportions reveal themselves more in the thought patterns and disposition of the person. This same hulk of a man was a mouse when it came to taking a strong, assertive stance on any issue. He would rather keep the peace and avoid confrontation. A gentle soul in a giant's body.

To continue this idea further, some typically masculine qualities include the following: active, energetic, resolute, daring, independent, dogmatic, forceful, business-minded, adapted for struggle or

Table 1. Body/Head Proportions of Historic Figures

Name	Head Type	Body Type
Leonid Brezhnev	Feminine	Harmonious
Jimmy Carter	Harmonious	Masculine
Sir Winston Churchill	Masculine	Feminine
Geraldine Ferraro	Masculine	Masculine
Gerald Ford	Masculine	Masculine
Mikhail Gorbachev	Masculine	Masculine
John F. Kennedy	Masculine	Masculine
Gen. Douglas MacArthur	Masculine	Feminine
Golda Meir	Masculine	Feminine
Napoleon	Masculine	Feminine
Richard Nixon	Masculine	Masculine
Gen. John J. Pershing	Masculine	Masculine
Nancy Reagan	Masculine	Masculine
Ronald Reagan	Masculine	Masculine
Nelson Rockefeller	Masculine	Harmonious
Franklin Roosevelt	Feminine	Harmonious
Teddy Roosevelt	Masculine	Harmonious
Anwar Sadat	Masculine	Masculine
George Sand	Feminine	Feminine
Elizabeth Taylor	Masculine	Harmonious
Margaret Thatcher	Masculine	Harmonious
George Washington	Masculine	Harmonious

competition; typically feminine qualities are communicative, sociable, tactful, friendly, diplomatic, religious/spiritual, domestic, affectionate, aesthetic, intuitive, pliable, hesitating, magnetic, sympathetic. From this list you can see that some people are a combination of the two, while others may be more masculine or feminine in disposition.

Some typically masculine vocations would be engineering, mechanics, construction, farming, mining, law, politics, travel, dance, sports; more feminine vocations (using feminine characteristics) would be medicine, sales, nursing, music, lecturing, ministry, art, poetry, fine work, advertising. As you can see, these vocations have nothing to do with "male or female" because women can go into politics and men can go into the ministry. It's important to see how the vocation ties to the body type.

COMPLEXION

Most of us can remember the question posed by the advertiser of a hair-coloring product that asked: "Do blonds have more fun?" Well, I'm afraid we still will not be able to answer that question since both blonds and brunettes enjoy life in their own way. Yet the question raises an important characterological point: there is a distinct difference between blonds and brunettes.

The color pigmentation of individuals shows their mental vibration or wavelength. Blonds have a more rapid mental vibration; brunettes have a slower but more thorough mental vibration.

Many factors have effects on the skin, complexion, hair, and eyes. Food elements, such as hydrogen, carbon, sodium, calcium, magnesium, oxygen, iron, sulfur, and silicon, and a colder climate are at the foundation of a light complexion. You will note that Scandinavians, Germans, and other races that come from colder climates tend to fair hair and light skin and eyes—with the exception of the American Eskimo, who eats a high-protein diet.

Food elements, such as organic nitrogen (contained in high-protein, fatty food substances), potassium, phosphorus, chlorine, manganese, fluorine, and iodine, and a tropical climate are at the foundation of a dark complexion. The South American and African continents predominate in the brunette races.

Other factors involved in skin, hair, and eye color are sedentary work, outdoor work, room heat, disease, smoke, fumes, gases, bacteria, work, bathing, wind, drugs, food toxins, food acids, body acids, emotions, temper, passion, habits, gluttony, starvation, soul states, evolution, heredity, karma, and so forth.

We identify the Blond and Brunette influences by the appearance of two out of three conditions among hair color, eye color and skin color. Blonds are typified by hair that can range from white to light brown, light red, "platinum" blond or gray. Eyes may be pink, light blue, gray, or light green or light amethyst. Skin is usually white or pink. In the brunette group, hair can be black, brown, or dark red. Eye color ranges from light or dark amethyst through dark amber, the brown shades, and black, as well as most hazel eyes. Skin color can be yellow, copper, or the black or brown shades.

If a person possesses two out of three of the descriptions for hair, skin or eye coloring, they are classified in either the blond or brunette group. Of course, there are different degrees of coloring. If we make an imaginary color scale and let it run from the darkest, blackest person on the earth—with black hair, black eyes, and black skin—to the other extreme: the albino with white hair and skin and pink eyes, we can classify all other people by degrees within that scale. Most individuals in the United States will fall in the range of 35 to 65 percent, with some exceptions, of course.

In terms of racial distribution on this imaginary line, the darker races will fall more on the brunette side and partake more of brunette characteristics and tendencies. The lighter races will fall more on the blond side of the scale and partake more of blond tendencies. An overlap will occur somewhere around 40-60 percent, where lighter complected orientals and blacks and darker complected caucasians will more properly be called intermediate in complexion.

As elsewhere in characterology, no rigid barriers exist, and other factors must always be considered, especially Temperament and individual faculties. These principles indicate group tendencies, which may be overcome or overridden by stronger factors in the personality. Extremely light, blue-eyed caucasians may develop sentimentality that comes naturally to brunettes. Extremely dark, brown-eyed blacks may be able to handle rapidly changing vocational circumstances and resist the natural tendency to concentrate on individual aspects. No racial, ethnic, or sexual bias is intended in these, or any other group of characterology principles. It must always be kept in mind that these are tendencies and not laws, and that there are ranges of color within racial groups to which the same principles can be applied. The black races range from a rich blue-black to a yellowish or reddish brown or tan. The oriental races range from almost caucasian as in the Northern islands of Japan, to the brown-olive skin of Okinawa. The white races range from pale white to sanguine brown.

Blonds have rapid mental vibrations, and are well adapted to work requiring a rapid change of ideas and circumstances. They can adapt to these changes without confusion. They can go out and meet new people and new challenges daily and actually prefer it that way. They have a variety of interests and are always intrigued with new ideas and new interests. If they do not have enough distractions and diversions, they will create their own.

Brunettes have concentrative mentalities. They should know more or less what they will be doing each day and should be able to do their work with a minimum of interruptions. They should always concentrate on one thing at a time, start one project and finish it before going on to the next thing, in order to perform their best work. Intensity of purpose and concentration are demonstrated in the Brunette, and they should specialize in their chosen vocations. Sentimentality is another leading quality of the Brunette.

In a conversation the Blond will touch on many subjects in a short space of time. The Brunette will concentrate on a minimum of subjects but is more thorough.

Blonds and Brunettes have a natural attraction for each other and frequently marry. In such a marriage the Brunette spouse will prefer to stay home and enjoy sharing the pleasures of the home, whereas the Blond requires more variety and diversity. The Blond's rapid mental vibration stimulates the Brunette, and the Brunette tones down and calms the Blond by a slower vibratory rate. The child of a mixed couple will go to the Blond parent for activity and to the Brunette parent for cuddling and loving.

In business we tend to find the Blond is the business builder, and the Brunette is the administrator. The Blond is all business. Salespeople should not try to waste his or her time but should immediately talk business and matters at hand with the Blond businessperson. On the other hand, the Brunette businessperson will respond to inquiries and comments about family and home. In fact, they will most often have photos of loved ones displayed on their desks.

The skin of the Blond has open pores and is susceptible to odors, atmospheric gases, harsh chemicals, soaps, detergents, and the like. Sun bathing must be done carefully because Blonds burn more easily and are more susceptible to skin cancer. They should avoid the direct rays of the sun and should think twice about that vacation to Florida, the Bahamas, or Arizona.

The Brunette can be exposed to the sun for longer periods without harmful effects as their origins are basically in warmer climates. Brunettes are generally healthier and happier south of the Mason-Dixon line. Brunettes are safer in occupations involving the handling of chemicals, sprays, and so forth.

HEALTH

You can judge a person's state of health by his/her general appearance. Specific health indications can be found in the line patterns of the hand and the various patterns and colors found in the iris of the eye.

Good health will, first and foremost, bring color to the face, the palm of the hand, beneath the nails, and all parts of the body in general. In light-skinned people, pink is the best color to be seen. Red shows excess and at times high blood pressure or alcoholism. White shows a lack of red corpuscles, poor circulation, kidney problems and coldness in the extremities. Yellow may indicate bile and other toxic substances in the blood and skin (such as uric poisoning). Blue in the lips, hands, and nails is the signal of heart problems. The color of the skin also brings its own personality quirks in addition to health indications; for example: pink, outgoing personality; red, intensity and excess; white, coldness and selfishness; yellow, moodiness, irritability.

These variations of color are perhaps more easily seen in light-skinned people. In the darker races, adaptations must be made. Even when the skin is dark, a palor or paleness (which might be called white in light-skinned people) is still obvious in poor health. Flush, vivid and clear skin tone is seen in health (which may be called pink). The palms of the hands will be pale or vivid, the lines in the palms pale or a rich dark brown, and so on. Yellow and red are easily visible in the white of the eyes in any race or nationality. The palms of the black races are considerably lighter in color than the rest of the skin, and a pink blush is easily discernable in good health. We are not looking at the surface color as much as the tint beneath the surface and its effect on health and personality.

When body chemistry is balanced, the skin is clear, soft, slightly moist, and somewhat pink. The hair is lustrous and full, with no indication of brittleness or excessive dryness. The eyes are bright and clear with no dark circles under them. The whites of the eyes are clear, not blue, red, or yellow. The muscles are firm and the body weight is well distributed. The posture is upright and the carriage pleasing. The nerves are steady, and the joints are limber and free from calcium deposits and stiffness. The organs function properly without sensations of heat, cold, pain, soreness, fatigue, uneasiness, heaviness, swelling, or pressure.

The person with a healthy body feels alert, active, vigorous, ready for action and *glad to be alive.*

This is the picture of good health in the body. This is the state we must all strive for by proper diet, exercise, mental relaxation, spiritual growth, good habits, proper periods of work and rest and a proper frame of mind. Let us all remain free of the doctor's poisons and the surgeon's knife. We must leave all death-food out of our diets and make our tissues alkaline. Stay away from food toxins, dyes, metallic acids, adulterants, and perservatives that go into modern processed foods. Remember, there is a ghost in every loaf of white bread or processed flour; acid venom in the candy box and sugary cake; ugliness in the frying pan; arthritis in the coffee cup; gas in corpse sausages; high blood pressure in salted foods; misery, pain, and disease in coarse proteins, fatty gravy, sugary dope-drinks, bleached noodles, pasteurized milk, table salt, and toxic medicines.

Let us retrain our warped palettes and eat for health and beauty. As Thomas Edison wrote, "The doctor of the future will give no medicine but will interest his patients in the care of the human frame, in diet, and in the cause and prevention of disease."

QUALITY

There is a condition or value expressed by men and women that requires our close attention and evaluation if we are to judge properly the potentials of our subject. This condition we refer to as Quality, although the word is broad and inadequate.

From burlap to silk we cover a wide range of fiber grades, working qualities, and structure. The human species exhibits an equivalent range of grades that tell us about their refinement, mental abilities, strength, and potential for greatness or anonymity.

All men are not created equal—physically, mentally, spiritually, or in quality. The presence of high Quality endows one with the mental, vital, or motive possibilities that can far surpass those people of lower Quality. This does not depend on the features per se but on the Quality or Power found coming through the features: modeling, membranes, skin tone, and so on.

Quality shows itself in many different ways. In some instances it shows extreme sensitiveness to outward conditions; in others it may show great mental ability with little sensitiveness or refinement in conduct—enormous power without refinement, or a ruggedness that is capable of resisting extreme burdens.

Determining the Quality of an individual will tell what realm that person will express themselves in, whether the coarse, low existence is theirs or if they will achieve great feats with their abilities and characteristics.

In judging Quality we depart from our pure analytical approach and must tune in to the individual on another plane, that of "impression" or "sensitivity" or "feeling." Each person gives off a vibration, radiance, aura, or life force that is consistent with their general Quality. In the brave we sense courage; in the timid, timidity; in the great, greatness. Making ourselves conscious of a person's Quality will awaken that intuition in us if practiced to any great extent. However, there are some visible aspects to this condition.

Often the character and tone of the modeling of a person's features betrays their Power and Quality. At times the features are rugged and deep, with meaningful plateaus, such as in the faces of Lincoln and Michelangelo. At times the appearance is not that powerful in its distinctness because it has finely finished contours with balanced and expressive features. It may be comparatively smooth in contour, but every margin and relief will be apparent, however delicate it may be.

If we look at the faces of historical figures, we can see what great Quality looks like. If we look at the faces of low-grade individuals, we see a careless lack of detail and structural development and a lack of finish to their faces. Instead of purpose, power, and refinement, the common face has a variety of contours, lines, and peculiarities that lack this essential unity and mental order.

There are also textural indices of Quality. Fine hair, refined features—especially the ears, nose, mouth, and skin—show an individual's Quality. In the skin and tissues we can see elasticity, structural tone, strength, or translucency. In very refined people this translucency is detected in the skin tone and especially around the nostrils, eyelids, ears, and mouth. Quality and refinement have no racial barriers, and can be witnessed in all peoples as a refinement of the basic racial structure, features, hair, and so on. Compare men and women of accomplishment with low-grade individuals of the same race. Quality determines what realm and how great the achievements of our subjects will be. Low-grade subjects cannot progress past a certain point, nor can they mingle with or experience the mental pleasures of higher-grade individuals.

In character analysis we say that certain patterns are existent in the individual at birth. These are coded in the DNA of the chromosomes through heredity and as a result of karmic patterns. Modern science is currently working in bioengineering and will soon be able to create certain types of individuals by altering the chromosomes. We feel that the end result of such manipulation will bring on "the

Brave New World" in which a person's place in life is predetermined before birth. It will be a class system from which there is no escape. We are opposed to any type of manipulation of genes because the end result will be catastrophic to humanity as we know it. The rich and powerful will naturally control and create this caste system.

Any thinking person should violently oppose this type of scientific investigation for its effects on humankind are as disastrous as atomic warfare.

PART 2:

ADVANCED STUDIES

What you are shouts so loudly, I cannot hear what you are saying.

—Ralph Waldo Emerson

By making samyama on the distinguishing marks of another man's body, one obtains knowledge of the nature of his mind.

—Yoga Sutras of Patanjalis

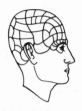

CHAPTER 7

PHRENOLOGY

We are now about to embark on the specifics of phrenology—the analysis of the organs of the head. This chapter will focus on making the student familiar with the groupings of the organs and the organs themselves. You should linger over this chapter to make sure you fully understand the material. The ability to locate the organs, to recognize whether they are highly developed or deficient, and to know their function in character development will be key to utilizing them as a tool to understanding human nature. The rest of Part 2 will focus on specific adaptations of phrenological methods, so it is important that the location and function of the phrenological organs become second nature to you.

CLASSIFICATIONS

The shape of the skull, shown in figure 20 on page 76, will determine the structure of the head and face. Since the brain fills the hollow cavity of the skull, there remains some yet undiscovered relationship between the mental makeup of a person and the physiology of the brain and skull. We will begin by looking at the groupings of organs. Students should go back and reread the Head Sections in Chapter 5, as we will begin with the three basic groupings described there. You should also be well versed in the Temperaments (Chapter 3), for this will be the first classification of your subject's nature that will be supported or modified by the phrenological organs that show activity or deficiency.

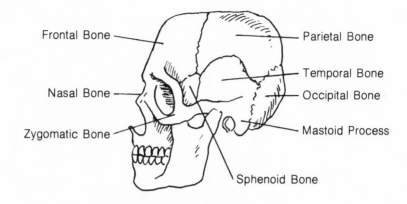

Figure 20. The skull, seen from the left lateral view, shows the different bones that will affect the shape of the head and face.

The organs are grouped into the Propensities, the Sentiments, and the Intellectual Faculties, and the phrenological organs fall within these groupings. Figure 21 on page 77 will show you the location of the basic groups. Figure 22 (pages 84-85) will show you the location of the specific phrenological organs. Before we turn to Figure 22, however, we're going to discuss the nature of each of the three major groups, and discuss the subgroups. Under each grouping, I have listed the classical name of the phrenological organ and its number, and have added some modern-day keywords in parentheses so you can begin to understand the aspects that each phrenological organ encompasses. You will note, if you continue your studies into phrenology, that I have kept the names and numbers consistent with what you will find in the traditional literature. You will eventually memorize these names, but as many of them are archaic terms no longer in common use, do become familiar with the modern meaning in parentheses.

THE PROPENSITIES

This group is made up of the Social Propensities and the Selfish Propensities. The Social propensities are responsible for the ties that connect us to family, friends, home, and country. The phrenological organs included in this group are:

1. Amativeness (sexual love)
2. Philoprogenitiveness (parental love)
3. Adhesiveness (friendship)
4. Inhabitiveness (love of home and country)
5. Continuity (one thing at a time)
A. Conjugality (love of mate, union for life)

The Selfish Propensities involve our responsibility for our own preservation by attraction to nourishment, self-defense, and future provision. The organs included in this group are:

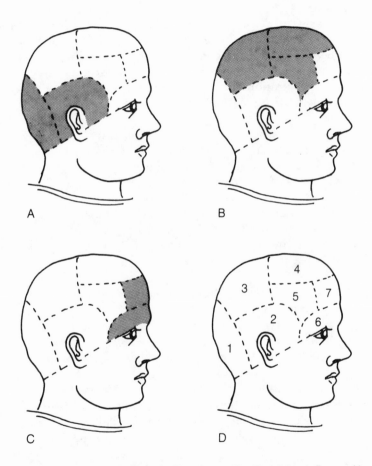

Figure 21. The Phrenological Organs. These are classified into a) Propensities, b) Sentiments, and c) Intellectual Faculties. d) These classifications are further broken down: 1. The Social or Domestic Propensities; 2. the Selfish Propensities; 3. the Selfish Sentiments; 4. Moral and Religious Sentiments; 5. The Semi-intellectual Sentiments; 6. the Perceptive and Literary Faculties; and 7. the Reasoning Faculties.

E. Vitativeness (tenacity, or hold on life)
6. Combativeness (resistance and opposition)
7. Destructiveness (executiveness, force)
8. Alimentiveness (appetite, love of eating) and Bibativeness (love of liquids, drinking)
9. Acquisitiveness (sense of economy and accumulation)
10. Secretiveness (sense of discretion, reserve)

THE SENTIMENTS

This group is made up of the Selfish Sentiments, the Moral/Religious Sentiments, and the Semi-intellectual Sentiments.

The Selfish Sentiments give us concern for our character, love of personal distinction and identity, and self-assertion. They are responsible for aspiration and have a ruling or dominating tendency. The phrenological organs in this group are:

11. Cautiousness (prudence, watchfulness)
12. Approbativeness (ambition, love of praise)
13. Self-Esteem (self-respect, dignity)
14. Firmness (stability, perseverance)

The Moral/Religious Sentiments elevate humankind and awake our higher and Spiritual Self. This group refines and sanctifies the action of all of the other groups when it is large and active. The organs included in this group are:

15. Conscientiousness (sense of equity, integrity, honesty)
16. Hope (expectations, anticipation)
17. Spirituality (intuition, faith, ESP, psychic ability)
18. Veneration (devotion, respect)
19. Benevolence (sympathy for others, philanthropy)

The Semi-intellectual Sentiments are concerned with self-improvement and production and appreciation of the beautiful. This group also has elevating qualities and is closely allied with the Moral Sentiments. The phrenological organs in this group are:

20. Constructiveness (building with hand or mind, shaping)
21. Ideality (refinement, love of the beautiful, purity)
22. Imitation (mimicry, following an example, copying)
23. Mirthfulness (sense of humor, wit, and appreciation of the absurd)

B. Sublimity (appreciation of the sublime and magnificent)
C. Human Nature (ability to perceive character and motives)
D. Agreeableness (pleasantness, suavity)

THE INTELLECTUAL FACULTIES

This group is composed of the Perceptive Faculties, the Literary Faculties, and the Reflective Faculties.

The Perceptive Faculties utilize the senses of feeling, sight, hearing, taste, and smell to bring us into direct communication with the physical world. Practical application of the information supplied by the Perceptive Faculties is the typical result. The phrenological organs in this group are:

24. Individuality (observation, examination)
25. Form (cognizance and memory of shape)
26. Size (cognizance of magnitude)
27. Weight (balancing, perception of the law of gravity)
28. Color (tone and perception of colors)
29. Order (methods, system, arrangement)
30. Calculation (estimation, mental arithmetic)
31. Locality (memory of places, scenery)

The Literary Faculties are basically concerned with communication and memory. This group includes:

32. Eventuality (memory and cognizance of facts and circumstances)
33. Time (cognizance of duration, punctuality)
34. Tune (sense of harmony and melody, love of music)
35. Language (vocal and written expression)

The Reflective Faculties take the facts presented by the Perceptive Faculties and compare and classify them. They also philosophize and originate ideas. The phrenological organs in this group are:

36. Causality (reasoning from cause to effect)
37. Comparison (analytical reasoning)

Inasmuch as these groups contain clusters of associated organs or faculties, it is possible to do a fair delineation of character without ascertaining the individual faculties that are present. These groups give shape to the head and either round it out, square it, or widen it and thereby form the appearance and conditions of the Temperaments. The Motive Temperament is shaped by the development of the Perceptives, the Selfish Sentiments (or Crown), and frequently the addition of Combativeness and Destructiveness. The Vital Temperament has the Domestic and Selfish Propensities large. The Mental Temperament is most developed in the Moral Sentiments, the Literary and Reflective Faculties, and the Semi-intellectual area.

LOCATIONS

After you've become familiar with the basic groupings and the terminology for the organs, the next step is beginning to learn how to locate these areas on the head. The Faculties are frequently difficult for the novice to locate because the natural geography of the head dictates that one organ blend into the next—there are no distinct boundaries on a living head. The best way to start is to practice on your own head. Table 2 on pages 81 through 83 takes you from cranial landmarks that are easy to locate and guides you along the head to the locations of other organs or faculties. We've also included the number of each organ in this table, so you can use it in conjunction with Figure 22.

The individual organs will range in strength and influence on the character of our subjects. The leading or most prominent organs will tend to dominate the character, with the organs of slightly less strength supporting the dominant ones.

The weak or small organs will hold no sway in the character, or they will be obvious because of the lack of certain traits in the personality. The quality or fineness of an individual will be the overriding factor in how the organs are expressed by the subject. It is always best for the student to look for exaggerated or obvious human examples of the organs, and then, by degrees, he or she will learn to judge just what proportion of those organs exist when they are not so pronounced.

Now take a look at Figure 22 on pages 84 and 85. Here we can see where the phrenological organs are located on the head, looking at the side, front, and back views of the head. We're now going to go in depth with a discussion of each organ and have provided some illustrations of how these organs have shaped the head—and the characters—of some famous individuals. You'll want to refer back to Figure 22 frequently to compare with the developed areas being discussed for each individual.

Table 2. Guide for Locating the Faculties

Faculty	Corresponding Number	Location
Individuality	24	First organ above the root of the nose, between the eyebrows
Eventuality	32	¾" up from Individuality, just below the center of the forehead
Comparison	37	From the center of the forehead to the slope of the forehead
Locality	31	1" outward on either side of Eventuality
Human Nature	C	Directly above Comparison, in front of Benevolence
Agreeableness	D	1" on either side of Human Nature
Causality	36	1" on either side of Comparison
Mirthfulness	23	About ¾" further out from Causality
Form	25	Outward from Individuality, just above and slightly between the eyes
Size	26	At the turn between the nose and eyebrows, over the inner portion of the eyes
Weight	27	Looking straight in the eyes, find the center of the iris; on the inside of this center line above and on the eyebrow is Weight.
Color	28	On the outside of this imaginary line
Order	29	On the outer corner of the eyebrow
Calculation	30	Beneath the outer corner of the eyebrow

Table 2. Guide for Locating the Faculties (cont.)

Faculty	Corresponding Number	Location
Tune	34	¾" above the outer angle of the eyebrow
Time	33	Inward from Tune and forming somewhat of a triangle with Time, Tune, and Mirthfulness
Destructiveness	7	Around and behind the middle top of the ear, extending upward about 1", commencing where the ears join the head; it is responsible for producing a wide head when largely developed.
Secretiveness	10	¾" above the top of the ear; above Destructiveness
Combativeness	6	About 1½" behind and above the ears; it extends upward toward Friendship.
Parental Love	2	Straight back from the upper portion of the ear, on the back of the head. There will be a prominence there when large.
Inhabitiveness	4	About ¾" above Parental Love
Friendship	3	1" on each side of Inhabitiveness.
Continuity	A	Directly above Friendship and Inhabitiveness
Amativeness	1	On the backhead below a line drawn back from the center of the ear; it extends down to the junction of the head and neck.
Cautiousness	11	Above Secretiveness where the head begins to round off
Alimentiveness	8	Forward and downward from the front of the ear, about ½"

Table 2. Guide for Locating the Faculties (cont.)

Faculty	Corresponding Number	Location
Acquisitiveness	9	1″ forward from Secretiveness
Sublimity	B	Forward of Cautiousness about 1″
Ideality	21	Forward of Sublimity about 1″
Constructiveness	20	1″ downward from Ideality (Cautiousness, Sublimity, and Ideality are found on the round of the head).
Firmness	14	Drawing an imaginary line straight upward from the center of the ear puts you on the forepart of Firmness.
Self-Esteem	13	About 1½″ behind Firmness
Approbativeness	12	On both sides of Self-Esteem, about 1″ outward
Conscientiousness	15	Found directly below and backward from Firmness
Hope	16	Directly below and in front of Firmness; below and back from Veneration.
Veneration	18	Center tophead, 1″ forward from Firmness
Benevolence	19	1″ foward of Veneration on the tophead
Spirituality	17	On either side of Veneration
Imitation	22	On either side of Benevolence
Vitativeness	E	Directly behind the ear on the bony protuberance found there
Conjugality	A	Above Amativeness on either side of Philoprogenitiveness
Language	35	Appears as a fullness beneath the eye, or pushes the eye outward, causing it to bulge.

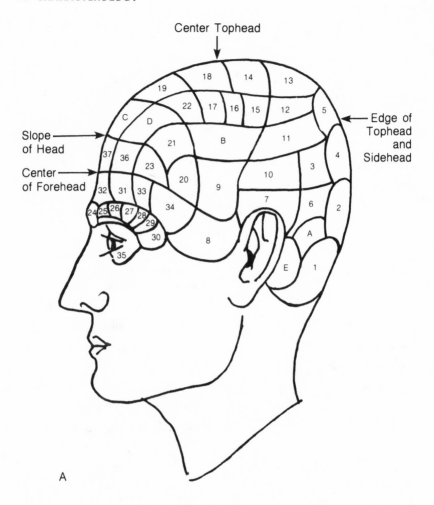

Figure 22. Location of the Phrenological Organs. There are no distinct boundaries on a living head—the individual organs are modeled and blended into the shape of the head. a) Side, b) back, and c) front show where the developed or deficient organs may be found. The organs are as follows: 1. Amativeness, 2. Philoprogenitiveness, 3. Adhesiveness, 4. Inhabitiveness, 5. Continuity, 6. Combativeness, 7. Destructiveness, 8. Alimentiveness and Bibativeness, 9. Acquisitiveness, 10. Secretiveness, 11. Cautiousness, 12. Approbativeness, 13. Self-esteem, 14. Firmness, 15. Conscientiousness, 16. Hope, 17. Spirituality, 18. Veneration, 19. Benevolence, 20. Constructiveness, 21. Ideality, 22. Imitation, 23. Mirthfulness, 24. Individuality, 25. Form, 26. Size, 27. Weight, 28. Color, 29. Order, 30. Calculation, 31. Locality, 32. Eventuality, 33. Time, 34. Tune, 35. Language, 36. Causality, 37. Comparison, A. Conjugality, B. Sublimity, C. Human Nature, D. Agreeableness, E. Vitativeness.

The student should note that this figure is labeled with both numbers and the letters A through E. This is in keeping with traditional phrenological charts, and you will find this system consistent with material you will read in your further studies.

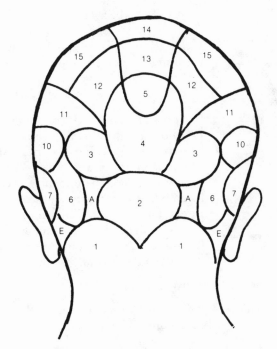

B

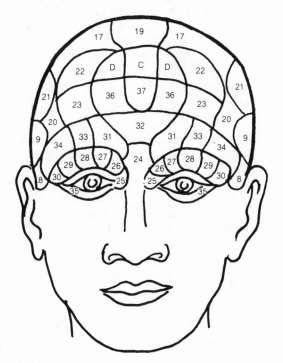

C

AMATIVENESS (1)

Pete Rose
Professional baseball player

Location: The organ of Amativeness is found at the cerebellum at the base of the backhead. It gives fullness to the head behind the ears and width to the neck.

Function: This is the organ of sexual love, whose purpose in the human family is to perpetuate life. It causes mutual attraction between the sexes and desire for union and marriage. The faculty becomes more manifest at puberty and causes women to exhibit the female charms and graces that make them attractive and lovely. It causes young men to become more noble, gallant, and tender toward women.

Excess: Licentiousness and gross sensuality.

Deficiency: A dryness and coldness of character. Lack of feeling for the opposite sex and humankind in general.

Remarks: Strong Amativeness and a strong cerebellum give one a love of nature and all that grows. Amativeness also has much to do with blood production. When abnormal or diseased in function, diabetes is the result.

CONJUGALITY (A)

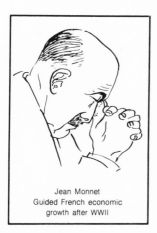

Jean Monnet
Guided French economic
growth after WWII

Location: Situated in the lower backhead above Amativeness and forward of Philo-progenitiveness.

Function: The mating or pairing instinct arises from this faculty. Mating for life is not dependent on Amativeness, which is a separate faculty of the head. This mating instinct is developed in such animals as lions, eagles, geese, and robins, which select mates and remain faithful through life; whereas horses, sheep, and cattle associate promiscuously.

People with deficient Conjugality look on marriage as bondage and slavery, but those who have it developed cherish their mates and provide for their family nests with love and affection.

Excess: Excessive attachment and dependence on one person.

Deficiency: No stability in marriage. No lasting union.

PHILOPROGENITIVENESS (2)

Location: This organ is located above the center of the cerebellum, about one inch above the occipital protuberance.

Function: The primary function of this organ is to impart feelings of love, affection, protectiveness, and provision for the young, and particularly one's own children. The natural language of this organ is soft, tender, and endearing, especially toward the weak, deformed, feeble and delicate. Often the children of other people are adopted, or there is fondness for pets and animals in general.

Harriet Beecher Stowe
Abolitionist, author

Excess: Overindulgence of children.

Deficiency: Neglect or disregard for children and animals.

Remarks: Parental love and ideality give one a strong sweet tooth; the candy appetite may be indulged.

FRIENDSHIP (3)

Louie Armstrong
Jazz musician

Location: At the posterior edge of the parietal bone on each side of Inhabitiveness and slightly above Parental Love.

Function: This is the basis of the social urge, an enjoyment of company and friends and a desire to exchange and indulge in friendly feelings. The organ has its effects in all phases of life and is indispensable in business pursuits. It is the basis of lodges, fraternal societies, clubs, church organizations, and other social gatherings. Its presence usually produces a warm, firm handshake. It has been noted that when dogs want to show attachment to their masters they will rub their heads at the location of this organ, against their masters.

Excess: Too great a fondness for social life; friendly without discrimination, leading to attachment to bad company or the unworthy.

Deficiency: The reclusive tendency; a desire to be alone as a hermit.

INHABITIVENESS (4)

John McCormach
Irish tenor

Location: At the backhead between Parental Love and Continuity.

Function: This organ provides attachment to and love of home and country—"there's no place like home" feeling. A love of one's country and birthplace and a desire for a permanent home come from this organ.

Excess: Any absence from home results in homesickness. An exclusive attachment to one's native place and no desire to travel.

Deficiency: Wanderlust and neglect of the home.

CONTINUITY (5)

Location: When large, the head is full below Self-Esteem; if lacking, a noticeable depression will be seen.

Function: This organ is primarily responsible for keeping the other faculties concentrated on a single subject until it is solved or completed. It gives concentration, application, unity, and completeness to mental operations. In a sense, it gives power over the distractions of the other Faculties while the mind must be held intensely on one subject.

Charles William Eliot
Educator

Excess: Prolixity, "beating a dead horse."

Deficiency: A superficial approach, excessive love of variety, lack of thoroughness.

VITATIVENESS (E)

Location: This organ is situated directly behind the ear and in front of Amativeness.

Function: Love of existence; tenacity for life; resistance to death, disease, and old age; great vitality. "All that man hath will he give for his life."

Excess: Great fear of death.

Deficiency: Yields to disease and death with little struggle.

Pete Rose
Professional baseball player

COMBATIVENESS (6)

John L. Lewis
Union organizer

Location: Combativeness is located directly above and behind the ears. It gives breadth to the head at that point.

Function: Regardless of this organ's name, it is not primarily a fighting faculty. It provides the will to overcome obstacles and resist oppression; it promotes self-protection, defiance, boldness, and bravery. It allows us to push and drive forward to our goal.

Excess: A quarrelsome and contentious personality.

Deficiency: A lack of force and courage.

DESTRUCTIVENESS (7)

Chiricahua
Apache brave

Location: It is situated immediately above the ear and gives prominence to the skull at that point. When developed, it is responsible for what we call a wide head.

Function: It was this faculty of the pioneers that was responsible for pushing back the forest, felling trees, starting new settlements, and bringing civilization into the wilderness. It imparts energy and executiveness to remove or destroy whatever is not beneficial to our welfare. It is given for self-preservation and to endure and inflict pain as, for example, in a surgical operation or in hunting for food. It permits us to take life to defend our own, to tunnel mountains, blast rocks, or face the storm. It is a beneficial faculty unless perverted.

Excess: Delight in destruction, cruelty, revenge.

Deficiency: Inefficiency, lack of executive ability, easily defeated.

ALIMENTIVENESS AND BIBATIVENESS (8)

James Beard
Gourmet chef

Location: Alimentiveness is situated directly in front of the upper part of the ear and occupies approximately 1 to 1½ inches, although that may vary. Bibativeness is situated between Alimentiveness and Calculation.

Function: The action of Alimentiveness is to create an appetite and the sensation of hunger. When not perverted, this Faculty is a safe guide for the selection and quantity of food we need. Bibativeness creates the sensation of thirst, desire for liquids, sauces, gravies, and drinks of all sorts. These organs should be large on gourmets and chefs. Swimming, washing, bathing, and love of boats are also shown.

Excess: Gluttony and drunkenness.

Deficiency: Lack of appetite and indifference to food, resulting in frail body.

Remarks: Strong Alimentiveness and Amativeness contribute to fat production in the body. Bibativeness is also the faculty of the eliminative functions. When low, the subject may suffer from blood diseases—diseases caused by gases, ferments, and yeasty substances in the blood causing autointoxication—bloating, diabetes, Bright's disease, liver ailments, and septic and toxic diseases. Weak Bibativeness may contribute to kidney ailments.

ACQUISITIVENESS (9)

Bernard Mannes Baruch
Financier and economist

Location: It is situated on the sidehead directly above Alimentiveness.

Function: It prompts us to store up or accumulate, to make provision for the future. It causes economy, frugality, and the saving disposition. It is found large in many professions and in collectors of coins, antiques, art, books, and so on.

Excess: Avarice and a grasping, close-fisted disposition; love of gain by any means, including dishonesty.

Deficiency: Prodigality and carelessness with possessions.

SECRETIVENESS (10)

Ho Chi Minh
Founder of Indo-Chinese
Communist Party

Location: It is situated at the inferior edge of the parietal bone directly above Destructiveness. When both organs are highly developed, it fills out and widens the sidehead above the ear.

Function: "A fool uttereth all his mind, but a wise man keepeth it till afterward." This organ gives self-restraint, reserve, cunning. It gives a sense of propriety as to when to speak and when not to speak, and the ability to hold a secret.

Excess: Cunning and deceptive ways.

Deficiency: Lack of tact, bluntness, inability to hold one's own private thoughts or those of others.

CAUTIOUSNESS (11)

Location: It is the next organ upward from Secretiveness in a line that goes from the opening of the ear to the organ of Self-Esteem on the Crown.

Function: The organ provides prudence, watchfulness, carefulness, self-protection, foresight, and avoidance of danger. It has a governing effect on all of the other faculties and prevents them from running to excess.

Excess: When too large and with only moderate Hope, it produces doubts, irresolution, indecision, unnecessary fear, excessive carefulness, and anxiety.

Deficiency: Recklessness and indiscretion.

George C. Marshall
Army officer, diplomat

APPROBATIVENESS (12)

Location: It is located on the upper and back part of the sidehead near the top and causes fullness and breadth at that point when the organ is large.

Function: This organ gives the desire for recognition, distinction, and praise. It causes one to be ambitious and acts to restrain selfish attitudes in order to please others. The good opinion of others, fame, eminence, and esteem are the motivations of this organ.

Excess: Self-praise, vanity, egotism, and a morbid oversensitivity to criticism.

Deficiency: Disregard for public opinion in such matters as manners, fashionable dress, and current attitudes.

Helena Rubinstein
Cosmetics tycoon

SELF-ESTEEM (13)

Friedrich Wilhelm Nietzche
Philosopher

Location: Situated at the back part of the top-head. When large and far upward and backward from the ear in that direction, it creates an upright and dignified carriage of the body.

Function: It inspires self-respect, dignity, pride of character, confidence, self-reliance and an aspiring and ruling disposition. It injects a tone of dignity and nobility into all of our actions.

Excess: Tyranny, egotism, arrogance, dogmatism, presumptuousness, and an insatiable love of power.

Deficiency: Excessive humility and a painful lack of self-confidence and self-reliance.

FIRMNESS (14)

Charles Robert Darwin
Naturalist (Theory of Evolution)

Location: On the top-head forward of Self-Esteem and almost directly on a vertical line drawn from the ear upward to the top-head.

Function: This organ imparts stability, decisiveness, and tenacity of will, as seen when one holds out till the end or sticks to it until accomplished. It manifests an aversion to change. Its influence seems directed to the other faculties; that is, coupled with Combativeness it produces determined bravery; with Veneration, sustained devotion; and with Conscientiousness, inflexible integrity.

Excess: Obstinacy, stubbornness, "mulish" resistance.

Deficiency: Fickleness, indecision, easily led.

HONESTY (15)

Location: At the posterior and lateral part of the coronal region, about three inches from the ear opening on the upper part of the parietal bone, below Firmness.

Function: This faculty grants us the perception of what is right and what it wrong. It is the great regulator of all of the other faculties and guides their expression. It adds a sense of accountability, honesty, regard for promises made, love of justice, truthful speech, sense of guilt, and moral strength. It makes a person appear earnest, sincere, and just.

Benjamin Harrison
23rd United States President

Excess: Too fault-finding and censorious; an uncalled-for sense of guilt and unworthiness.

Deficiency: Lack of moral principle, penitence, and circumspection.

HOPE (16)

Location: Situated on the side top-head on a perpendicular line drawn upward from the front part of the ear.

Function: Hope always anticipates the best, expects success, prevents depair. It helps prevent the failure of various projects, business or marriage. United with Approbativeness, it expects to rise to distinction; with Acquisitiveness it believes riches will come; with Spirituality it forms faith, trust, and belief in a future state and the goodness of God.

Pete Seeger
Songwriter, singer

Excess: Expectation that exceeds the realm of probability, unreasonable anticipation.

Deficiency: Despondency, worry, pessimism, and a lack of enterprise.

SPIRITUALITY (17)

Pope John Paul II

Location: In the lateral part of the anterior top-head below Veneration and above Ideality.

Function: This organ gives the intuitive knowledge of states of existence other than the material, the perception of spiritual things and other extrasensory perceptions, including immortality, God, and many unseen realities.

Excess: Superstition, fanaticism, and credulity to the point of being led astray by modern cults and religious fakes.

Deficiency: Tendency to operate solely on a material plane, skepticism, unimpressionability.

VENERATION (18)

Charles Kingsley
British clergyman and novelist

Location: Slightly forward of center in the coronal region, almost immediately above the junction of the frontal and anterior parietal bones.

Function: This faculty produces feelings of reverence, especially for religion and that which is held sacred. It grants devotion, adoration of a Supreme Being, and the disposition to pray and observe religious rites. But it does not form ideas concerning which objects to direct adoration toward.

Excess: Religious fanaticism and monomania, idolatry, undue deference, spiritual servility.

Deficiency: Lack of respect or reverence.

Remarks: Veneration makes one true to principles and family relations.

BENEVOLENCE (19)

Location: Directly foward of the parietal-frontal sutures and before the top-head turns to meet the forehead.

Function: Its office is that of kindness, sympathy, and the desire to relieve suffering and unhappiness. It is self-sacrificing, produces liberal sentiments toward human-kind, and dwells on their virtues rather than vices.

Excess: Giving and doing for others without discretion or guidance as to where it will do the most good, and without keeping enough for one's own needs, thereby losing the means for future benevolence.

Sir Moses Haim Montefiore
British Philanthropist

Deficiency: Lack of concern for fellow humans; with other signs, such as large Destructiveness and small Conscientiousness, it may show cruelty.

Remarks: Benevolence makes one equality-minded.

CONSTRUCTIVENESS (20)

Sir William Bragg
Physicist

Location: At the outer part of the frontal bone above the sphenotemporal sutures. When high, it gives breadth to the head above the zygomatic arch.

Function: People were made in the image of God. God creates and constructs the Universe in all its sublimity and magnificence. Constructiveness in people permits them to invent and produce shelter, machines of all sorts, instruments of all kinds, furniture, clothes, drawings, writing, engraving, sculpture, and so on. Constructiveness is given to some of the animal kingdom in a smaller way, such as birds, beavers, ants, and honey bees.

Excess: Attempting to invent impractical contrivances such as perpetual motion machines and similar devices. With low or deficient Conscientiousness it may be used dishonestly, such as in forgery, counterfeiting money, or similar endeavors.

Deficiency: Lack of skill and mental inventiveness.

IDEALITY (21)

Location: Along the temporal ridge of the frontal bone directly above Constructiveness.

Function: This organ elevates and refines the character; it grants a love of the beautiful, a sense of propriety and an appreciation of art, poetry, polish, and elegance.

Excess: A distaste for the mundane and everyday life; overfastidiousness.

Deficiency: Bluntness of manner, lack of taste, "rough around the edges."

Pete Seeger
Songwriter, singer

Remarks: Ideality desires perfection. Ideality and Amativeness give one a strong bathing instinct.

SUBLIMITY (B)

Location: On the sidehead, with Acquisitiveness below and Conscientiousness above. When large, it gives width to the upper and lateral portion of the head.

Function: Sublimity appreciates the vast and grand in nature, art, and literature. It rejoices in that which is startling, terrible, majestic, and sublime, such as the tornado, the cyclone at sea, the grandeur of the thunderstorm, mountain vistas, the clash of armies, and so forth. It is Ideality that recognizes the exquisite and beautiful, but Ideality and Sublimity cooperate in the artist and poet. Sublimity cooperates with Veneration and Spirituality in religious worship, the thought of eternity, and the concept of the vastness of God.

Pablo Casals
Cellist, conductor, composer

Excess: Extravagance, bombast, love of exaggeration.

Deficiency: Little interest in the magnificent, grand, or sublime.

IMITATION (22)

Location: On either side of Benevolence, just back of the hairline. When large, it tends to fill out and square off the top of the head as seen from the front.

Function: It produces an aptitude for copying or mimicking almost anything. The artist, mechanic, designer, actor, orator, and sculptor all need it large. It allows one to make patterns and imitate people or things.

Manfred B. Lee
Half the *Ellery Queen* writing team

Excess: A great tendency to imitate others.

Deficiency: Inability to conform with others.

MIRTHFULNESS (23)

Woody Allen
Comedian, author, filmmaker

Location: This organ is located at the corners of the forehead below the hairline and gives width, fullness, and squareness to that part when full.

Function: Laughter and the causes of laughter do not seem to exist in the lower animals to any great degree, and thus it is one of the distinguishing characteristics of humans. To laugh and be happy gives us great pleasure and is conducive to good mental and physical health. Mirthfulness enjoys the witty, the comical, the ludicrous, the incongruous, and the eccentric. Charlie Chaplin and Woody Allen have this faculty large.

Excess: Inappropriate humor and the so-called practical joke; making fun at the expense of others.

Deficiency: Lack of humor, too serious, too sober, too dry.

HUMAN NATURE (C)

William Shakespeare
English dramatist and poet

Location: It is situated directly on the median line of the forehead between Comparison and Benevolence.

Function: Highly developed, this organ furnishes us with an intuitive knowledge of the character, intentions, state of mind, and feelings of another. It allows us to adapt ourselves to them and even to operate on their feelings. It adds sagacity in dealing with others and was possessed large by North American Indians, Napoleon, and General U. S. Grant.

Excess: Too suspicious, too great a disposition to scan, pry, predict.

Deficiency: Inability to read motives and character of others.

AGREEABLENESS (D)

Location: Sometimes called Suavity, this organ is located in the area that is the first to lose hair in a receding hairline. It is near the corners and median line of the forehead.

Lee Harty
Maitre d'

Function: This organ gives the ability to win over others by pleasant manners and speech. It allows us to be persuasive and to put across our ideas without giving offense, to win friends easily and be welcome at social gatherings.

Excess: Affectation. It is seldom excessive.

Deficiency: Lack of agreeable behavior and a certain inflexibility in dealing with people.

INDIVIDUALITY (24)

Location: This organ is situated in the center of the lower part of the forehead immediately above the top of the nose. It gives projection and breadth between the eyebrows.

Che Guevara
Revolutionary

Function: It gives an immense delight in observing objects of all types without regard to their function, purpose, or character. This is the first organ in the perceptive group. It gathers material for the other faculties to analyze and classify. It gives the desire to see and examine; it gives form to all ideas entertained by the mind; and it tends to personify abstractions such as ignorance, wealth, wisdom, folly.

Excess: A great curiousity and inquisitiveness.

Deficiency: Failure to observe the things around us.

FORM (25)

Joe Frazier
World heavyweight champion

Location: At the internal corner of the orbit of the eye. When large, it gives breadth between the eyes.

Function: This faculty allows us to see and remember all of the peculiarities of objects. With the aid of Constructiveness it permits us to reproduce, make patterns, models, pictures, statues, and such, and it helps us to describe people, places, and objects seen. It disposes us to give shape to our ideas and concepts. It is essential to mechanics, builders, artists, architects, and, of course, phrenologists and character analysts. It is also useful in reading, spelling, and memorizing and gives assistance in balancing.

Excess: (No negative implications exist for an excess of this faculty.)

Deficiency: Inability to remember the shape, proportion, or form of an object.

SIZE (26)

Robert Broom
Paleontologist

Location: At the internal corner of the eyebrow on each side of Individuality.

Function: After Individuality recognizes an object, Size must determine the magnitude, proportion, length, breadth, height, and depth. It compares objects as to size and measures distances correctly by eye.

Excess: (No negative indications.)

Deficiency: Inability to make the judgments associated with this organ.

WEIGHT (27)

Location: The organ of Weight is located directly over the inner edge of the iris, next to Size, on the eyebrow.

Function: This organ gives a perception of the laws of gravity, motion, and a sense of balance. It gives the ability to estimate the weight of objects. People who possess Individuality, Size, Weight, and Locality large are talented in the natural sciences, engineering, motion mechanics, and feats that require balance and agility such as skating and dancing.

Robert Broom
Paleontologist

Excess: No negative indications, except when it makes one prone to dangerous feats of balance.

Deficiency: Poor judgment of weight and balance.

COLOR (28)

Location: In the middle of the eyebrow immediately above the iris.

Function: This is the leading faculty in artists, milliners, dyers, weavers, designers, and many others whose vocations depend on a sense of color harmony, blending, and shading. It permits us to distinguish colors and gives great delight in the contemplation of them. It also permits good taste in their usage and combination.

Jean Sutherland Boggs
Director of Philadelphia
Museum of Art

Excess: (No negative implications.)

Deficiency: Insensibility to colors; color blindness.

ORDER (29)

Fredrick Gowland Hopkins
Biochemist

Location: Situated over the outer corner of the eye between Color and Calculation.

Function: We view order as the natural Law of the Universe, for we see order, system, and arrangement everywhere in nature. This faculty adds method and order to all we do and is a co-worker with the reflective faculties in the conception of system and classification.

Excess: Makes the subject painfully aware of disorder and drives them to constant neatness and fussiness about everything.

Deficiency: Slovenliness and the mayhem of disorder.

CALCULATION (30)

Albert Einstein
Physicist (Theory of Relativity)

Location: This organ is found at the outer angle of the eye and swells the frontal bone at that spot. At times it creates a hood or crest over the outer angle of the eyes at the extreme end of the eyebrows.

Function: This organ may be termed Estimation for it gives the ability to gauge or estimate whatever concerns unity and plurality. Mental arithmetic, comprehension of numbers, figures, groupings, and the recollection of numbers are given to this faculty.

Excess: (No negatives.)

Deficiency: The inability to comprehend and remember numbers.

LOCALITY (31)

Location: On the forehead over the inner corners of the eyebrows, above Size and Weight.

Function: It gives the memory of place, scenery, location, roads, and the position of objects. It creates a desire to travel and see the world, explore, voyage, rove.

Excess: The rover, the drifter.

Deficiency: No sense of direction; those who easily lose their way.

Dr. Konrad Adenauer
1st Chancellor of West Germany

EVENTUALITY (32)

Location: In the center of the forehead just above eyebrow level and Individuality.

Function: This is the storehouse of memory and receives its information from the senses. It imparts memory of facts, occurrences, events, and this history of oneself and others. It desires to know through experience and is fond of receiving information from the senses and other organs.

Excess: (No negatives.)

Deficiency: Inability to remember the details of what has happened, even in the recent past.

Sir Ronald Fisher
Geneticist and Statistician

TIME (33)

Sir William Bragg
Physicist

Location: On the forehead above the center of the eyebrow.

Function: The sense of duration and the passage of time. The memory of dates and of when and in what sequence events have occurred. It gives the ability to keep time in music, rhythmic sense, keep in step while walking, dancing ability and accuracy in sequential actions of all sorts.

Excess: (No negatives.)

Deficiency: Lack of regular habits, sense of time, and sense of rhythm.

TUNE (34)

Enrico Caruso
Italian tenor

Location: On the side of the forehead just above the outer corner of the eyebrow next out from Time. It enlarges the lateral parts of the forehead.

Function: This is the musical ingredient. It allows for the perception of melody and the harmony of sounds. It remembers and learns tunes. When coupled with Time it gives the perception of musical intervals. It also tunes us in to natural sounds and the sound of machinery. Many good mechanics and equipment operators can tell when their machines are running "right" by the sound they make.

Excess: (No negatives.)

Deficiency: No love or ability to appreciate sounds, music, or harmony.

LANGUAGE (35)

Location: Considered to be situated on the back part of the orbitary plates, which would cause the eyes to be prominent when the organ is large.

William Morris
English poet and artist

Function: This is the communication Faculty. It gives the ability to express oneself by the spoken or written word, good verbal memory, fluency of expression, and the capacity for learning languages and signs of all types. When not supported by a good intellect, the subject will babble on indefinitely to express a few ideas or no idea at all.

Excess: Talkativeness to the point of being tedious, rapid use of words, circumlocution.

Deficiency: Monosyllabic, hesitation in speaking.

Remarks: The appearance on the under eyelid of a sac or roll or of a swollen appearance is also a sign of strong Language. This is not the so-called dark circle under the eye, which is an indication of a health problem and not of Language. The indication itself has been disputed by Dr. Holmes Whittier Merton, who places the Faculty of Language on the side of the forehead near Tune. However, we have found prominent eyes to be a fairly reliable indication of this faculty.

CAUSALITY (36)

Charles Worthington
County prothonotary

Location: Situated in the upper fore-head on either side of Comparison, which occupies the center above Eventuality.

Function: This is the why and wherefore faculty. It gives perception of the cause-and-effect principle. It recognizes the general relations between objects and penetrates the way in which effects and their causes are linked. It produces originality, forethought, new thoughts, new ways of doing things. It plans, reasons, and adapts means to ends.

Excess: Can become too theoretical and lose practicality.

Deficiency: Lack of originality and the ability to reason from cause to effect.

COMPARISON (37)

Immanuel Kant
German Philosopher

Location: On the middle line of the fore-head, extending from just below the hair-line to about the center of the forehead.

Function: This is the analytical ability; it classifies, separates, compares, detects differences and resemblances, draws conclusions, and judges.

Excess: Criticism and fault-finding qualities, even nit-picking.

Deficiency: The inability to apply knowledge and perceive qualities of things.

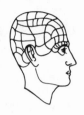

CHAPTER 8

BENHAM'S SEVEN TYPES

Scientific hand analysis is the most intricate and accurate method of character analysis that we know of. The developer of scientific hand analysis was Dr. William Benham. During fifty years of study, research, and development he separated fact from fortune-telling and put the information in organized form in his book *Scientific Hand Analysis*. This is the bible for any serious student of the hand.

Dr. Benham's seven types can be identified by their physical appearance or by seeing only the hand. Indeed, many combinations of the types can exist in one individual, and often it takes an examination of the hand to distinguish the primary, secondary, and tertiary influences of the types in one individual—and also to determine what influences are lacking. The seven types were known before Dr. Benham's time but were not so thoroughly delineated.

The seven types as represented by Dr. Benham are described as they appear in the caucasian race. At the time and in the locality in which Dr. Benham worked and taught, the other races had not achieved their rightful place as equal brothers and sisters in a great nation. His work and experience did not bring him into contact with other races.

Since then, we have had the opportunity to include the darker-skinned races in our observations and have found the types well represented in oriental, black, and brown races, and the universal pattern of the seven types can be applied to them in terms of character, health, and vocation. Individual facial features and brain faculties will give you the variations from the pure types. In the physical descriptions of the types given, you will note that skin, hair and eye color refer basically to whites, since the terminology comes directly from Benham's original work. These are the only three aspects that cannot be applied universally. All other physical characteristics apply within the limits of racial structure.

The reader should understand that when the type is referred to as "pink," "red," "white," or "yellow," these are colors that can be seen tinting the skin, ears, nails, and palms of light skinned peoples. However, the real significance of these colors is in their influence on the types: pink types are spontaneous, warm and genial; red types tend to excess; white types are more controlled and more emotionally cold; and yellow types are moody, despondent and occasionally criminal. Just as the word "Jupiter" should evoke an image of certain qualities, abilities, characteristics and appearance, so also should the word "white" evoke an image of the absence of human warmth. It is possible to have a black Lunarian and still consider their color to be white in terms of blood supply and emotions and health. Always remember, too, that "color" is another type tendency and that not all individuals of a type will necessarily partake of that tendency.

Dr. Benham worked basically with the hand and was not knowledgeable in diagnosis from the head and features. However, he did recognize and describe for us the physical appearance of the pure types. This information, coupled with what we know from preceding chapters, will enable you to identify and read the seven types. As you progress, you also will begin to identify the combinations of the types.

You will notice that the seven types have planetary names. Those readers knowledgeable in astrology should readily see the relationship between the seven types and their planetary counterparts. I will not attempt to correlate the planetary names since astrology is not my field of expertise. Dr. Benham used the planetary names because of their early association with palmistry and because the names Jupiter, Luna, Mars, and so on will, after constant use, evoke an immediate memory of that type and what it stands for. In that vein, it would be just as easy to name the seven types the Leader, the Fighter, the Artist, etc. However, those titles do not present a complete picture of the type in question. That is my reason for retaining the traditional names. Perhaps it would give more credibility to these observations of character if we developed scientific names for them, but the planetary names will be easy for you to remember and will not make your observations less valid.

It must be remembered at all times that the following descriptions refer to people as types and not to any particular individual. Although people within a type are all subject to these tendencies, no individual has them all. Every person can and should rise above the level of his or her own type. It also should be noted that specific facial characteristics, secondary type characteristics, and other factors can soften some of the severe types or increase the power of the more subdued types. Apply your understanding of human nature to the types, and you will achieve an excellent understanding of your client. All of the seven types have both men and women in their ranks. For the purposes of fluidity, I have used a masculine or feminine pronoun in the following outlines, as appropriate.

JUPITER

You will know the Jupiterian by his noble bearing and dignified presence. You will feel and sense that here is a person you can trust, who will stand by his word and take charge of the situation. Jupiterians are generous and caring. They recognize the Creator in their fellow man and always appeal to the best part of us. If he (or she) is not a member of the clergy, then at least we must call him a spiritual person. At some point in a Jupiterian's life he will identify with his God.

Whatever sphere the Jupiterian occupies in life, he is always a leader or rapidly rises to a position of leadership. He is ambitious, but fortunately with a strong sense of responsibility and honor. He must sincerely believe in what he is doing, and if he does, there is little that can stand in his way. The Jupiterian has a strong ability for organization, has a strong and persuasive speaking voice, and takes a deep interest in foods as one of his primary vocations. Figure 23 on page 112 will provide you with some examples of Jupiterian people.

Jupiterians have no real weaknesses. Their weaknesses, if they can be called that, are mostly a result of the overdevelopment of their strengths. They may become too proud, overdominant, too ambitious, or they may overindulge their appetites. As you study the outline that follows, you will build a firm picture of the Jupiterian type and their attributes.

APPEARANCE

Temperamental Combinations: Vital, Vital-Muscular

Head: Wide head denoting the presence of Destructiveness, Alimentiveness and Bibativeness, and frequently Acquisitiveness. Also high in the Crown area, especially in Self-Esteem and Approbativeness, which adds pride and ambition to the character. The backhead and Moral sections are also high, especially in the area of Benevolence and Veneration.

Vincent de Finis
head of hotel catering service

Carol Gruber
promoter for music fair

Average Grade Jupiterian
using talents in the food
industry

Joe Gentile
President of restaurant

Figure 23. The Jupiterian. These illustrations provide us with good examples of this type, engaged in vocations that are typical of Jupiterians. The keywords for Jupiter are ambition, leadership, spiritual thrust, honor, and dignity.

Face: The skin of the face is usually clear, smooth, and fine in quality. The color is healthy-looking. The eyes are large and expressive and have an honest, kind, and mild look. The upper eyelids are thick and swollen in appearance, with long curled lashes. The eyebrows are arched, with the hair growing evenly. The nose tends to be large, straight, and well formed. The mouth is somewhat large with full lips. The upper lip projects over the lower and is slightly larger. This is partially due to the position of the teeth. The two front teeth are longer than the rest, resulting in an overbite. The cheeks are well rounded, and the cheekbones are not visible. The chin is long and firm with a dimple in it. The ears are regular and well formed, lying close to the head. The neck is thick and strong and of medium length. The hair is brown to chestnut, wavy, abundant, and fine in quality, especially in women of this type. The Jupiterian male grows bald early in life, partially because of his eating habits and because he perspires freely during exertion, especially on the top of his head. The Humanitarian mouth bracket will be seen full between the parentheses of the mouth, with the parentheses themselves being well marked, as this is a sign of Dignity. The lower cheeks and jaw area are also full, denoting executive ability.

Color: This is a spontaneous type, and the natural color is pink. Pink will be seen tinting the skin, the nails, and the palm of the hand. The Pink types are always better suited to work with the public.

Body Structure: He is of medium height and inclined to be heavy, but his flesh is solid rather than fat and spongy. He has broad shoulders and a well-developed chest that helps give his voice a rich tone that can command, influence others, speak in public or sing. He has large, strong bones, and shapely strong legs.

Walk and Stance: The Jupiterian walks with authority and dignity and is inclined to come down firmly on his heels. His walk, posture, stance, and appearance inspire confidence in others. He walks and stands as a prince and a leader, full of self-confidence, pride, and dignity.

CHARACTER TRAITS

Ambition: Ambition and self-motivation characterize the type through the entire range of quality, from coarse to fine. Ambition pushes him and urges him on to the higher positions in his business or profession, regardless of the obstacles that must be overcome. Divine discontent urges Jupiter on to greater and greater achievement.

Leadership: This is a warm type that keeps his friends and becomes a favorite of all classes. Because he is well liked and respected, he is often pushed into or offered desirable positions. His strong speaking voice, dignified appearance, and desirable qualities strengthen the confidence of his fellow man. He has a strong influence on others and tends to mold and control their opinions. He may brag and bluster a bit through vanity, but basically he is kind, warm-hearted, and a real humanitarian. He takes an interest in how people get by, how they live, how they manage on their income, and how they get along together. He is the champion of the underdog and speaks out for their cause. He prefers to make his own mistakes, and rather than rely on the advice of others he relies on his own judgment.

Spiritual thrust: Jupiter is one of the basic religious types. He salutes the Godhead in his fellow man and is especially cognizant of God when he views the magnificence of the Maker in Nature. He also has a strong love of nature, flowers, and all growing things. He has a fondness for dogs and horses.

Pride: In the proper amounts, Pride is a good quality to have. It gives one a sense of self-worth and makes on want to do his best. It makes Jupiter anxious to succeed and realize ambitions; it spurs him on to greater effort and brings out his strength. Pride can be too strong in the type, in which case it will become an interference leading to excessive vanity and a view of oneself that is beyond actual capabilities.

Honor: This is a well-marked characteristic that extends through the complete range of the type from coarse to fine. He is a confidant who can be trusted and relied on. It is because of this that he is qualified to be in charge of large sums of money and important secrets.

Dignity: Dignity fits the type well with his strength of character, fine appearance, size, and the positions he attains. He is aristocratic and conservative.

Organizing Ability: He can organize himself, his affairs, his business, social groups, and those around him. He is the consummate organizer.

Politics: Although this is more properly a vocation and not a character trait, it is a natural outgrowth of his other qualities. He is an aristocrat and independent, but his sense of fairness often leads him to be a champion of the plain people, and that endears him to them. He fights for the underdog and the underprivileged, and this assists him in becoming a successful politician. His leadership qualities, fine physical appearance, excellent speaking voice, strong ambition, honor, and benevolence all stamp him as a natural politician. Whatever his grade, he is always a vote-getter and a capable political boss. Ambition prompts him to seek high offices, which he fills to the credit of himself and his party.

MARRIAGE

He is a pink, spontaneous type and does best when mated with one of the other spontaneous types, such as Apollo, Venus, or Jupiter. He must be able to exhibit high pride in his mate and family. She should possess a commanding presence, physical beauty, charm of manner, and intelligence. He usually prefers to marry one of his own type or a Venusian, as these types embody more of the qualities he admires than any of the others. If his mate should become careless of her appearance or character, his pride is wounded; however, because of his pride he seldom enters the divorce court. He cannot admit defeat or failure. His sense of honor makes him live up to an agreement or contract once it has been entered into.

HEALTH

This is a vigorous individual with a large frame and a great deal of energy. Because of this, he requires a considerable amount of food, which he enjoys and consumes in immense quantities. As a result of this overindulgence he suffers from a disordered stomach. Indigestion and other defects (such as gout, eczema, and skin rashes) that come from overly rich and acidic foods will affect him if his tendency is not controlled. Jupiter's big chest sometimes contains rather weak lungs, and respiratory problems are an additional problem. Pneumonia, flu, allergies, tuberculosis, and emphysema are sometimes experienced. Some of these defects come from Jupiter's habit of indulging in drinking, eating, and smoking to excess. Jupiter is also prone to high blood pressure and stroke.

VOCATIONS

Religious Field: His natural spiritual thrust and love for humanity assist him here; **Drama:** A commanding presence and good speaking voice give him excellent stage abilities; **Politics:** (mentioned above); **Social Work:** He is the basic humanitarian type, sharing this quality only with the Venusians, interested in how others get along and giving in such a way that the recipient is not belittled; **Sales:** He has contact and sales ability, cementing others to him and thus building a fine, well-paying clientele. Because of his ambition and organizational abilities he soon becomes the sales executive; **Foods:** As a gourmet, all businesses that have their roots in food are his forte—chef, salesman of food products, food demonstrator, restaurateur. His understanding and appreciation of food make him well adapted to these vocations; **Beauty Culture:** Women of this type are especially gifted in this area. They can excel as cosmeticians, hairdressers, or models because of their perfect skin pigmentation and luxurious hair. Also, their fine figures, firm flesh, and natural sales ability assist them in the area of foundation garment sales.

Other vocations include the military, public speaking, executive positions, the professions, journalism, diplomacy and public contact.

BAD SIDE

It is unfortunate that we cannot have all good Jupiterians, for the world would be made a better place to live in if it were so. In the bad grade we find that the appearance is changed, and in place of the noble and commanding presence we have an undersized man. The eyes are lacking kindness; the skin is bad and lacks a healthy glow. The hair is straight and stiff, the nose is poorly shaped, and the mouth is very large, full, and sensual with long dark teeth. This negative Jupiterian retains his love of command but lacks the power and ability to enforce it except on the weak and those unable to resist him. He is a tyrant and despot who can abuse his family and make them miserable by his overbearing pettiness. He is grossly extravagant but only to satisfy his own pleasures and appetites. He is selfish and a sensualist, and debauchee. His family is subjected to many indignities and forced to submit to his tyrannical will. He is unsuccessful in life. His desire to rule is constantly thwarted, so he turns to drinking and debauchery, making himself a further burden on his family.

REMARKS

Jupiter has a kindly, generous, and charitable nature. He tends to be extravagant. He makes large sums of money but does not hoard it. He likes the best in all things and is very fond of lavish ritual. The Jupiterian type is a force for good in this world.

SATURN

If the wife of a Saturnian were to drag him to a party, he would be the tall, lanky one with the somber face, nursing his drink in the corner or thumbing through the host's library. The Saturnian is not a mixer. His very presence brings a note of seriousness to any gathering. He is born with the desire to know, and within the limits of his inquiry, there is no end to his seeking. He penetrates his subject deeper and deeper until his absorption becomes complete. To others, he seems to lead a bleak, colorless existence, but he is satisfying the hunger of his soul in a wonderful realm of knowledge and internal experiences.

In extreme cases, the Saturnian can become antisocial, a hermit, a rebel against society, a true loner, even a criminal or twisted mass-murderer.

The Saturnian subject is easy to recognize but difficult to comprehend. His feelings are deep, profound, serious, and somber. There is never a frivolous moment in the life of a Saturnian.

Figure 24 on page 118 provides us with a page of Saturnian faces. Can you honestly say that there is a happy face among them? I do not want to mislead you into thinking that a Saturnian can never be happy. I have met many warm and generous Saturnians, but I have never met a frivolous one! Dr. Benham emphasizes in his introduction that the plan of the seven types is divine in origin and that each type is necessary to carry on the work to make this world complete. The Saturnian was made to keep us from being too reckless and carefree. He brings us back to earth, lest we fly too high and scatter our energies in useless ways.

As you review the type outlines, you may recognize someone you know. My hope is that you will understand them better and send your love, which they so sorely need.

APPEARANCE

Temperamental Combinations: Motive, Motive-Mental, Mental-Motive.

Head: The head is long and rectangular in shape. The backhead is usually weak in the pure types. The frontal section is usually strong but can be found in all degrees of development. The Crown can be high or low. When low, it emphasizes the lack of self-confidence and the self-depreciating qualities of the type. When the Crown is high, there is more force and power in the character traits. The Perceptive

William Holmes McGuffey
Educator, author, lecturer

Anwar Sadat
Egyptian President and
Statesman

Igor Stravinsky
Composer

Henry David Thoreau
Writer, naturalist, strong moral
convictions

Negative Development Saturnian
convicted murderer

Figure 24. The Saturnian type. Here we see the typically long face and serious expression of this type. Their beliefs, their vocations, and the manner in which they lead their lives clearly point out their Saturnian natures.

region and Intellect are usually pronounced. In some of the highest specimens, such as Abraham Lincoln, we will find Benevolence and the Moral region developed.

Face: The hair of this type is typically black, straight, and lank. The Saturnian male loses it when quite young, adding baldness to his other unattractive qualities. Light hair can be found on Saturnians, in which case it will modify the melancholy of the type to some degree. The face is long and harsh, what we commonly refer to as hatchet-shaped. It is thin, making the cheekbones prominent and high. The skin is yellowish or saffron-colored and drawn tightly over the skull and bones. The cheeks themselves are sunken, with the skin frequently flabby and wrinkled or marked with one or more deep crevices. The eyebrows are thick, dark, and stiff. They turn up at the outer corners of the eye and grow together over the nose, looking like one long eyebrow. The eyes are deep set, showing the inability to communicate. They are dark in color with a sad, melancholy, or severe expression. Because of his biliousness, the whites of the eyes are tinged with yellow. The nose is long, thin, and pointed, bending down like a beak over the lips at times. The nostrils are large but closed and inflexible; they do not seem to dilate as he breathes. The mouth is frequently large, but the lips are thin and pale, with the lower lip more prominent and firmly set. The teeth are long and white in youth, but they are soft and so they decay early. The gums are not healthy; they look pale, sickly, and bloodless. The chin is prominent, large, and tends to project forward. If he has a beard, it is dark, stiff, and straight, growing thick on the chin and lip but very sparsely on the cheeks. The neck is long and lean, with the cords and Adam's apple prominent and the blue veins very visible.

Color: The distinctive color of Saturn is yellow. Yellow tinges his skin pigmentation, the palms of his hands, the nails, and the whites of his eyes. Yellow is caused by bile and toxins in the bloodstream. It causes moodiness, irritability, repression, and possibly criminality.

Body Structure: The typical Saturnian is tall, gaunt, and thin. He has rough, dry, wrinkled skin that is tinged with yellow. It will hang in flabby folds or be drawn tightly over the bones. His chest is thin from front to back, tending to crowd his lungs and make the voice coming through his thin lips harsh and unpleasant. His shoulders have a noticeable stoop, and his long arms dangle lifelessly by his sides. His entire appearance looks unhealthy and poorly nourished.

Walk and Stance: Saturn stands and walks as if he had the weight of the world on his shoulders. He has no lively step but a shuffling gait with head down. His feet are large and awkward, and his mind is frequently on weighty matters so that he is often clumsy.

CHARACTER TRAITS

Balance Wheel: Saturn has an awareness of the tragic side of life. He slows down the spontaneity and steadies the other types. He is a repressing influence that keeps the other types from going too fast and being too reckless. His physical appearance and attitude make him the balance wheel of humanity.

Soberness: Saturn is a cynic who looks upon life as a series of sad and unpleasant experiences. His face rarely lights up with a smile or warmth. He does not engage in frivolous and light joking conversation with his fellow man. His recreations are found in his studies. He retires himself rather than advancing himself. He has that indrawn personality that psychologists refer to as introverted. He sees the serious, the ironic, the depressing, and the darker side of life. All of this weighs heavy on him and has a sobering influence.

Sadness: Sadness tinges his every activity. His writings, his humor, his musical compositions are all expressive of his sadness. There is little of joy, exuberant spirits, lightheartedness, or gladness about him in his gloomy thoughts, sad eyes, repressed walk and feelings.

Superstition: Saturn is often a victim of superstition. He is inherently a mystic who is intrigued by all of the mysterious forces of nature, the occult, the compounding of drugs and chemicals, the miracles and other religious mysteries, the abstract and the supernatural. He fears death and observes the superstitions that are intended to delay a visit from the grim reaper. When the balance wheel qualities are lost in Saturn, he becomes a hopeless victim of superstition.

Wisdom: In whatever realm Saturn is found, he brings knowledge to bear on the subject at hand. When you see a Saturnian you should think of STAR: Student, teacher, analyst, researcher. He can lose himself in his textbooks, his test tubes, his investigations, theories, creations, and scientific studies. He can teach in any of the fields in which he has ability, and he can write on these subjects as well. He is slow but a patient and indefatigable worker.

Prudence, Caution: This fits the Saturn disposition. He is suspicious of other people—their motives, their honesty, their loyalty. He does not like to go into business enterprises with them. He would rather invest in less risky enterprises such as real estate, farms, and buildings. The stock market and mercantile businesses are too much of a gamble. He is very conservative and does not rush into anything. He builds endless mental bridges by asking himself "what if . . ." In this way he conceives of every angle and possible variation before making a decision. His prudence also makes him save everything, and at times he becomes miserly and stingy.

MARRIAGE

His yellow color gives us the key to his attitude toward marriage. His physical heat is below par, and so there is little attraction to the opposite sex. He inclines toward coldness and biliousness, and sexual magnetism plays a very minor role in his affairs. He prefers to live by himself so as not to be interrupted in his studies. He avoids social gatherings and contact with other people as much as possible. However, Saturn does marry, and many times he makes a sad mistake in so doing. He is naturally atracted to his opposite, the Venusian woman. She has everything that he lacks: magnetism, personal charm, radiant health, friends, and popularity. He reaches out for her love and warmth, whereas she admires his seriousness and knowledge and academic degrees. After they marry, they do not change their basic natures. He wants to be alone, and she wants friends in to enjoy social life. She loves attractive clothes, and he cares nothing for personal appearance. Marriages does not change her Venusian joy for love and life, nor does it change his cold, undemonstrative qualities, and so they drift apart.

If Saturn is well matched with, for example, a Saturn-Venus combination, then he stays mated for life. As if to attract what he fears, he usually has a large family. He is a strict disciplinarian but will provide for his family to the best of his ability.

HEALTH

His yellow color comes from the malfunctioning of the liver. This is an inherent defect that brings on many of his other health problems. The biliousness makes him exceedingly nervous. In extreme cases paralysis is the result; it usually affects him from the hips down. The extent of his nervousness can be detected in his nails, which develop flutes and ridges, becoming brittle and turning back at the ends. Sometimes they become flat, showing nervous exhaustion.

Rheumatism also affects him, along with other hazards to the bones and joints. Back problems, hemorrhoids, and varicose veins can be problems with him. His hearing can be defective, and in some cases deafness is the result.

He is accident prone, especially with problems to the ears, legs and bones. Sometimes he is preoccupied to the point of not paying attention. Older writers on the subject stated that Saturn was prone to accidents in forests and caves because of his solitary existence.

Of all his potential health problems, he is most prone to mental quirks. He falls victim to self-pity, extremes of dejection, morbidness, and melancholia. He retires and isolates himself rather than advancing himself. He is under the influence of the suicidal pull and commits suicide as a solution to this problems. Luna is the other type in the human family that is under the suicidal influence. Jupiter and Mars will drink their problems away. Venus and Apollo seldom take such a serious view of life.

VOCATIONS

Saturn is a profound student. His physical appearance does not make him feel at ease with other people, and so he is happier with his books, instruments, and test tubes. It is for this reason that he becomes proficient in many areas that invoke deep thought and serious consideration.

Earth Sciences: He prefers the country to social life and has a natural aptitude for things having to do with nature. All growing things and all of the contents of the earth, such as oil, minerals, rocks, precious jewels, coal, are under his realm of investigation. All the fields of agriculture, agronomy, soil management, animal husbandry, fertilizers, dairy products, insecticides, feed, seed, floral culture, reforestation, flood and drought control, drainage, milling, irrigation, surveying, tree surgery, landscape work, sewage, and sanitation are but a few of the many vocations that have their roots in the Saturnian type.

Science: He is a true scientist. Saturn can study, teach and apply all of the sciences mentioned above. He can research them and write on them as well. This applies to all the sciences: astronomy, geology, chemistry, medicine, nuclear physics, computer sciences, and engineering, to name a few.

He does excellent research work in biology, medicine, pathology, psychology, and the develoment of medicinal remedies and medical products. Saturn can train and serve in all of these areas if he gets the proper technical education. He is an excellent student; however, he is also freedom-loving and rebellious. Young Saturnians must be guided carefully or they rebel against school, teachers, and parents.

Engineering: This type has a technical mind and is a natural mechanic and machinist. With wide wings to his nose and low-set thumbs he will also have the hand skills to do precision work. Civil engineering, chemical, aeronautic, mechanical, electrical, automotive, and mining engineering fields are all open to this type, who has an instinctive knowledge of what makes the wheels go round. Radio, television, telephone, heating, ventilation, and air conditioning are all in Saturn's realm.

Occult fields: He is intrigued with whatever is mysterious and has an investigative and inquiring mind. He delves deeply into subjects such as ESP, clairvoyance, clairaudience, precognition, hypnosis, mesmerism, spiritualism, astrology, hand analysis, numerology, phrenology, and all branches of psychic phenomena.

Psy fields: Fields such as psychology, psychoanalysis, psychiatry, and psychosomatic medicine are also the haunts of the Saturnian. He can teach, write about, or do research on any of these subjects and any other subjects that are in his realm. In lower grades he can work in asylums and with mental patients in other institutions.

Teaching: Saturn is our basic teacher of the human family. In whatever field he engages in, *he brings knowledge to bear on the subject.* He is the student, teacher, analyst, and researcher and can pass on his knowledge to any who are willing to learn. He may seem dull and unexciting in the social realm, but he is factual and profound as a teacher. He is technical, thorough, and painstaking and can teach a wide variety of subjects but especially science, math, religion, psychology, and all of the other fields for which he has special aptitude.

Writing: He is an introvert and expresses himself more easily on paper than in speech. He is the researcher and analyst, and he is of the type that writes all the textbooks in the world.

Theater: Strange as it may seem, Saturn makes our best comedian. His sense of irony and sarcasm, his gawky, clumsy, and humorous appearance can be turned to profit in the field of comedy. At times his humor is biting and serious, as in the case of Lenny Bruce, or tragic and pitiful, as in the case of Emmett Kelly.

With the addition of some of the other types in his character he can play many other roles. He is often seen in many serious roles that fit him well. He is seen in horror movies or as the heavy in other stories.

Law: When Saturn studies law, he becomes a serious lawyer. He is not usually a trial lawyer; Mercury is the basic lawyer and much better at this. Saturn prepares the briefs and does the research and investigation.

Music: Here as elsewhere Saturn is the student, teacher, analyst, researcher. He studies music and is particularly attracted to cold and formal classical music or to the intellectual technicalities of jazz—the kind of music one must study and analyze to appreciate. He is particularly fond of the organ and the stringed instruments. Remember, he can write. In music that allows him to compose.

The three music types are Saturn, Venus, and Luna. A mixture of these types can produce exceptional musicians, composers, musicologists, instrument repairers and instrument makers, music teachers, music critics, or music researchers.

Music is close to math and science in many ways. This appeals to the Saturnian mind. When he works alone, he composes profound classics.

Religion: He investigates the various religions and cults. He is attracted to the miracles and other mysteries of religion. He is frequently attracted to cold, stern, and severe religions or to intellectual and philosophical religions.

Crime: His yellow color contributes to his attraction for crime. Bile has poisoned his bloodstream and clouded his mind. His picture is often found in the "wanted" posters at your local post office. Saturnians have engaged in every type of criminality from petty thievery to bank robbery and murder.

BAD SIDE

When we witness a Saturnian with coarse skin, skant and lifeless black hair, stooped shoulders, yellow, wrinkled skin, crossed eyes, and sapped vitality, we have a creature who is low, mean, jealous, and capable of hideous deeds. They can plan your death and then coldly execute murder while gloating over your death agonies. They are cold, solitary, selfish, and reserved. No more malevolent creature exists. They can be poisoners, mass-murderers, butchers, vipers, and fiends.

REMARKS

He is opinionated and does not like to be contradicted. He is independent and dislikes any restraint unless he imposes it upon himself—for instance, if he becomes a hermit and goes on long fasts.

Saturn in the finer grades can do remarkable work for humanity. Abraham Lincoln was a perfect Saturnian of a more evolved state.

Anwar Sadat and Kurt Waldheim are also high-grade Saturnians. It is interesting to note how much Sadat and Lincoln fall into the same pattern and how both were assassinated.

APOLLO

If you were at the same party where we earlier saw the tall, lean Saturnian, be prepared for quite a contrast in human types as the vivacious Apollonian enters the room with her Apollonian escort! She enters the room with a broad smile—you notice her teeth are strong and white, her mouth healthy and red. She is energetic— the life of the party. Her clothing is the latest thing, and her escort is equally dressed to the nines. As he talks to you, he makes you feel like an old friend. You would swear he is witty and intelligent and understands your business as if it were his own. Of course, they dance all night—they know the latest tunes and all the latest dances.

If you turn to Figure 25 on page 126, you will get a sense of the handsome figure presented by the Apollonian type. They appear to be models, and indeed many are just that. As you review the list of vocations, you will find them involved in many art-oriented careers. They predominate in the entertainment fields and anywhere a personable, congenial, and likable personality is needed—as in sales, diplomacy, or promotion.

The Apollonian has a free and easy attitude about life, coupled with extravagant tastes. They seldom take life as seriously as our Saturnian friend, yet they are subject to volcanic emotions that pass as quickly as they appear.

As you read through the type outline, you may begin to get the impression that beauty is only skin deep and that the Apollonian is superficial. Again I remind you that you may find individuals of this type who possess a depth uncommon to the type as a group. Always remember to apply all you know to see just how the features will upgrade or drag down the type qualities.

APPEARANCE

Temperamental Combinations: Mental-Muscular, somewhat harmonious; they are not big-boned but have a definite masculine head and body structure.

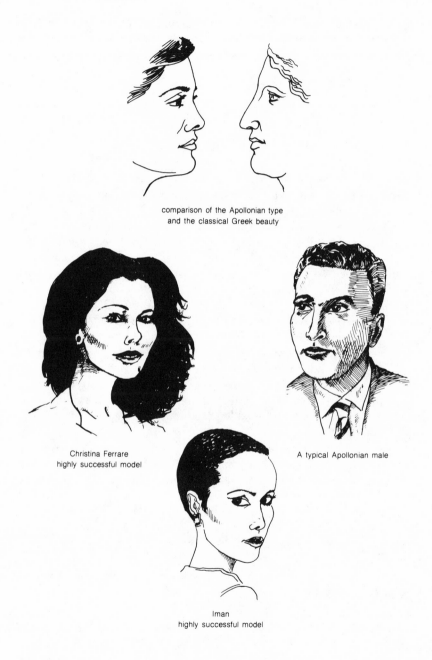

comparison of the Apollonian type
and the classical Greek beauty

Christina Ferrare
highly successful model

A typical Apollonian male

Iman
highly successful model

Figure 25. The Apollonian. If there is such a thing as "luck," it was given to the Apollonian type! Natural beauty, charm, artistic taste, and pleasing personality combine to attract success with ease.

Head: High in the Crown area, especially Approbativeness. The faculties of Form, Color, Language, Suavity, Tune, and Imitation are also well developed. The forehead is usually wider than it is high.

Face: The complexion of the Apollonian is clear, with a fine firm texture. It is white with rosy cheeks. The hair can be golden and flaxen, auburn, or black, but it is always fine and silky in quality and abundant and full in quantity. The forehead is broad and full but not high. His eyes are large and almond-shaped, with long lashes that curl up at the ends, making the eyes most attractive and appealing to look at while adding the Faculty of Language. The eyes have an honest and sincere expression that can arouse sympathy or sweetness when the emotions are in play. They sparkle with brilliancy and life, reflecting the brain that is behind them. The cheeks are firm, well-rounded, and fairly high set, with no pronounced hollow. The nose tends to be small but finely shaped. The nostrils are beautifully proportioned and dilate sensitively under the play of emotions. Frequently, the nose is slightly upturned so that the nostrils are visible from a frontal view of the Apollonian. This is a personality type and a fun-loving type, so the large nose of productivity is not found on a pure specimen. The mouth is fairly large but graceful in outline. The lips are full, curved, and evenly set but not excessively large. The teeth are white, even, and healthy-looking and are set in pink, healthy gums. The chin is shapely and rounded and protrudes slightly beyond the plane of the face. The ears are of medium size, well formed and pink. The neck is long and well shaped. It does not show a prominent Adam's apple nor the cordlike muscles at the sides of the neck.

Color: Pink is the natural color of Apollo. It is found tinting the cheeks, ears, fingernails, and palms of the hands. Apollo is a spontaneous type and usually healthy.

Body structure: The graceful neck is connected to an equally graceful and masculine pair of shoulders. The chest is full and expansive, which assists in purifying the blood and producing their pink color. The voice is musical but not full and resonant as Jupiter's is. The women also partake of the andromorphic body structure and do not have overly large bosoms, but they are shapely and proportionate. The lower limbs and buttocks are muscular, firm, graceful, and finely proportioned. They are never fat. The feet are of medium size with high arches. This aids them in spring and elasticity as they walk or dance.

Walk and stance: Apollo is the picture of health, beautiful proportions, grace, and symmetry of body. This is not affected or derived by conscious effort; to the Apollo it comes naturally. The walk is a distinguishing characteristic. When they walk, they have spring and elasticity in their step, making them appear happy, lithe, and graceful.

CHARACTER TRAITS

Brilliancy: To such a type as Apollo, with its natural grace, symmetry, and beautiful proportion we must link similar attributes of the mind and mental characteristics. The mind vibrates at a rapid rate, and these people can do more with a little knowledge than any of the other types. They are often brilliant, alert, quick—some are very superficial. They do not have to labor to learn, as the Saturnian does. They can grasp an idea intuitively and use it to their advantage. They are inventive as well as imitators. Their versatility allows them to use their knowledge in unique ways and they often get credit for knowing a great deal more than they actually do. They can adapt easily to people and circumstances. Without preparation they can surmise what is going on and astonish those present with their seemingly deep understanding of the subject; it matters not whether they are with scientists, doctors, lawyers, anarchists, philosophers, or any class or profession of people.

Artistic impulses: Apollonians are fascinated by beauty—in women, home furnishings, art, nature, or clothing. Anything that lacks beauty they find repulsive. They are artistic in eveything they do. Apollonians are not always painters, sculptors, or poets, but they appreciate, understand, and adore art in every form. At the very least they are dabblers or art critics—lovers of fine clothes, luxurious surroundings, jewels, and fine automobiles. With high quality, taste in these matters will be excellent. In low quality Apollonians, the taste becomes loud, garish and shoddy. They wear bright colors and too much loud, heavy jewelry, pendants, big bright rings and so forth.

Daring: At certain times we find the ring finger (the Apollo finger) to be almost as long as the Saturn or middle finger. A person with this formation is a plunger. This causes them to gamble and take chances. This instinct is not limited to cards and horses, but extends itself to business, marriage, and even life.

Apollonians are daring to begin with. They are the personality type and take many chances that frequently push and further their success. They advance quickly in this way with little actual effort.

Personality: When we say that Apollonians are the personality type, we mean that they get by and succeed by their personalities. They are handsome, dashing figures with the ability to mix and mingle easily. Personality, artistic ability, brilliance, dash, versatility, showmanship, and spontaneity combine to make them successful. Of all the types they are the most ingratiating. Ingratiating means "to win or secure a favorable reception for oneself," which the Apollonian does with natural ease.

They are the life of the party, the heros of the athletic field, the daring and successful plungers in the stock market, gold market, or roulette table. Even if they have but a thin dime in their pockets, they look like a million dollars. People are taken in by their successful appearance and are glad to give them what they want.

Basically, they are good people with good health. They are drawn to and feel kindly toward people, and manage to cope with them easily. The Apollonian has many friends, but tends to be changeable and not constant, and therefore has few real lasting friendships. Apollonian brilliance attracts and enslaves temporarily, but does not create a lasting friend and does not inspire true friendship in others. The Apollonian does not hold a grudge, and in the end can even win over his enemies.

Because of their brilliance, they are inclined to make enemies among those less endowed who are envious of Apollonian good fortune and ease. Despite this, they are generally well liked, and their interests are forwarded by many admirers. They attain good positions and are great moneymakers, although they are never economical. Their tastes are luxurious, and they spend freely to satisfy their tastes. They think in large sums of money and never consider the single dollars.

Showmanship: Apollo subjects are not afraid to speak out and make themselves heard. As a matter of fact, they love to be heard and seen. They have a great faculty for expression. They are not deep but are easily understood. They love to be in the public eye and have their approval. They desire celebrity, and they attain it. They are natural entertainers. They have a flair for doing things in a dramatic way, and they are one of the basic theater types.

Versatility: They are truly the jack-of-all-trades, and this can become a hindrance at times. They seem to grasp all things intuitively and can turn a mishap to an advantage. If they would only use a little more effort and depend less on luck, they could accomplish much more.

Among their many accomplishments they can become involved in business, religion, politics, and occult subjects. They grasp these subjects by intuition rather than deep study.

They love pleasure and gaiety, but they are not debauchees or sensualists when a high type. Apollonian men enjoy women for the beauty of their dress and the quality of their appearance rather than for baser reasons. They enjoy the banquet for its decorations, music, after-dinner wit, and companionship more than for the opportunity to stuff their faces. They do not fall into dissipation easily, but enjoy pleasure in any form when it is tasteful and with the proper accompaniments.

The type ranges from those who appreciate art and the beautiful in life to the true creative artist. (Creativity comes from Luna.) Many are dabblers in some form or art, but all exhibit their artistic taste in clothing, home decorations, jewelry, and general sense of style.

To Apollonians, success is natural. It comes with seeming ease just by the force of circumstance. People admire them and gladly forward their interests. They make money easily and are rarely criminal. If they do turn to crime because of a Saturnian influence, they are confidence men or crooked gamblers and use personality here as elsewhere.

MARRIAGE

The pink-handed Apollonian will want to mate with one of the other pink types, and will be attracted to the Jupiterians, Venusians, or his own type. He or she does not mate successfully with the colder types. Remember that Apollo loves the limelight, and so desires an attractive and presentable mate who will complement his public image; but because of strong ego he does not want his mate to shine more than he. This is the type of man or woman that the opposite sex desires because they have charm, beauty, and all the social graces; however, the Apollonian sweetheart may suddenly be attracted to someone more dramatic and scintillating. In this sense they are fickle. Apollonians have a poor track record as far as marriage is concerned. Many of the so-called Hollywood marriages are marriages between two Apollonians.

HEALTH

This is a naturally healthy type, and to this we may attribute much of their success. They are entirely free from bile and its irritating, depressing influence. This shows in their health, temper, and character for they are healthy, happy, and, even at their worst, not a criminal. They do not overeat and tax their stomachs. They do not drink too much and ruin their livers.

When health problems are present they frequently affect the heart, which is irregular and Apollo's most serious health defect.

Apollo is subject to weak eyes, color blindness, styes in the eyelids, and other eye problems. He is liable to sunstroke, fevers, and skin irritations from wind, sun, soaps, and cosmetics.

VOCATIONS

Remember that this type is endowed with a true and strong color sense when his eyesight is normal. This is the basis for almost all artistic fields, and many of his professions have their roots in the arts.

Artist: Oil painting, watercolor, and other color mediums; designer of clothes, home furnishings, textiles, interior decorations, millinery, rugs; decorator, graphic artist, illustrator, and on a lower place, house painter, bridge painter, etc. When Apollo is blended with Saturn, the engineer, we have the architect, architectural engineer, designer of beautiful cars, bridges, tunnels, arches, buildings.

Theater: This is the natural theater type. Their love of being in the limelight, their beautiful physical appearance, personality, and brilliance all equip them to appear before the public. They have natural dramatic ability but are more often found in the entertainment field where they can dance a little, sing a little, tell pleasant stories, and make a beautiful appearance. Jupiter gives true dramatic ability. Saturn can study and play heavy roles or comedy. Mercury is the character actor, and Apollo is the personality actor or entertainer. He or she is always a glamorous figure.

In radio and especially in television, we have a large number of Apollonians. If you watched television for an hour, you would see a large number of Apollo types in that time.

Diplomacy: Apollonians are so pleasing, so ingratiating, so easily adapted to other countries and peoples, and make friends so quickly that they are well placed in the realm of diplomacy. Of course, they must be of a high grade and should be supported by Mercurian characteristics. Apollos are the "diplomat par excellence," as Doctor Benham called them.

Business: This is the true sales personality. There are no better, smoother, and more natural salespeople in the world. They sell best if they sell things in harmony with their type endowments: art, luxury lines of jewelry, clothes, and automobiles (in sales, customer relations, and distribution).

Apollo is a glad-hander. They sell themselves and their place of business, so they really excel in the hotel business. In promotion, as an executive, or at the front desk they are equally at ease. They will extend hospitality and make each guest feel they are the most important. Also, selling sense, dramatic sense, and showmanship all help the Apollonian excel in the advertising field. In the business end of theater, radio, and television Apollonians also do well. Their dramatic sense and contact ability are assets here as elsewhere.

The Apollonian wears clothes like a model; in fact he or she is the model. Apollonians design, sketch, advertise, sell and promote clothes. They do everything except manufacture them. That is in the realm of Mercury. Observe the models in all the fashion magazines; they are almost all Apollo types.

Cosmetics is another art-associated field. It is a practical, commercial phase of art. The Apollo color sense and love of beauty, style, and fashion are put to use in this field. Remember Apollo's perfect skin texture and coloring, luxurious hair, well-shaped teeth, kissable lips, and attractive eyes. They are a walking advertisement for all cosmetic lines and grooming merchandise.

Window display is frequently one of the most highly paid fields of art. Apollo will put to use dramatic and artistic endowments in some of the topnotch department store windows in the country. Many have been artists and actors before turning to this field. Their sales sense, display sense, business and merchandise sense also assist in this field.

BAD SIDE

Lower-grade Apollonians are not as attractive as the higher grades. The features are more common, the body undersized, the hair and skin dingier, and sometimes the eyes will be crossed.

These individuals will be vain and boastful. They have a good opinion of themselves and their abilities. They are interested in notoriety; they crave it. They'll do almost anything to have people look at them and recognize them, but they have none of the taste of their higher brethren. They wear loud colors, gaudy jewelry, and exotic clothing. They are fond of show and display. They have all the extravagant taste of the type but without the brilliant means for making money; thus, they are improvident and poor.

They overestimate all their abilities and fancy themselves great actors or talented artists. When they are repulsed, they become hurt and bitter and think they got a bad deal—that everyone is conspiring against them. They stop at nothing to make themselves conspicuous and wind up looking quite foolish. But although unhappy and unsuccessful, they are never criminal if of a pure type.

REMARKS

Apollonians are found in many more vocations than we listed here. Remember, they are the jack-of-all-trades and often "the master of none." Too often they are dabblers and cannot concentrate their efforts. Salesmanship can assist them to sell insurance, stocks and bonds, futures, etc. Personality and contact ability can assist them in banking or other financial areas. As a matter of fact, at times they can secure ample loans based solely on wealthy appearance and personality.

MERCURY

As a type, the Mercurian is the most versatile, adaptable, shrewd, and financially successful member of our family of seven. He may be a scientist, doctor, merchant, inventor, lawyer, or metaphysician or be involved in a thousand and one businesses. Whatever he is involved in, from criminologist to criminal, he is always active, industrious, quick, inventive, and one step ahead of the competition. Whatever he is involved in, he turns it into a financial success. He may not have the fame and notoriety of the Apollonian, the power and control of the Jupiterian, but he always has the monetary rewards of his labors.

The Mercurian is as active and quick mentally as he is physically. His frame is on the small side because of the Mental Temperament influence, but his ideas and abilities make him a giant. You will never get the best of the deal when you "horse-trade" with a Mercurian. He is always one step ahead and can read you like an open book even if he never took a course in characterology!

Mercurians are devoted to their families and make loyal friends. Much of their untiring work is to provide their families with the best as they see it. Many Mercurians with secondary Venusian influences will teach in kindergarten or work with children in some way.

Albert Einstein
Physicist

Henry Kissinger
Diplomat

Paul Browning
Inventor

Dr. Frantz Halberg
Professor of medicine and
chronobiologist

Figure 26. The Mercurian. These types are an incredible force in whatever realm we find them. Typical Mercurian faces and vocations are illustrated here. From concert master to con man, no type is as versatile as the Mercurian.

Because they are generally small in stature, the children relate to them even more readily.

Look at the Mercurian types illustrated in Figure 26. If you give some thought to the life and career of Henry Kissinger, his phenomenal diplomacy in the Middle East, and the fact that he was one of the few survivors of the Nixon administration, you can grasp the incredible qualities that we call Mercurian.

APPEARANCE

Temperamental Combinations: Mental, Mental-Vital, Mental-Muscular.

Head: Sometimes pyriform or long-oval in shape. Most prominent are the reasoning faculties, also Language, Calculation, Imitation, Human Nature, Acquisitiveness, Parental Love, Inhabitiveness, Secretiveness, Cautiousness, Construction, Self-Esteem, and Continuity. Not all of these faculties are equally developed in all Mercurians.

Face: His face is oval in shape. The features tend to be regular. His expressions change rapidly because of the rapidity of his mental processes. His skin is smooth, fine and transparent, olive in color. Facial color ranges from red to white when he is excited, embarrassed, or in fear. His forehead is high and bulging at the Reasoning and Semi-Intellectual Faculties. The Perceptives are also in evidence. His hair is chestnut or black and curls on the ends. His beard grows easily and is generally darker than the hair, if it is any color other than black. (He likes his beard trimmed close and neat in appearance.) His eyebrows are not overly thick. They are regular in outline and run to fine points on the outer angles and lie over the eyes. His eyes are dark, restless, and sharp in expression. When he looks at you, it is as if he can see through you and read your mind and motives, as indeed he is capable of doing. A tinge of yellow is frequently seen in the whites of the eyes. His nose is thin and straight, sometimes fleshy on the end; or else he has the mercantile nose, large and full, with a high bridge and slight dip at Scrutiny in the tip. His nervousness causes him to breathe quickly and often through the mouth so that the lips are often a little apart. The lips are thin, evenly set, and frequently pale or bluish in color. They may droop slightly at the corners. The upper lip may be thicker and project forward a bit more than the lower lip. The teeth are small, white, evenly set in medium pink gums. The chin is long and pointed, sometimes turning up slightly at the end, which completes the oval contour of his face.

Color: He is the second bilious type. His skin is yellow or olive or honey-colored. Bile in the system usually leads to nervousness, stomach troubles, moods, and even criminality.

Body structure: The Mercurian is represented on the hand by the little finger. This is the shortest finger on the hand, and the type is also small in statute. They average about 5 feet 6 inches. They are compactly built, trim in appearance, and tidy-looking, with a strong and penetrating expression of countenance. The neck is fairly strong and muscular and is attached to shapely shoulders. The appearance is lithe, sinewy, and graceful in outline. The chest is large and well muscled for his size, and the lungs themselves are large. The voice is of medium timbre and has good carrying quality, but it is not exceptionally strong. The limbs are graceful and agile and permit the quickness of movement for which he is noted. Taken as a whole, the Mercurian presents an image of a well-proportioned, agile, strong, and shapely figure but not necessarily always one of beauty.

Walk and stance: The Mercurian is the quickest and most active of all the types, not only in physical movement and agility but in the mental strata also. He is proficient in games that require coordination of mind with dexterity and skill. At times, nervousness and the rapid flow of ideas will not permit him to sit still; however, when he moves with purpose he exhibits lithe, graceful, and direct motion.

If the Mercurian keeps his hands hidden, it should make you suspicious of his motives, for certain grades are criminal in nature and all are crafty, shrewd, and adroit.

CHARACTER TRAITS

Shrewdness: Mercury has many characteristics, some of which are good and some bad; and many can be used in either direction depending on the quality and what mental faculties are developed. Thus, he is a many-sided person. It is seldom that any of the other types can gain an advantage over him. He is inherently a schemer and is constantly laying plans in which he can gain the advantage over some other person. In the finer grades this characteristic does not take the form of dishonesty or unfair advantage, but the lower grades will stop at nothing. In the lower grades we find the common or petty thief, liars, swindlers, fortune-tellers, palmists, and devious businessmen. He can grasp an idea quickly and turn an opportunity in his favor, bringing him out ahead. He has keen powers of persuasiveness, oratorical abilities, tact, shrewdness, and adroit methods of approach. He understands human nature and can use his powers to get others to carry out his plans if it becomes necessary.

Industry: He is never lazy; consequently, he never loses an opportunity but seizes every moment and makes it count. Whether he is engaged in the most beneficial of occupations or in the lowest crime, he will work hard and tirelessly; he spares no effort for the successful outcome of his venture. He is constantly on the go and can accomplish what he sets out to do before his slower-moving brethren are aware that he has put one over on them.

Quickness: None can keep pace with him. Before you know what he is thinking, he has laid his plans, executed them, and is on his way to another field of operation. He is quick mentally as well as physically, and this characteristic extends through all of the grades. His intuitive faculty records in a flash, and he enjoys anything that puts his quickness to a mental or physical test. It is this same quickness that allows him to turn every opportunity to account and to have a rapid retort in conversation. He makes an excellent after-dinner speaker.

Oratory: The faculty of language is well developed in this type. He is fond of oratory and is eloquent in any area in which he has interest. It is power of oratory combined with his shrewdness that allows him to be very influential.

Intuition: He is an excellent judge of human nature. He mentally estimates everyone he meets and uses his quick mind and tactful way to make a friend and accomplish what he wishes. He is a clever manager of people because of his ability to understand them. Not only does he understand people, but he also has the ability to mimic them.

MARRIAGE

On the good side the Mecurian is not vicious or criminal, only shrewd and keen. He is even-tempered, and he loves children dearly. He is a devoted family man and a constant friend.

His pleasures are basically mental; he is not a sensualist. He is fond of beauty in women, but he is not an amorous type.

In the marriage relationship he is frequently a matchmaker. He marries fairly early in life, choosing a mate of his own age and frequently one of the same type. He admires neat, trim, and stylish women who are full of life and fire. Essentially, it is the Mercurian woman that fits this description. He is proud of his family and likes to see them well dressed, well fed, well educated. If he is of a good grade, he is an excellent provider. Many Mercurian women become heavy later in life, but this is never a cause for divorce with this type.

HEALTH

The Mercurian is of the Mental Temperament, which means that the nervous system predominates. His quickness and energy unmistakably show the great stimulation of the nervous system. This nervous energy prevents him from being lazy, and it makes him love to travel. Nervousness can become excessive and interfere with the action of the liver, causing him to become bilious. His liver trouble improves when the nervous trouble is relieved. Stomach trouble, dyspepsia, indigestion, and similar disorders plague him. In extreme cases he suffers from paralysis in his arms and upper extremities.

He is primarily a healthy type, and we do not look for illness as much as we look for peculiar mental characteristics.

VOCATIONS

Science: The Mercurian has a love of study, especially along scientific lines. He is the born mathematician and can solve the most intricate problem. He is more successful as a physician than any of the other types and is always a moneymaker in this profession as well as any other he engages in. Energy, studiousness, scientific aptitude, combined with an insight into human nature, make him an excellent diagnostician as well as practitioner. His scientific frame of mind causes him to realize the value of laboratory assistants, so he is a safe doctor to employ.

He does well in other areas of science also: biology, mathematics (Albert Einstein was a Mercurian and considered the greatest mathematician of our day), engineering, and the like.

Law: He is the basic legal worker. All of his characteristics assist him in this field. He is shrewd; he is an intuitive judge of character; he is keen and quick; and he can see through things readily. He takes his opponent off guard, and with his power of oratory he makes an excellent trial lawyer. He also makes an excellent criminal lawyer. (It takes a thief to catch a thief.) The same type produces the criminal as well as the criminal lawyer. The only difference is the grade or quality of the individual and the plane of operation. One is negative and destructive; the other is positive. Doctor, lawyer, merchant, thief—that is the Mercurian.

Writing: The Mercurian is fond of reading. He is not much attracted to romance; he prefers books that are true to life, nature, and humanity. He is an orator, but he can express himself equally well on paper. He can write on any subject for which the type has ability. His particular talent in writing is different from the other types in that he expresses himself in dialogue. (The writing trinity is Saturn, Luna, and Mercury.) He is the character reader and the one who understands human nature and human failings. He translates this understanding into his plays or books. His characters are always "in character" and true to life.

Dialogue is the basis of radio, television, and theater and he does well there; but he also writes on science, finance, business, law, and world events.

Teaching: He can teach all of the subjects for which he has ability. He knows how to reach his students. He has "buymanship" as well as salesmanship, and so he can teach marketing, merchandising, retailing, business courses, advertising, science, math, economics, labor economics, collective bargaining, labor relations, law, and public relations.

Finance: He is the financial, money-conscious type. He makes his enterprises pay or he gets into another business that will. He makes money not only for himself but for others as well. His preference is for a business that permits him to handle cash or its equivalent. He works in insurance, business loans, banking, appraisals, credit, collection, and all types of financial work, including accounting, cost estimating, and so on.

Diplomat: The Mercurian makes an excellent diplomat. If he is of the Mercury-Apollo combination, there is no finer diplomat to be found. In this profession as elsewhere his intuitive understanding of people, his inherent shrewdness and adroitness add to his potential success. Almost all diplomats have a strong Mercurian influence. Henry Kissinger is a fine example of the Mercurian diplomat.

Actor: Mercury is the character actor. He portrays people. He has the ability of mimicry or imitation. He can express himself and likes to talk. He does not make the glamorous appearance of the Apollo; but his characters are played to perfection, whereas Apollo looks the same in any role. Apollo is the entertainer, personality, theater actor; Jupiter is the dramatic actor; Saturn the heavy or comedian. Mercury can also be found doing impersonations or magic (sleight of hand). Doug Henning has strong Mercurian development coupled with Apollonian traits. Johnny Carson, with his quick retort, has strong Mercurian development and appearance. He also began his career doing magic. Dustin Hoffman has strong Mercurian development, and is a tremendous character actor.

On occasion Mercury is an artist. Here again he is the character analyst, and that means portraiture. He can capture the soul qualities and paint a true likeness of his subjects, whether people or animals.

Occult: There are three occult types in the human family as described by Dr. Benham. Luna is the true psychic, medium, spiritualist. Saturn is the scientific occultist, as for example, Dr. Benham, Dr. Spencer, Holmes Whittier Merton, and countless others. Mercury is what we consider the intuitive occultist, although he also has a strong bent for the scientific side. He has that intuitive ability to size up people. He has an uncanny ability to judge character, motives, and conditions. His business instinct is always present, and so in this field as in others he knows the importance of a paying clientele. He also had medical ability and can be a metaphysician working on spiritual healing and spiritual therapy.

Being fond of making money, many conscienceless Mercurians are found in the ranks of phoney clairvoyants, fortune-tellers, and palmists. When Dr. Benham was gathering information for his study of scientific hand analysis, he met a number of alleged palmists who claimed to tell your name from your hand, or the names of friends or enemies. He found them to be specimens of the bad Mercurian type who admitted they knew little about palmistry but resorted to sleight of hand and their ability to judge human nature in order to fool their clientele and extract their money.

Basic Businesses: The type can succeed in several hundred different businesses so we mention only those most typical. He has an instinctive sense of values of merchandise, style, and human nature and can combine time, money, and raw materials and come out with a profit. Remember, as a trader he never comes out second best. He is clannish and frequently has his relatives in business with him.

He manufactures almost anything but especially clothing, household appliances, furniture and machinery of all sorts. He is inventive and can think up and produce new products or gimmicks or improve old ones. He is the buyer and seller as well as the manufacturer. Delicatessens, department stores—and countless other retail businesses—luxury items, toys, musical instruments, oriental rugs, drapes, clothing stores are found with Mercurian proprietors.

He is found particularly on the managing or financial end of hotel work.

Insurance, real estate, stocks, loans, and other types of investments are in his realm, as are banking, money exchange, and pawnbroking.

In working with children, he excels in entertaining, caring for, training, and teaching children; pediatrics, adoption services, children's clothing, and other work with children are in Mercury's realm. The addition of Venusian qualities is an important asset to Mercury in this area and supplements their natural love of children.

BAD SIDE

This is the second bilious type, and as such it is responsible for producing many of our criminal fraternity. Many are found in our jails and prisons convicted of petty crimes, larceny, con games, mail fraud, forgery, and so forth. Remember, Mercury is the thief of the gods in Greek mythology.

The type also produces a class that has not yet reached our penal institutions but deserve it even more than those who already have. The Mercurian walks a narrow path between shrewdness in business and actual dishonesty. His natural endowments make it easy for him to outwit his fellow man, and the temptation is so great that he cannot always resist it. He can become the businessman who cheats his customers with facility and ease, the lawyer who is one step ahead of the law, or any other type of unscrupulous professional.

In the lower grades they are bank robbers, pickpockets, sneak thieves, con artists, crooked gamblers, gypsies, and other deceptive characters.

REMARKS

This subject is a many-sided person, having many excellent capabilities and qualities to help him get by in life. He is also a lover of nature, natural scenery, horses, dogs, and art, especially when the art depicts real life, nature, or portraiture. Nature appeals to him more than anything artificial.

He is restless and needs diversity and change; therefore, he loves to travel. As often as not, he will travel on business or in some way take advantage of his trip if only to provide him with new ideas and frontiers.

Mercury could be a powerful ally and a source of good for humanity, but he also can be dangerous. We look for pronounced olive or yellow color, twisted little finger, hands in pockets, shifting eyes, closed buttons, pointed ears, or any other sign of deceit, secrecy, or hidden motives whenever we are dealing with a Mercurian subject.

MARS

The Mars type may not seem to be anybody extraordinary on first appraisal. He could be a neighbor of yours who works on a construction crew as a carpenter or mason. He enjoys a drink with the boys after work and may consider an exciting evening to be sitting in front of a ball game on television with a beer. He seldom reads a book, and his wife may have to drag him to the community art show, but when it comes to practical matters, the Martian is the man to get the job done. Martians may seem lackluster—but when an emergency arises, a Martian will spring into action. He will be the one who disregards life and limb and dashes into your burning home to rescue your children. It will be Martian firemen who rush to the scene to fight the fire, and Martian rescue workers who drive you to the hospital and apply first aid to keep you alive on the way. Emergencies call out the Martian qualities of bravery, courage, strength, and aggression. As Ann Koernig so frequently put it, "He has the courage to dare, to do, and to conquer."

In the finer grades, the Martian type accomplishes great deeds of valor. His is the world of accomplishment, and it is great acts of conquest that are meaningful to him. If you will look over Figure 27 on page 144, you will recognize the type quite easily. Much of history abounds with examples of the Mars type.

The Mars type is basically a masculine type and has many rough edges in the lower grades. They may even frighten you with their heavy-handed approach, but beneath it all they have hearts of gold and make loyal and true friends who will defend you with their lives. Most are very attached to their families and truly loyal mates, although the strong appetites of the type make pure hedonists out of some of them!

APPEARANCE

Temperamental Combinations: Muscular, Muscular-Motive, Muscular-Vital.

Head: The head is usually andromorphic, with a high Self-Esteem. Almost always the Martian will be wide-headed, showing Destructiveness, Combativeness, Vitativeness, Alimentiveness and Bibativeness. The backhead will be thick and full at Amativeness, Adhesiveness, Conjugality, Inhabitiveness, and Philoprogenitiveness. Construction is almost always present, whereas Language, Secrecy, Sublimity, and Ideality may be below normal. The Perceptive Faculties are always prominent.

Face: Because of the faculties mentioned, his head is short and square, somewhat bullet-shaped, with an unusually large development at the base of the brain making the neck thick and broad. In pronounced specimens it almost appears as if the head runs into the upper back and shoulders with no neck. In reality there is a great deal more neck than with the other types. The face is short-square or rounded-square, with thick skin that is red or red-mottled, especially in and around the ears. The hair is auburn or reddish shades, often cut short, and is curly and coarse in texture and thick or abundant. The beard is also thick, short, and harsh. The eyebrows are similar and grow low over the eyes. A line of intensity or the two lines of Judgment are usually seen between the eyes. The overall effect is to make the face seem to scowl. The eyes themselves are large and bold-looking, with a fierce or fixed stare, or are bright and sparkling. The whites of the eyes are frequently red and bloodshot, showing the intensity of the blood supply. The nose runs from medium small to quite large but usually has a high bridge or bumps, showing the Defense qualities present. The mouth is medium with the lower lip fuller than the upper lip. The mouth is firmly set. The teeth are small, regular, strong, and yellowish. The ears are small and project slightly from the head. They are red to purplish in color. The chin area is usually the dominant section of face, the chin being large, firm, and strong-looking, often turning up at the end. Perseverance, Independence, Mobility, and strong Will are all seen in the chin section of the Martian.

Color: Mars is the only type that has red as its natural color. Red is their distinctive color, and their ruddy, sanguine complexion is easy to identify. The red color should tell you something about their health, energy, and tendencies. Red shows excess.

Body structure: His short, thick neck is connected to broad, muscular, and well-developed shoulders, with large muscles running down the back and a large, expansive chest. The chest contains a large, strong pair of lungs that give him a powerful commanding voice. His legs are relatively short but thick and muscular. All of his bones are big and strong. His feet are broad, with the instep inclined to be flat. He has an overall rugged appearance that impresses you with its strength, force, and vitality.

Ulysses S. Grant
General and strategist

Sally Ride
first American woman in
space

Douglas Fraser
United Auto Workers president

Average Grade Martian
athletic coach

Figure 27. The Martian type. This figure shows the strong, conquering Martian spirit and forceful features of the type. No other type has the capacity to force through opposition, conflict, hardship, and turmoil as does the Martian.

Walk and stance: The Martian is flat-footed, but he walks in a proud, determined manner. He puts his feet down in a firm and purposeful way and carries himself with a self-confident air. He walks boldly to his objective.

CHARACTER TRAITS

Courage: First of all, the Martian subject is brave. Conflict does not scare him because he has no thought of danger, no acceptance of defeat. To the Martian soldier it is victory or death. Dr. Benham felt that Leonidas at the pass of Thermopylae had a band of true Martian soldiers.

He does not give up. Whether he is fighting a foe with guns or fists or fighting the problems of a large corporation, he resists discouragement and pushes forward. He is a strong, capable person, able to cope with the problems of the world. His robust constitution equips him well to deal with adversaries from without and within.

Endurance: Because nature equipped him with robustness, he can endure more hardship than any other type. He has the thickest skin of all the types. His heavy jaw and large chin will tell you that he has endurance, vitality, and a strong hold on life. He can fight privation, hardships, and all of the calamities of nature, war, and life.

Coolness: In hand analysis we differentiate between the Aggressive qualities of Mars and the Defensive qualities. In the Resistive or Defensive aspect, we have the subject who is calm and cool in the face of danger. He is not provoking the situation but is poised and prepared to fight back. It is this resistance that fights off discouragement and obstacles on the path of life. Suicides do not have any Mars in their character to fight life's hardships. Mars has the mental poise and physical strength that make him self-possessed in moments of danger.

Activity, energy: Of course from our description you have surmised that his is an active constitution. He is always on the go, doing and accomplishing what seems to him to be the real in life. His daring and energy cause him to climb mountains, explore the unknown, battle the foe, fell the forest, dynamite a tunnel, hunt the wild bear and boar. In his home you may find skis, diving suit, weights, baseball glove, firearms, knives, and strong whiskey.

MARRIAGE

His natural color is red. That means excess in all areas that deal with Mars, and the conjugal and sexual aspects of Mars are included. He is red-blooded with a strong sex drive. He is a strenuous lover and is intense in his likes and dislikes. He is never sentimental or mushy but assaults his love object with fire and dash. He has an abundance of health and great physical energy. He is drawn to the opposite sex early in life. He is predisposed to early marriage and will marry again if something happens to his mate.

The finer specimens can hold their drives and passions in bounds; with the coarser grades the passions become more intense and violent. The Martian is a jealous type and can commit murder in the heat of passion.

He likes the feminine women. It is the Venusian that attracts him. She is a clinging vine, feminine in every way, and strongly sexed. Only a woman of the spontaneous type, with vigorous sexuality, can mate well with him. He also mates well with Jupiterian women and women of his own type. He makes a devoted husband when well mated.

Martian women are unusual when found. They become a strong force in their home, environment, community, or business.

HEALTH

His natural red color is also the key to his health. First it shows that he has an abundance of red corpuscles in his blood. He is a heavy eater and drinker. He is a meat-and-potatoes man. His preference is for red meat, pork, veal, game of every kind, fish, crabs, lobster, and all sea foods, eggs, bread, and heavy vegetables. That is his main diet, all of which he can wash down with strong drinks. His great consumption of food eventually taxes his stomach and makes him liable to the ills of heavy eating.

He is inclined to have fevers and is predisposed to intestinal disorders as well as throat troubles, bronchitis, laryngitis, and other respiratory disorders. He is also subject to high blood pressure. He is of the vigorous type that will suddenly die of a severe stroke.

Most of Mars' problems stem from excess. Excessive drinking, eating, or living can ruin the natural gift of health that God has given him.

VOCATIONS

Emergency worker: Mars is well equipped to fight nature's upheavals such as storms, floods, tornadoes, drought, fires, forest fires, earthquakes, and other disasters.

Navy: Ships both military and privately owned are manned by Martians, each according to their grade and education. From longshoremen, who are the physical workers, to the captain and crew we will find many specimens of the Martian type. Visualize the disasters at sea and think of how Martian capabilities would handle those tests. Not too long ago an offshore oil drilling rig collapsed in the North Sea, sending men into freezing cold water. It was said that a man could survive for only five minutes in those extreme temperatures, but four hours later they rescued several of the men. These men were Mars types. Their thick skin, their vigorous constitutions, their strong hold on life, their fight and refusal to give up saved their lives.

Military: He is found from private to general in the military. He is a natural soldier—courageous, brave, and with a strong fighting instinct. General Pershing, U. S. Grant, Mussolini, General MacArthur, and General Ridgeway were all Martian specimens. President Eisenhower was a splendid example of a high-grade Martian. The military life is ideal for him. He is the most masculine of all the types. He uses short crisp sentences that are natural for military orders. He is the warrior.

Mechanical: Mars is the second mechanical type, the other being Saturn. He has an understanding of machines and tools and does well in mechanical trades such as auto repair, machinist, press operator, etc.

Sports: He is a natural athlete and loves rugged competitive sports such as football, rugby, soccer, boxing, wrestling, and ice hockey. The Martian thrives on competition. He wants absolute fairness, and may the best man win.

Animals: He has a great adaptability for working with animals. He handles working dogs, sporting dogs, cattle, horses, or wild animals. He can work in zoos, on cattle boats or ranches, breeding farms, racetracks, or as a game protector or game warden.

Business: The Martian has an objective and practical mind. He can put all of his natural endowments to use in the business world. He makes one of our best salesmen. Many businesses fail because just when victory is in their grasp, they give up. But the Martian never gives up, so he succeeds where others fail. He pushes his product and his business and overcomes any obstacles on the way.

The Martian businessman should have a physical outlet as well. He should jog, walk, hunt, or belong to a racquetball club or athletic club of some sort.

Action fields: He is the most strenuous of our family of seven types and is best placed in fields of action where his type qualities can be expressed. He makes our best soldier, marine, merchant marine, sailor, aviator, policeman, traffic officer or traffic manager, guard, fireman, explorer, prize fighter, athlete, job foreman, construction engineer, labor union organizer, or space pioneer. It is he who goes forth to do, to dare, and to conquer.

BAD SIDE

The Martian's negative side also stems from excess. Everything that tends to coarsen him makes him more brutal. He can become lascivious, a drunkard, or even a murderer. He is not inherently criminal, but he will steal to gratify his passions. He does not steal because the act of stealing itself is gratifying but merely to use the proceeds of his crime to appease his appetite.

The lower types live to gratify their low passions, and to this type brutality is a way of life. He may beat his wife or children, or he may rape. When crossed in love, he murders. He may use his fists, a knife, a club, or an ax; and even in the act of murder he brutalizes as much as possible. The Saturn-Mars combination in the criminal world makes one of our lowest and most vicious types of criminal.

REMARKS

Fortunately the Mars type is basically good, warm, and sympathetic. He is generous with his money, sometimes too much so for his own good. He loves friends and companions and he makes a true loyal friend who will fight for you as well as spend his money on you. He is loud and blustery and tends to brag but mostly in what he considers good fun.

Whatever he may be, he presents the same strong, ardent, heroic figure. His achievements in the eyes of the world are of the most significance to him. His strong characteristics are felt in the mental world, the business community, the military, the church, politics, and every other realm. To him the philosopher and student are small and insignificant because they are not out in the world accomplishing great deeds.

At times, his taste tends to art. If so, he will love battle scenes, hunting scenes, or paintings depicting games or sports. As a reader or writer he chooses stories of war and strife or of heroes and great men. As a musician, he favors brass bands, military music, march music, and the drums.

He is hot-tempered and can flare up rapidly, although he may not hold a grudge after he cools down. He is considered a good type, and basically he is. He needs only to keep his passions and excesses under control.

LUNA

The influence of the moon on the human psyche has been validated by modern observers but has been known for centuries. The Lunarian is more strongly influenced by lunar changes than any other type, even becoming the "lunatics" listed among the greatest failures of psychologists and psychiatrists.

Lunarians are a complex type in that they range from the depths of dejection, perversion, depression, lethargy, and repulsion to the most imaginative, creative, spiritual, and sensitive people we know. This type must be handled with care and understanding. They are strongly influenced by suggestion in thought, word, and deed, and they may magnify a careless comment until it consumes them.

Lunarians tend to be physically heavy. Reasons for this can range from hydrosis or water retention or lack of a strong will (a strong will always firms the body) to a disposition that lives in the feelings and imagination rather than in the real world. Any aspect that will strengthen the Lunarian is an asset. A strong, bony nose, high crown, practical hands with a firm handshake, improved color and skin tone will benefit the type greatly and permit the creative ability to find an outlet and achievement.

Figure 28 on page 150 clearly shows the influence of Luna on the physiognomy, disposition, and health. Dreamy, other-worldly, mystical, deep as the primal waters themselves are the Lunarians. They are not made for physical work. One look at them will tell you this. They need physical exercise in moderation, but they hate it. They need real love and understanding but often cannot accept or hold onto it. They imagine they are not worthy or that their lovers desire

Richard Parsons
engineer, hypnotist, metaphysician

Manly Palmer Hall
President of Philosophical
Research Society and author

Reverand Timothy Lull
Theologian, professor, writer,
lecturer

John Gacy
Convicted of the murder and
abuse of 29 young men

Alfred Hitchcock
Writer, producer, and film
director

John Hinkley, Jr.
Attempted assasination of
President Ronald Reagan

Mark David Chapman
Convicted of the murder of
John Lennon

Figure 28. The Luna type. The complex and diverse patterns created by the Lunarian element are seen in this illustration. A newspaper article on the "eerie similarity" between Hinkley and Chapman does not surprise those knowledgeable in human analysis—here we see that the Lunarian influence in both is obvious. The Lunarian is a sensitive type who can range from high spirituality in the higher grades to lunacy in the lower grades. You should note the strong nose of Manly Palmer Hall, not usually common to the Lunarian type.

another, or they themselves are fickle. They need practical, solid companions but do not choose their friends wisely.

As with the other types, those of a higher grade can become great linguists, authors, methaphysicians, playwrights, composers, and spiritual healers. So much depends on their individual features and quality. We recommend that you look carefully before a final opinion is formed and that you guide with sensitivity and discretion. Do not expect rapid or dramatic results with the Lunarian client.

APPEARANCE

Temperamental Combinations: Lymphatic, Lymphatic-Vital, Lymphatic-Mental.

Head: The faculties of Ideality, Spirituality, Sublimity, and Language are dominant. Tune, Construction, Causality, and Comparison are frequently developed, as are Veneration and Human Nature. They are generally low in the sidehead faculties except for Alimentiveness and Bibativeness. Bibativeness is usually more a factor than Alimentiveness.

The head is round or a rounded rectangle and broader at the upper temples, showing Ideality. It bulges over the eyes, and the forehead is low.

Face: The hair on this type is fine, soft, and a colorless white blond or possibly chestnut. The hair is never thick nor abundant and is usually straight and scraggly. The eyebrows are very lightly marked and usually grow together over the nose. The eyes are round and bulging or projecting. They have a distant stare and are usually very liquid.

The color of the eyes is blue, gray, or pale colorless. The pupils have a luminous gleam. The eyelids are puffy in appearance and look swollen. The Lunarian nose is short and small and often turns up at the end, with the nostrils showing plainly in a "pig" or "pug nose" appearance. The mouth is small in size but full and pouting and rarely held completely closed. The lips are pale in color. The teeth are large and long but yellowish and irregularly placed in pale gums. They are soft and decay while the subject is still young. The chin recedes from the plane of the face. It is heavy and hangs in folds (double chin). The ears are small and set close to the head.

Color: Luna's distinct color is white. White indicates coldness and selfishness in the character but is even more suggestive of a great many health problems, which will be discussed in the proper section.

Body structure: He is tall in stature and fleshy in build. His limbs are thick, and his feet are large and clumsy. He is frequently stout, even obese. His flesh is soft and flabby; it lacks tone and firmness. It feels spongy to the touch. His complexion, of course, is dead white. He has a ghostly pallor that marks him as a possible victim of anemia, kidney trouble, or dropsy. His abdomen is large and bulges forward. His legs lack grace and have a dropsical appearance. Lunarian women are often very big from the hips down, having a large buttocks and upper leg area, making them look like the early paleolithic figures of women. The shoulders are sloping in the gynomorphic fashion, adding intuition to their character.

Walk and Stance: Because of their large feet, swollen, dropsical ankles, large hips and rump, they tend to waddle, duck-like, when they walk. There is certainly nothing graceful or charming about it. Dr. Benham says they walk like a sailor after he gets to dry land. His posture and stance are awkward, retiring, and clumsy, lacking self-confidence, assertiveness, and energy. He looks, and frequently is, physically lazy.

CHARACTER TRAITS

Imagination: The Lunarian lacks physical strength and beauty so that instead of entering the world of activity or sociability he is left to sit and develop his imagination. Imagination is one of his foremost characteristics. Imagination is one of the most important characteristics possessed by the human race. It is the basis of language, art, invention, progress, and faith.

The Lunarian type is under the domination of imagination. They can conceive of plans. They can understand the meaning of words. Without imagination we would have no power of speech or words. It is because of imagination that we can form a mental picture of the appearance and attributes of objects to which we give a name.

The Lunarian expresses himself fairly well and enjoys the pleasures of the imagination. A person with no imagination cannot visualize anything of his own accord and must see concrete objects before him. A Lunarian with excessive type development goes to the opposite extreme and becomes flighty, mystical, and dreamy. He can even lose control of his mind entirely, becoming quite insane.

A healthy imagination lifts the world from dull materialism into the realm of fancy, creativity, and beauty. This is the gift of our greatest linguists, musicians, composers, artists, and writers.

Fancy: The Lunarian dreams to such an extent that at times he loses all sense of practicality. He is introspective, and his mind wanders to realms of mystery and fancy. He creates sand castles of the mind that have no place in reality. He believes in signs and omens and has wonderful visions and hallucinations which grow to be real to him.

Coldness: His physical heat is below par, and his color is white. His hands and his flesh are flabby, so coldness becomes another strong characteristic that pervades his personal life and work. He is slow in his movements, phlegmatic in disposition, and extremely sensitive to others and his environment. He imagines slights when none were intended, and so he withdraws into himself and avoids company. He would prefer to be out of touch with reality and retire to the woods to commune with nature—birds, flowers, and anything else that tends to elevate the senses and stimulate the imagination. To him "self" is a great word.

Intuition: He is of the gynomorphic body structure, which in itself suggests the feminine quality of intuition. His head faculties of Ideality, Sublimity, and Spirituality also assist him in this area. This is the basis of all his extrasensory abilties. He is the true psychic of the human family. Often though, he may become mystical, melancholy, and even superstitious. He believes in signs and omens. He receives visions and prophetic dreams. Many times his visions and hallucinations become very real to him and influence him to the point where his reality is dominated by them.

MARRIAGE

Although Lunarians are not strongly drawn to matrimony, they do not avoid it entirely. Because of their white color they are cold by nature and incapable of true affection. They are not inflamed by the fires of passion but stimulated by the imagination. They are fickle and capricious, undependable, and changeable. They make strange alliances. Many times they are involved in May-December marriages in which the partner is much older or much younger than themselves. I had one Lunarian subject who was a willing partner to a man she knew was a bigamist. Whatever the circumstances, it will almost certainly be a peculiar match.

The Lunarian is always seeking, seeking; he knows not what. If one mate does not satisfy him, he might look elsewhere for someone he believes will understand him better. They make poor husbands or wives, and many unhappy marriages spring from Lunarian partnerships.

HEALTH

His color is a ghostly white. This is a big clue to the state of his health. First, it shows that his blood supply and circulation are poor. He has flabby muscles. He lacks physical motivation and strength. These conditions make his body a fertile field for the propagation of bacilli. The abdomen is also paunchy and distended because it is in the same spongy condition as the rest of his body. The Lunarian is a victim of peritonitis, inflammation of the bowels, appendicitis, kidney problems, bladder difficulties, problems in the reproductive organs in women and the prostate in men. He is a victim of flu and of all types of intestinal disorders.

The Lunarian is also subject to gout and rheumatism. He has many difficulties, and these are compounded by the fact that he can also be a hypochondriac. He imagines he has more diseases than he does have and worries about them as if they were real or until they become real by psychic suggestion.

With the Lunarian subject there is also a liability to insanity. In a fine specimen it may manifest as some form of neurosis, but in excessive developments of the type the insanity takes many forms, and some may be dangerous to themselves and others. Changes of the moon strongly affect all Lunarians. Lunarians work almost exclusively through the feminine body, which makes them highly sensitive to atmospheres, vibrations, psychic impressions, planetary changes, and the like. Psychiatric help is seldom of any avail for the Lunarian as they are inherently "crazy" by nature. This is the type that develops psychoses, neuroses, and complexes of all sorts. They suffer from psychic disturbances and psychic obsessions. The annals of psychiatric research are filled with case histories of Lunarian patients.

Women of this type who are suffering from gynecological problems are always more or less mentally disturbed, growing gloomy and despondent when the condition is severe and especially at the time of menstruation. Their minds, which may otherwise be clear, become cloudy temporarily so that they may suffer from all sorts of imaginings and hallucinations. Many suicides are a result of this temporary imbalance of the mind. Luna is the second suicidal type. When Saturn is also a strong influence or in combination with the Lunarian subject, the danger of suicide is more prevalent.

VOCATIONS

Writing: Their imaginative and creative abilities find expression in this area. If they possess good quality, the type can become authors of poetry, fiction, and history as well as advertising copy and other practical writing if the type runs to practicality.

Much Lunarian writing is fanciful, mystical, or about some exotic place far away. They like ghost stories, mysteries, and stories about boats, water, and travel.

They can study literature and also teach it, but romance, poetry, and fiction are their favorites.

Language: The Lunarian has linguistic ability for the reasons we mentioned earlier. This is a real asset to him in many ways. He is a traveler, and his linguistic ability certainly helps him there. He is sensitive to all organized sounds, which include language and music. Many businesses on an international level require the services of multilingual individuals, interpreters, and translators. He also can translate and learn the lost languages that archeology uncovers.

Composer: His music is serious, sad, or fanciful. It tends to be classical and is produced in seclusion. There is none of the gay, popular melodies that attract the Apollonian and Venusian subjects; nonetheless their music has a beauty all its own. As composer, musician, or conductor they can excel with the right type of combinations and mental faculties.

Mystic: The Lunarian is frequently lazy physically and mentally. He loves to dream and explore imaginative realms. Even the look in his eyes is dreamy, cold, and distant, as if looking at another dimension rather than at the reality before him.

He is sensitive to everything and everyone around him. He is hurt easily, even by unintended slights, so he becomes melancholy and mystical. He is the true psychic, mystic, and occultist. He possesses genuine extrasensory ability. He makes a good character analyst and is involved in all occult and spiritual realms. He also can teach these subjects or write about them. You will also find him involved in many metaphysical and spiritual churches for he is often religious.

Travel: He is restless, changeable, and fickle. He is never happy in one place long. His restless disposition prompts him to seek new scenes and localities. He travels by air, land, and sea and can use this natural restlessness as a vocational outlet. He can fill positions having to do with travel: travel agencies, shipping, transportation, and courier or messenger services.

Other vocations include seaman, navigator, maritime researchers; manufacturer of sweets such as ice cream, candy, cakes, soft drinks, and other confections; psychiatrist; minister; proofreader; artist, designer; literary editor; playwright.

BAD SIDE

When the negative side of the Lunarian is developed, he will usually be shorter in stature with gray watery eyes and dead-white skin, and a noticeable and disagreeable perspiration and odor coming from his skin. He is talkative and often lets his imagination run rampant, making him a liar. He deceives others but deceives himself as well. He is mean, selfish, deceitful, hypocritical, and slanderous, as well as lazy, insolent, and unchaste. This type has no physical heat or passion, but they need constant sexual gratification to satisfy their imagination. From this class of Lunarians we get our nymphomaniacs and much worse; we find real perverts in this category. John Gacy, who raped, tortured, murdered, and buried twenty-nine young boys in his basement, belonged to this class of Lunarians. With this grade of Lunarian the mental state is always on the brink of becoming totally unbalanced.

REMARKS

Each of the family of seven has a place in the theme of things, and the Lunarian is no exception. This would be a dry world indeed if we had no imagination, no perception of the beautiful, and no connection with the spiritual realms.

It is traditionally believed that the Lunarian has a great affinity for water and travel on water. In my practice I have found two conflicting attitudes about water among Lunarians. There are those who do indeed love water—the ocean, sea, lakes, boats, and swimming—and there are those who abhor water and only admire it from a distance.

The type in general lacks self-confidence, perseverance, and energy. He feels and is unfit for most of the active pursuits of life in general and the business world in particular. The common grade has a difficult time getting along in reality; however, the high grade can use all of the positive aspects of their natural characteristics and abilities to make their way in the world.

VENUS

So far, we have discussed types that show push and drive, analytical and scientific minds, flare and daring, mysticism and coldness. The Creator could not have rounded off His work without the element of love. It is said that love makes the world go round, love heals, love is blind. Love is the essence of poetry, music, art, and religion. Love makes us human and complete. The Venusian is the Love type. She is soft, voluptuous, loving, and kind. She is the loving mother, devoted wife, sympathetic friend, sensuous lover who heals us, body and soul. She is dance, music, poetry. When she turns to art, she becomes Cassatt, Renoir, or Degas. She is always gentle and receptive.

As Mars expresses masculinity, Venus expresses femininity. Two opposite poles of a magnet, it is no wonder they attract and cling to each other. With the Venus type, as with Luna, there is a strong need for other elements in order for the Venusian to produce results that will be noticed by the world. Without more forceful qualities, the Venusian is still a factor by adding love, peace, and harmony in her own quiet way, without heavy responsibility, intensity, or purpose.

In Figure 29 on page 158, we have illustrated some Venusians who have made an impact on the world, so that you can identify the strong Venusian influence that is present. The typical Venusian is attracted to carbon foods. In other words, she has a strong sweet tooth, and her body chemistry is strong in the elements of carbon and phosphorus. This constitution always lives more in the emotions of love and sentimentality and avoids that which is difficult, severe, bitter, or harsh. But who can condemn her loving ways? One look from her could melt the soul of even a hard Saturnian.

APPEARANCE

Temperamental Combinations: Vital, Mental-Vital, Vital-Mental.

Head: The Venusian possesses the feminine head structure. The high faculties are Agreeableness, Benevolence, Hope, Mirth, Tune, Spirituality at times, Alimentiveness and Bibativeness to some degree. Also Language, Form, and Color. In the backhead the Venusian is developed in Inhabitiveness, Adhesiveness, Conjugality, Philoprogenitiveness, and Amativeness. The low faculties are Destructiveness, Combativeness, Acquisitiveness, Self-Esteem, Firmness, and Secretiveness.

Itzhak Perlman
Violinist

Renata Scotto
Soprano

Caniglia
Operatic star

Jackie Gleason
Comedian

Figure 29. The Venusian. The realm of Venus is art, music, poetry, dance and love. The Venus type softens and completes the variety found within the Seven Types.

Face: Venus is the most feminine type in the family of seven; this femininity pervades her character as well as her appearance. It is for this reason that we refer to the Venusian type as "she" even though there are also male specimens of this type.

The Venusians have round faces or full oval faces. The face is finely proportioned and is not interrupted by high cheekbones, thin cheeks, or square jaws that would make it angular and mar its soft beauty. The cheeks are rounded and ornamented with dimples when the subject smiles. The hair is usually auburn in color and long, silky, and wavy. It is abundant and full bodied, as the Venusian does not naturally go bald. The forehead is of medium height, well proportioned, and gracefully rounded, with delicate azure veins at the temples. The skin on the forehead is tightly drawn and does not seem to wrinkle. The skin of the face is soft and velvety to the touch and is a transparent white through which glows a delicate pink. The eyebrows are well marked, abundant, and dark, and they form graceful curves on the forehead. They do not usually grow together over the nose, but if they do it will coarsen the type. The eyes can be round or almond shaped and are brown or dark blue in color, with a tender and sympathetic expression. The eyes are usually large, clear, moist, and prominent, with large pupils. The eyelids are delicate, well formed, and blue-veined. The eyelashes are long and silky, curling up on the ends.

The Venusian's nose is shapely, full, and tends to be rounded at the tip. The nostrils are broad and flexible, contracting and expanding when the subject is excited.

The lips are like a cupid's bow in shape, full, with the lower lip more prominent. At times the right side of the lower lip is slightly larger than the left, and a small dimple appears at the corners of the lips when the subject smiles.

The teeth are white and strong and set in beautiful, healthy pink gums. The chin is round and full with a small dimple in it. The face as a whole, with its expressive eyes, dimpled cheeks, and beautiful teeth makes a perfect and beautiful picture when she smiles.

Color: Her natural color is pink. She is spontaneous, vibrant, healthy, and happy.

Body structure: The Apollonian and Jupiterian are types of manly beauty, but the Venusian is feminine, soft, voluptuous. Male subjects of this type also partake of this feminine beauty. The body shape is gynomorphic, with soft rounded shoulders. They are of medium height or slightly on the short side with graceful curves from head to foot.

Their necks are long and shapely and connected with gracefully rounded shoulders that are not muscular but show breadth and health. Their chests are round, full, and expansive, which helps to give them rich musical voices. Their legs are graceful; their hips high and round, with the thighs proportionately long. Their feet are small and shapely with high insteps. The entire appearance of the Venusian is attractive and pleasing to the eye.

Walk and stance: She is the very picture of grace and beauty as she walks and moves. There is elasticity and spring to her step. Whether she is standing, walking, dancing, or sitting, she is the picture of refinement, happiness, and grace.

CHARACTER TRAITS

Love: The Venusian is pink in color, showing a good supply of clean blood. This, in fact, is the reason for her good health and happy nature. Health and happiness also produce the freshness and attractiveness that mark the handsome Venus type. We find that each type is endowed with the color that accompanies their health and characteristics in order for them to manifest those particular elements that the type represents. The Venusian was created for love and was given health, warmth, and physical attractiveness in order to inspire love wherever she may be. There is no gloom, biliousness, coldness, or selfishness in her nature. She is all warmth, beauty, and magnetism and is beset by many temptations. She is attracted to, and attracts, the opposite sex, and she is endowed with strong sexual passions. Refinement and will power are necessary for this type to control such urges. In coarse types these impulses are neither checked nor controlled. But in refined specimens there is a higher grade of morality; love is more platonic and directed more toward those of equal refinement. Love of flowers, nature, art, music, and dance is indicated.

Sympathy, compassion: Love expressed in a higher form is philanthropy or humanitarianism. Along with Jupiter, Venus is the other humanitarian of the human family. This is work of her instinctive love for all mankind and extends itself to the lowly, hurt, sick, and burdened in life. The Venusian feels most for those whose path in life has been difficult and filled with obstacles. She is entirely unselfish. When she hears a story of distress and woe, she forgets herself and seeks only to aid the sufferer. In the hour of despair the Venusian never deserts a friend but tends them with an open hand and open heart.

She is sometimes known as a "soft touch" and taken advantage of by those who wish to con her for her generosity and sympathy. She is imposed on with ease, for she is always ready to help others even after she has been used.

Grace: The quality of grace is quite natural to her. It is the expression of her mind. Refinement, poise, manner, graciousness, and grace all come naturally to her and are never affected. Her mental state is carried through and reflected in the grace of her body, which is lithe, attractive, and charming, adding to her irresistible nature. She is the personification of grace as she walks, dances, plays, or sits. She is feminine charm from head to toe.

Melody: The very soul nature of Venus responds to music. The area in the hand that represents Venus has often been referred to as the Mount of Melody. Her music is not somber and melancholy as with the Saturnians; rather it is filled with the joy of life, as she is. Her music has melody, harmony, plenty of rhythm and sparkle. She likes songs about life and people. Her music is light, "popular," or "country-western," where she can draw on your heart strings. She also is found in light operas or in a dance chorus. Her music makes you want to move the feet, as a Strauss waltz can do.

Remember that Venus, or any type for that matter, may not have had the opportunity to develop their intrinsic abilities so do not be surprised if you find subjects that are not musicians; however, all Venusians will love music.

The addition of Luna to the Venusian subject will assist greatly in the field of music. Lyricist Ashton Springer is an excellent example of this combination.

Gaiety: To the Venusian, living is a joy. There is no bile or toxins to poison her blood and disposition. Good health makes the world look brighter and fills Venus with gratitude and happiness. Everything looks rosy to them; they see the good, positive, and hopeful side of any issue and spread their brightness on whomever they encounter. They are not serious about life and will pursue pleasure to the exclusion of business. They do not value riches or assume responsibility; consequently, they seldom become wealthy. They are carefree and improvident, but they are happy. They are neither profound nor studious but are content to enjoy life to its fullest. They love color, dress, home, art, flowers, and beauty wherever it may be found. They prefer the beautiful to the practical.

Venusians are basically honest and truthful for they neither scheme for money nor are they ambitious for high places. They are loyal and constant friends, true and faithful mates. They dislike conflict and strife and would rather suffer an injustice than engage in an argument. They want merely to give pleasure, to amuse themselves, and to be appreciated.

MARRIAGE

Venus is pink and therefore spontaneous. She is full of fire, passion, and attraction for the opposite sex. She almost always marries and at an early age. In modern times there is a widespread tendency to enter the intimacies of marriage without the marriage ceremony. The young Venusian is aroused sexually at an early age and may be drawn into a "living together" arrangement even without actual marriage. The young Venusian should be given a good sex education at an early age. Her discrimination should be perfected so that she may choose a partner of equal refinement and quality. It also may be beneficial to direct her passions to music, the arts, and social services, where she may find more noble outlets.

Venusians are attracted to strong, healthy, warm partners. The vigorous Martian or robust Jupiterian attract the feminine Venusian and are best capable of sharing mutual conjugal pleasures. They do not mate well with the cold or bilious types although they are subject to the attraction of opposites in that they sense that the Saturnians, for example, have what they lack.

The suitor who regards love casually and expresses his love feebly can never win the Venusian woman. She loves strong men who come urgently, press their suit with heat, and if necessary actually sweep her off her feet and carry her away. Their passion is intense. They love romance, courtship, and ceremony. The mild approach is not for them.

Venusian women do not belong to the birth control league or the various "women's lib" groups. They love children and family life. Their home is happiest when filled with youngsters; they may even adopt additional children. When well mated, Venusians seldom divorce their mates. When they lose their mates, they continue to marry, regardless of age.

Venusian men as well as women have a great capacity for parenthood. The Venusian wife is not always provident or the tidiest homemaker, but her home is always filled with happiness and warmth, color, flowers, and good cheer.

HEALTH

Venus is found to be one of the healthiest types in our family of seven. Her color is pink, and her philosophy, although not deep as some others, is one of optimism and happiness. She never commits suicide. She finds too much in life to be thankful for and little to discourage her.

She is not subject to the chronic diseases that accompany the other types, but she may fall victim to some of the acute conditions that affect people in general, such as febrile diseases, colds, hay fever, rose fever, and such. She is frequently of a nervous disposition and worries much about her loved ones and family.

In low-quality Venusians we may find venereal diseases. They are frequently marked by black dots or brown patches (not age spots) on the back of the hand and on the Venus mount at the base of the thumb.

VOCATIONS

Music: This is one of the most prominent endowments of the Venusian. All Venusians love music and some are capable of careers in this area. The other two music types are Saturn and Luna.

Dance: Visualize the grace of the Venusian. Many of our professional dancers are Venusians or are strongly endowed with Venusian qualities. In this vocation it is an asset to identify the type while still young. Three years of age is not too young to train in dance. Careers in dance frequently span only a brief period, and it is well to have an auxiliary career in the offing.

Theater: With the natural grace, beauty, and charm of the Venusian it is easy to see why this type does well in the limelight. Venus is lovely to look at and succeeds well in musical comedies, revues, light opera, or as a show girl. They do well in parts that touch the heart or bring the audience to tears. They speak to the soul and excel in human interest stories. They play the ingenue with ease.

Social work: Here is the humanitarian that is strongly motivated to alleviate suffering, hardship, and heartache. The Venusian has the capacity to work patiently with the handicapped, the underprivileged, amputees, or the retarded.

Cosmetics: With her perfect pigmentation, luxurious hair, clear skin, and healthy appearance she is a walking advertisement for her products. Her ability to reach out to people enables her to develop a clientele of her own easily. Hair preparation and treatment, hairdressing, beauty culture, barbering, and related fields are open to the Venusian.

Clothing: Although style comes from the Apollo type, Venus is also considered a beauty and clothes type and looks beautiful in whatever she wears.

She also can do sales and contact work, especially in infants' wear and maternity clothing shops and in specialty shops. Articles such as crystal, gifts, greeting cards, children's furniture, lingerie, luxury lines, and so forth are in the vocational realm of Venus.

Marriage: Perhaps we should place this as a vocation first. It is perhaps the most important career in the world, and yet few are so well adapted to it as the Venusian. The Venusian is a natural mate, parent, homemaker, and friend to all creation. She makes her home attractive and comfortable. She is the ideal hostess, charming and gracious. She dresses herself and her family well even on a limited budget. She is a strong and positive influence in her community.

BAD SIDE

In the lower grade of Venusians the baser instincts and desires rule. They are shorter in stature and stouter, with prominent abdomens. All grace and beauty is eliminated from them; the eyes appear bloodshot and the nose upturned. Excess is stamped on their form and character. The lips are thick, red, and sensual, and the hands are swollen in the area of the base appetites.

They enjoy life in a coarser fashion, being dominated by the desire to gratify their pleasures. They do not distinguish between a refined pleasure and a low one, so they debauch themselves. Vulgarity, obscenity, and ribald talk give them pleasure. They are libertines and reprobates who disgust decent people. You will find all grades of Venusians from the debased to the splendid and elevated type. It is the task of the character analyst to distinguish between them.

REMARKS

The Venus type is not a strong force in the world unless supported by a Mars or Jupiterian development, or balanced by Saturn or Mercury. There is no ambition, industry, perseverance in the face of hardship, combativeness, or force in the Venusian. They merely beautify and enjoy life and are basically passive by nature. Love, sympathy, tenderness, generosity, beauty, melody, gaiety, joy, health, and passion are the tools they employ to get by in this world.

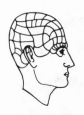

CHAPTER 9

THE MERTON SYSTEM
OF VOCATIONAL COUNSELING

From 1859 to 1884, Alesha Sivartha issued work on his discoveries on the Physical and Spiritual constitution and the ideal society based and organized upon the same twelvefold principle that is represented by the evolved person. His work, *The Book of Life*,[4] became the basis for much of the radical thought throughout the age; he viewed 1881 as the numerological and mystical turning point for humanity.

His discoveries on the human mental construction were thought to revolutionize and modernize all previous work, from Gall to Spencer. He had an adept and astute student in Holmes Whittier Merton, who carried these discoveries to an astounding level of perfection. The background of Merton is summarized in the introduction to this book, and his subsequent development and application of Sivartha's principles as they relate to vocational abilities also can be found there.

The Merton System will prove an invaluable tool for the counselor who wishes to be of service to his or her clients. The System is complete in itself and can be used without knowledge of any other technique, with the exception of Temperaments, which must be mastered as a basis for any worthy system of character analysis. Figure 30 on pages 168 and 169 illustrates the complete Merton System. The individual faculties and their corresponding subfaculties are shown separately in figures 31 through 50 in this chapter.

I suggest strongly that you review Chapter 3 on the Temperaments and that the information contained in that chapter become second nature to you. There are four major systems that carry on the

---

[4]Alesha Sivartha, *The Book Of Life*. Holmes W. Merton, New York, 1884.

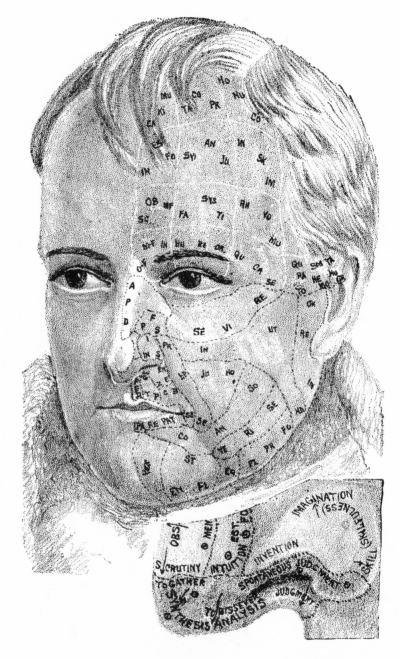

Figure 30. The major Faculty areas. Reprinted in its original form from Merton's course in "Vocational Counselling and Employee Selection," this illustration shows us the labeling of the subfaculties on the face. These subfaculties will be further elaborated in Figures 31 through 50.

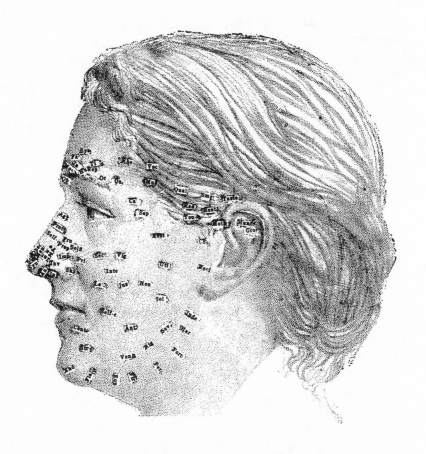

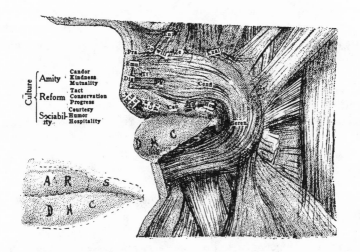

life processes in the human body—and those are the Vital, which are the viscera, intestines, bowels, bladder, stomach, etc.; the Motive, or Osseous, which is the body framework; the Muscular, which are the muscles and other fibrous parts of the body; the Mental, which includes the brain and nervous systems. Each of these systems influences character in its own way, depending on which system predominates in the body. A review of Chapter 3 will give you the needed information.

You should also review the Basic Section of this book where we have devoted space to the condition known as Quality. This strongly affects our rating of any individual's abilities, potentials, and basic character. Regardless of how large the signs are on our client's face, it is the Quality of the organism that gives it power. There are plenty of dunces with long and high foreheads. This merely shows that in proportion to all that such a person is, or has in himself or herself, the Mental Temperament predominates. It is by judging the inherent relative workmanship, refinement, strength, modeling, and vibratory rate that Quality is determined. First, we classify the Temperament of an individual, then the Quality, and then the Signs. The importance of the signs is determined by their relative distance from the ear openings. The largest sign in the face will hold personal and vocational dominance.

HOW TO USE THIS MATERIAL

The Merton System of Vocational Counseling follows the pattern we have set down in all the preceding chapters. It is not possible to isolate one feature and adequately assess abilities and personality. The entire face must be charted and the strong and weak points noted.

The material has been laid out by Location, Function, Development (which is indicated as either High or Low), Subfaculties, and Vocations for each faculty. An illustration for each faculty has been provided under each heading to show the reader where that faculty can be found on the face. The material under the heading of Function will suggest the activity of each faculty. It will discuss what the purpose of the faculty is, what it is concerned with, or what it does in terms of its work in the mentality. The descriptions of high and low supply additional information about how the developed or deficient faculty will affect the personality. In most instances, I have tried to illustrate clearly how the face would appear if the faculty were "high" (meaning developed or raised on the face) and how it would appear if the faculty were "low" (lacking or deficient in development). The caution here is that the rest of the face must be taken into consideration to see which of these qualities would apply to the individual you are looking at. "High" means that the facial area in question is large, long, highly developed. This also suggests that the Function will be strong. *A higher development equals a more active function.*

"Low" implies that this facial sign is not developed. Because of the geography of the face it can never be missing entirely, but its contours will be low, flat, or inconspicuous. The Function also will be low, lack power, and be unusable as a vocational tool. The qualities listed for Low will apply also, where warranted. Not all of the qualities listed under High and Low will apply in every instance. Common sense and observation will guide you in interpretation. This also will account for any seeming contradictions.

Subfaculties are finer divisions of a faculty, or more properly, they are the components of a faculty. They are always three in number. (The logical, systematic, orderly approach of Merton can be seen in portraits of him, where the sign of Analysis, in the septum of the nose, is quite large.) I would suggest that the student read the faculty as a whole and not attempt to distinguish between nuances of areas that are sometimes only millimeters apart. Read the faculty as a whole and be aware of its components. At times when a subfaculty is obviously more pronounced than the faculty area as a whole, you can consider judging the subfaculty development. Each illustration or figure will show the entire faculty area and the location of the subfaculties within the faculty boundaries. The subfaculties are indicated by abbreviations. These are the first two letters of the name of the subfaculty.

The list of Vocations indicates your client's vocational *potential* when that faculty area is developed or high. Natural aptitude, capability, and adaptability for certain vocations are shown. The necessary training, intelligence, health, and persistence are always required in addition to suitability. What we can safely judge is vocational potential, inherent strengths, natural capability, trainability, and aptitude. Many vocations require faculties in combination. This is more common and probably the rule rather than the exception. When you find a vocation followed by the names of several faculties and subfaculties, you will realize that these are combinations best suited to that particular vocation.

In addition to the above categories, you will occasionally find a listing for "Against." Simply put, the faculty in question will not permit the characteristics it is "against." An easy example would be Friendship, which is "against" a go-it-alone disposition. Obviously, Friendship needs a recipient and therefore prevents the subject from being a recluse.

FORM

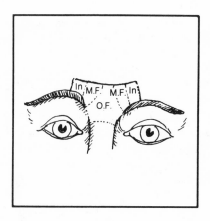

Location: The inner edge of the eyebrows just above the root of the nose. It appears wedge-shaped or like a keystone when developed. When this area is large, the brow will appear quite prominent and project forward.

Function: Form is the faculty or sign that sees and remembers with clarity the sizes, shapes, textures, structures, harmonies, proportions or disproportions of objects in which it is interested.

Development: High development, shown in Figure 31a, indicates vanity and a desire to see all. When development is low (Figure 31b) the subject can see as well as any other, but has no memory or takes no specific pleasure in what he sees.

Subfaculties

Object Form: This specific ability allows for the noticing of length, breadth, and thickness of objects; the size of spaces and orderly arrangements; perspective. It remembers the outlines of changing forms, their contours, and is of great value in remembering faces and

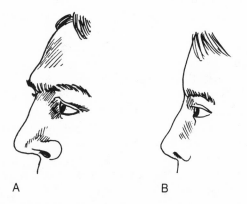

A   B

Figure 31. Form (Merton System). a) When the faculty of Form is highly developed, the individual is visually oriented. b) A low development of Form indicates no unusual excitement over visual experience.

recognizing people. The arts, mechanical trades, and crafts require large Object Form.

Motion Form: This specific gives the capacity to see or sense the path or route of moving objects, such as the path of a ball or flight of a bird or moving parts of machinery. It can judge speed, direction, or change of course. For the Motion Form of the pugilist, see Form, page 107 in Chapter 7.

Individuality: Individuality is the aptitude for observing the peculiarities of objects and their actions. It is of great assistance in the inspection and close examination of objects where it works together with the faculty of Scrutiny.

Vocations: Form is important wherever the dexterous cooperation of hand and eye is necessary, and so it is found in many simpler vocations such as carpentry or farming. It gives the recollection of shapes and memory of persons and faces. With the aid of Construction, it gives the ability to make patterns, models, pictures, statues, and so forth. It disposes us to give shape to everything, including our mental conception of such abstracts as God, Death, Hope, and such, all of which are given mental form.

It is essential to sculptors, designers, draftsmen, patternmakers, dressmakers, silversmiths, cutters, engravers, sign painters, opticians, weavers, inspectors, lathe operators, toolmakers, cartographers, jewelers, glassblowers, architects, and or course it is very important to the phrenologist, physiognomist, iridologist and hand analyst.

COLOR

Location: The Color signs are located in the brow, just outward from Form. They extend from directly over the inner side of the iris, to directly over the outer side of the iris, on and slightly above the brow. See Figure 32 on page 174 for clarification. When this sign is large, there is a long projection of the brows as compared with the forehead above these signs.

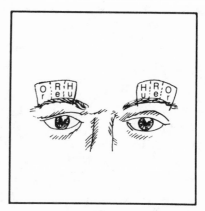

Function: The three members of the perception group are Form,

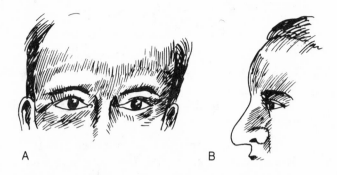

A   B

Figure 32. Color (Merton System). a) When the faculty of Color is highly developed, the individual is sensitive to color and color combinations. b) A low development of this faculty indicates a lack of color sense or appreciation.

Color, and Number. Normal sight registers things through these three faculties. We observe an object's form, its color, and its number or quantity (whether it is one, many, or a large number). You cannot observe any object without seeing these three things. Try seeing only two of the three, and you will find out it is impossible.

Color perception is one of our greatest sources of pleasure. It gives beauty to objects, gratifies the aesthetic sense, and has many utilitarian functions. Color aids in Memory and in a great many arts and sciences.

Development: High development indicates vanity; a love of seeing, remembering, and basking in color. (See Figure 32a for high development.) Low development indicates little memory or appreciation of color; also a tendency to dress, decorate, and live with drab, nondescript colors. (See Figure 32b.)

Subfaculties

Hues: This area of the Color sign gives the ability to judge tones, tints, and shades and to contrast values and luminosities in colors. People with low color faculties see color but are not concerned with the color relationships that might drive others to distraction. They hardly notice delicate shades and blends of colors and seldom remember colors they have seen.

Representation: This area gives the ability to represent various scenes, views, visions, and imaginings. It permits the memory to recall the color and color relationships one has experienced in the past and to grasp the changing spectrum of nature—in a sunset, for example.

Order: This sign notices the order and arrangement of physical objects and gives the ability to recall these arrangements. When Order is small, the brows retreat or slope backward sharply from the midbrow. The large Order does not give the desire for tidiness and neatness but is merely interested in seeing things as they are. It is more interested in artistic placing or color harmony grouping rather than practical arrangement.

Vocations: Color is also a factor in most of the arts and in many industries and sciences—sciences such as chemistry, physics, pharmacy, spectrum analysis, botany, zoology; industries such as dyeing, bleaching, printing, paint making, pottery, tapestries, rugs, furniture and clothing. A list of additional vocations with combinations required follows. Lithographer: Color, Form, Imagination, Skillfulness, and Dexterity; Wallpaper designer: dominant Color, essential Form, supporting Imagination, Skillfulness, Independence; Decorator: dominant Color, essential Form, supporting Imagination, Skillfulness, and Observation; Dyer: dominant Color, essential Attention, supporting Caution, Mobility; and Impression; Art dealer: dominant Color, essential Object-Form, Imagination, Observation, Intuition, and Sociability. He or she also will need the salesmen's Language, Integrity, Aggression, Economy, Laudation, and Aspirations; House painter: Color, Mobility, Dexterity, Industry.

NUMBER

Location: The signs of Number are located in the sidehead in the lower part of the temple at and above the outer corner of the eye. The strength of the sign is measured by the width between the temples from side to side in this area.

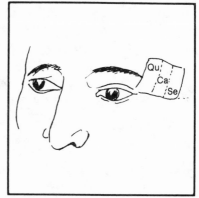

Function: It is the business of Number to count and estimate quantities. Number answers the questions how much, how many, how divided or separated. Sight, hearing, and touch are all employed in answering these questions.

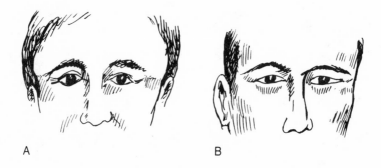

A   B

Figure 33. Number (Merton System). a) A high development of this faculty indicates a good ability to estimate and to assess value or quantity. b) A low development indicates that the individual is inaccurate at rapid appraisals.

Development: High development indicates systematic, commercial vision. (See Figure 33a for an example.) A low development (see Figure 33b) does not lend itself to accurate rapid appraisals.

Subfaculties

Quantity: This is the type of estimation used when exact measurement or accounting is not possible or needed. It may be called a guess, an estimate, an appraisal, a supposition, or a valuation.

It is notable that most good gardeners, nursery men, cooks, and many farmers have a large Quantity sign because their vocations call for estimates rather than measurements. Woodsmen become capable in the estimation of timber, hunters in the estimation of distance, and so forth.

Calculation: This part of Number works with arithmetic. It deals with computations of the common order: for example, addition, multiplication, division, and subtraction; tables, measures, and scales.

Separation: Just as Quantity masses thing to estimate their whole amount, Separation divides things that cannot be counted as they are. It separates groups, varieties, or subspecies of a mass and forms a good judgment as to their relative proportion. It does not count or enumerate them.

Vocations: All businesses where estimates of prices, quantities, and proportions are required or businesses dealing with weights and measures. Higher forms of mathematics are reflective in their mental requirements or are carried on by analysis.

Accounting, systematizing, insurance brokerage, credit, storekeeping, dispatching, navigation, surveying, etc., are vocations where Number is required.

ATTENTION

Location: The specifics of Attention are located in the end of the nose. The nose end projects outward for Observation, spreads in the crest for Mental Focus, and droops for Scrutiny.

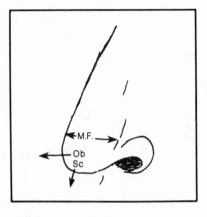

Function: This is the mental faculty that acts as the lookout for abilities farther along in the thinking process. It pays attention to what has been seen by the Perceptions, heard by the Language, or felt by the senses.

Development: Keywords for high development are: argumentativeness, critical, systematic, dexterity, fond of travel, tact, absent-mindedness, accuracy. (See Figure 34a for an example of high

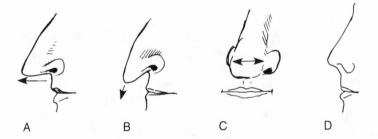

A   B   C   D

Figure 34. Attention (Merton System). a) A nose that projects outward at the tip indicates a high development of Observation. b) When the tip of the nose droops, a high development of Scrutiny is indicated. c) A nose with a wide spread across the crest indicates a highly developed Mental focus. d) When the faculty of Attention overall is not developed, this usually indicates that the individual lacks the ability to be attentive and has a poor capacity for concentration.

development.) Low development, as shown in figure 34d, indicates a person who is distracted easily, indifferent to order.

Subfaculties

Observation: This is called the automatic attention ability. It is alert to the unexpected and the unknown. It gives an immediate grasp of matters that bear directly on a person's working field. It detects means and opportunities. Because of these qualities, Observation stimulates many of the other faculties, notably Vigilance, Perceptions, Aesthetics, and Memory.

Small Observation notices only the striking effects of things around the person; its interest is superficial, irregular, lacks good memory, and is easily distracted from its work. Details and defects are easily overlooked.

Mental Focus: This faculty is opposite in nature from Observation. The assignment of Mental Focus is to eliminate all outside distractions that could interrupt the chain of thought being carried on by other specifics. This sign causes the term "absentminded" to be applied, as the subject does not seem to be paying attention to what is going on around him. In truth, the subject is engrossed in deep concentration on the matter at hand to the exclusion of all others.

Scrutiny: The activity of this specific is to pay voluntary attention to details, minutiae, imperfections, and other facets that are not readily seen by general observation. It implies carefulness, close perception, and prolonged inspection.

Remarks: The Observation specific tends to be commercial in application. The Scrutiny specific, when the hook or beak is especially noticeable, tends to be cautious, meddlesome, and suspicious but has many vocational applications.

Observation and Analysis are frequently confused because of the similarity of their results. Where Observation can answer a question by noticing the details of what is going on, by noticing variation and remembering the order of events, then Analysis is not needed.

Vocations: Observation: printing press operators, sewing machine operators, freight house foremen, tallymen, glass workers, messengers, nurses, janitors, paper makers, weavers, tobacco workers, candy makers, club managers, hotel managers, truck drivers, dispatch clerks, trainmen, riveters, signalmen, inspectors, file clerks, airplane pilots, pottery makers, seamen, forest rangers, etc. Attention is also a secondary factor in numerous vocations.

Mental Focus favors many types of routine work and occupations that require close attention with a minimum of distractions.

Scrutiny is seldom required as a dominant in any vocation but is necessarily of large development where the work is fine and close as instanced in textile fields, botanical and histological sciences, entomology, and the finer forms of mechanics such as watchmaking, engraving, and fine die cutting.

MEMORY

Location: These signs are found directly above those of Color in the cranial part of the forehead. They are measured by their length forward from the ear opening in comparison with the rest of the forehead.

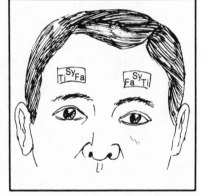

Function: The memory specifics bring back the past for present use by keeping track of the main items of other faculties and bringing them to mind when needed. All of the faculties have their own type of memory, but the Specific Memory signs store and supply particular items or groups of facts and information as they are needed.

Development: Keywords for high development are: organizing, systematic, commercial vision. (See Figure 35 on page 180.) Low development indicates someone who is slow in recollection, and has an indistinct or confused memory.

Subfaculties

Fact Memory: This specific registers facts for easy recall. The time, sequence, or relationship of the facts are not taken into consider-

Figure 35. Memory (Merton System). A good memory will project the forehead forward at the point indicated by the arrow. A low development of this faculty will show as a flatness or slight depression here.

ation. Only the facts stick, and a mental note is made as to where in the mentality the message was sent.

There are people who have countless facts at their fingertips, but this does not guarantee the ability to reason or act with a systematic method.

System Memory: This specific links together similar ideas, facts, or manner of actions. It organizes matter that have been found to go together and can furnish this information to Reason, Construction, or other faculties with the needed associations, methods, or systems.

Time Memory: This specific keeps track of the passing of time and is involved in sequencing or "timing," and remembering matters set for the future. It is responsible for synchrony, acting together, meeting at the right instant, moving with the right speed, judging speed of movements and so forth.

Time Judgment is important in many trades, to help avoid injuries or make perfect work.

Vocations: Purchasing agents, circulation managers, information clerks, medical clerks, warehousemen, librarians, statistical analysts, trial lawyers, and storekeepers all need good Memory, although it need not be the dominant faculty in the face.

LANGUAGE

Location: Located in the cranial region above the Number signs in the temple of the forehead, and outward from Memory. In long-forward, narrow heads the region lies more on the side of the forehead. When Language is dominant, the forehead is uncommonly broad at the temples. This is especially true when literary ability is present.

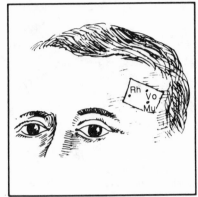

Function: Its main powers are those of remembering words and music, distinguishing them as sound symbols (words) and sound vibration (music), organizing sentences in logical order, and associating words with their objects and acts.

The ability to master languages, grammar, rhetoric, and spelling, to remember names of people and places, verbal statements, lectures, rules and answers, verbal or written instructions, and musical nuances comes from the specifics of language.

Development: Keywords for high development are: affableness, argumentativeness, complaining, persuasive, loquacity, evasiveness, fluent talker, sarcasm. (See figure 36a on page 182.) Low development indicates taciturnity. (Figure 36b.)

Subfaculties

Vocabulary: This specific remembers words chiefly by sounds and next through sight, and stores the words and their meanings.

Large Vocabulary does not always imply talkativeness; Sociability would be needed as a propelling factor. At times we hear a loquacious talker with a small vocabulary and even smaller supply of ideas.

Rhetoric: This gives the ability to express oneself in a convincing and precise manner by arranging one's thoughts and conversation. It has to do with logical arrangement and impressive presentation, rather than correct grammar or the meanings of words. The sentences have persuasive power, charm, clearness of theme.

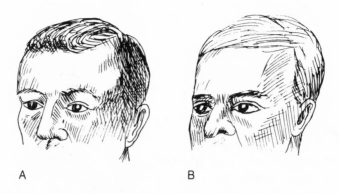

A   B

Figure 36. Language (Merton System). a) When the entire area of Language is highly developed (note wide upper temple), the individual has a pronounced potential to be an author or musician. b) The narrow temple shows low development of this faculty—no power of speech is indicated.

Music: This specific allows the accurate perception of sound differences. It is the basis for musical ability, but is also helpful in accurately perceiving and registering word sounds. It can allow one to pick up a foreign language "by ear." In musical directions it perceives pitch, time, stress, harmonies, rhythm, voice, overtones, as well as discords.

Vocations: The following vocations need Language as a primary faculty, and other faculty requirements are listed in order of importance. A lecturer needs Language, Aspirations, Memory, Laudation, Industry, Sociability, and Imagination. Life, fire, marine, or accident insurance brokers need Language, Calculation, Amity, Sociability, Imagination, Synthesis, Firmness, and Defense. Language also is important to the stenographer, typist, multigraph operator, salesman, minister, lawyer, postman, and some natural science vocations that involve extensive lists of names to be remembered.

Vocations for Vocabulary: Actor, abstract clerk, telephone operator, waiter, printing solicitor, radio operator, advertising manager, publicity manager, mail clerk, auctioneer, bookseller, copywriter, private secretary, author, translator, teacher, editor, historian.

Vocations for Music: Instrumentalist, piano tuner, conductor, vocalist, composer, telegrapher (Morse Code).

REASON

Location: The specifics of Reason are located in the lower side of the end of the nose. It is the part of the end of the nose and its alae that is in shadow when a strong light falls from directly above.

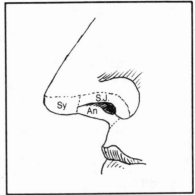

Analysis is shown by the drooping septum. Synthesis is seen in the fleshy part of the under nose, and judgment is seen when the rim of the nostrils are full.

Function: Reason must be called on any time there is a need for reflective efforts, analysis, or synthetic judgment. Problems that are not simply habitual thought or repetition of former judgments usually require Reason.

Development: Keywords for high development are: argumentativeness, changeableness, consistency, critical, organizing, persuasiveness, sagacity, skepticism, systematic, commercial vision. Low development of this faculty indicates a lack of good reasoning power.

Subfaculties

Synthesis: This specific gathers facts from memory, or new facts, in order to make a judgment on them as soon as a conclusion can be reached. Synthesis is the executive, administrative way of reasoning and is present in most forms of supervision and management. It is impatient with details. It masses impressions, memories, and ideas and makes judgments based on them. It acts with greater speed than analysis and is prone to error if the facts or information it uses are faulty. (See Figure 37a on page 184 for an example of high development of Synthesis.)

Analysis: This form of reasoning separates problems into their parts. The mental business of analysis is to discover the modes, methods, and laws concerning things or people. It searches for causes, components, measurements, and functions and leads to the discovery of these aspects. (See Figure 37b for an example of high Analysis.)

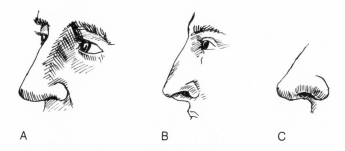

A   B   C

Figure 37. Reason (Merton System). a) When the subfaculty of Synthesis is highly developed, the individual has the ability to gather facts in order to draw conclusions. Synthesis is represented by the shaded area under the tip of the nose. b) When Analysis is highly developed, the individual has the ability to separate problems into their parts, components, causes, etc. Analysis is seen in the drooping septum. c) When the subfaculty of Spontaneous Judgment is highly developed, the individual has the ability to make quick judgments or decisions. This subfaculty is even more heightened when the subfaculty of Synthesis is also highly developed.

Spontaneous Judgment: This sign is a valuable adjunct when quick or rapid judgment must be made. The quality of these judgments depends on the quality of information available. It works best with Synthesis but can also speed up Analysis. It makes for quick decisions in emergencies and the so-called snap judgment. (See Figure 37c.)

Deliberate judgment works best with Analysis and gives the tendency to deliberate a considerable time before making a judgment. Deliberate judgment causes development at the root of the septum.

Vocations: Reason is required in countless vocations, trades, occupations and professions as a secondary sign.

Vocations for Synthesis include marketing, science teacher, sales manager, welfare worker, exporter, president of savings bank, store manager, weather prognosticator, superintendent of schools, corporation president, merchant.

Vocations for Analysis include surveyor, topographical expert, hydrographer, paymaster, pathologist, executive, veterinarian, engineer, pilot, osteopath, chiropractor, civil engineer, pharmacist, claims adjuster, optometrist, architect, nutrition expert, statistics analyst, chemist, psychiatrist, astronomer.

Vocations for Judgment include policeman, fireman, emergency worker.

CONSTRUCTION

Location: The Construction signs occupy the entire wing or alae of the nose above its lower margin, which is reserved for Spontaneous Judgment. The outer border is the ravine between the wing and the cheek and upper side of the nose.

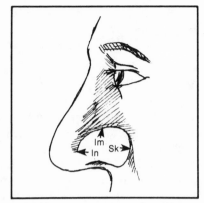

Function: This is the chief mental organ utilized in creating all types of structures, inventions, and images. It manifests in some new form, different manner of working, new objects or new forms of action.

Development: Keywords for high development of this faculty are artistic temperament, changeableness, idealistic, organizing, progressive, variety-loving, versatile, dexterity, exaggeration, fluent talker, initiative, optimism, rugged outdoor life, mechanical skillfulness, commercial vision.

Subfaculties

Imagination: This subfaculty is measured by the height of the alae. The business of Imagination is to visualize new impressions, sensations, mental visions or ideas, or to remake or recombine ideas. It combines, elaborates, and changes what is available. It foresees what is needed to accomplish a purpose and how things will fit or relate to each other. It works equally as well with the tangible and the mental or emotional. Figure 38a on page 186 shows high development of this subfaculty.

Invention: This aspect is concerned with mechanical action. It works chiefly with objects, changes in machines, and experimentation. It deals with power and energy and their relationships, new phases of social and commerical life, and trial-and-error methods. (See Figure 38b.)

Skill: Skill can follow models, forms, or designs closely, but it does not attempt to vary or change them. Its work is best when it is repetitious. It will duplicate accurately. Figure 38c shows Skill highly developed.

When combined, Skill and Imagination result in *Skillfulness*, which is the capacity to use a variety of means and methods to create a variety of ends. It gives dexterity.

Vocations: Draftsman, engineer (also needed are Analysis, Judgment, Synthesis, Form, Number, Memory, Stability), manufacturer, electrician, plumber, building construction worker, orthopedic surgeon, concrete or iron worker, foreman, foundry worker, sculptor, and other artists.

Vocations for Imagination include milling machine hand, real estate dealer, bridge engineer, punch press operator, printer, ornamental iron worker, electrician, power plant engineer, purchasing agent, transportation manager, building contractor, instrument maker, toolmaker, surgeon.

Vocations for Skillfulness include electrician journeyman, airplane mechanic, steel erector, dentist, auto repair, electroplater.

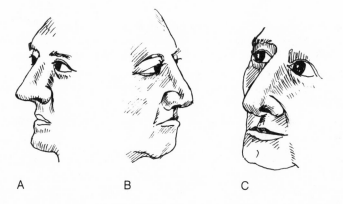

A   B   C

Figure 38. Construction (Merton System). a) When the subfaculty of Imagination is highly developed, the individual has a good ability to form ideas. b) When the subfaculty of Inventiveness is highly developed, experimentation, discovery, and invention are indicated. c) When Skill is highly developed, the individual will show control and dexterity in the hands.

INSPIRATION

Location: This faculty occupies a very narrow strip at the edge of the crest and the alae, or between Mental Focus and Construction.

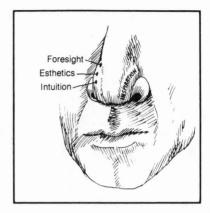

Function: In the Merton Method this is the only aspect of Human Nature that is not credited with originating in the physical senses. It is, as the name implies, the influx of knowledge or understanding from a higher realm than the physical senses.

Development: Keywords for high development are: artistic temperament, changeableness, idealistic, originality, progressive, radical, rashness, vanity, variety-loving. Psychic and creative ability are usually indicated.

When this faculty has a low development, there will be no ridge in this location, and the individual will show traits of cynicism and skepticism.

Subfaculties

Intuition: It is the nature of this specific to receive impressions from the vibrations of others and thereby to sense something of their cast of thought, ideas, or purposes. It is the extrasensory faculty. It gives us a conception of otherwise unrevealed intentions, the nature of living things, the mental atmosphere of a place, a group of people, or a person. It deals directly with impressions rather than going through intellectual processes.

Foresight: Foresight, as the word implies, looks into the future. It aids Reason in planning for the future and discovering natural laws. It "predicts" future possibilities and the results of various influences.

Aesthetics: This faculty gives us a sense of the sublime and beautiful and the desire for harmony in conduct, personal relationships and visual and emotional atmospheres. It wants to avoid commonness.

Vocations: No vocations arise from or require dominant Inspiration; however, the faculty has its place in artistic and literary endeavors as well as business and science.

FRIENDSHIP

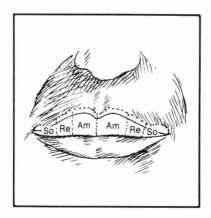

Location: Located in the red part and the margin line of the upper lip. Amity occupies the central one-third portion, and Reform and Sociability occupy one-third each of the remaining area.

Function: These signs represent abilities that allow us to make and hold friends. They influence toward social and cultural changes for the better.

Development: When the faculty of Friendship is highly developed, it indicates an individual who is concerned, friendly, and social. When this faculty has a low development, the individual is likely to be dry, cynical, and friendless. Figure 39 shows high and low development of this faculty.

To truly assess the overall development of this faculty, you must look at the subfaculties, for they will more accurately indicate the components of friendship. Keywords for the development of each subfaculty will be listed below.

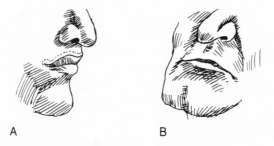

A   B

Figure 39. Friendship (Merton System). a) A high development of Friendship, and b) low development of Friendship.

Subfaculties

Amity: Amity is expressed by candor, kindness, expressions of admiration, chivalry, honesty, and sincerity. High Amity is interested and alive in social intercourse. Key words for high development: affableness, benevolence, optimism, courteousness, frankness, honest tendencies, good mixer, sensitiveness, sincerity, friendly disposition. Keywords for low development are: domineering, unsympathetic, vindictive, despondency, ingratitude, irritability, bluntness. (Low development results in the thin, tight upper lip.) Amity is **against** a go-it-alone disposition.

Reform: This specific is expressed by tact, conservation, and progress. Tact allows us to move gracefully and agreeably among friends or strangers. Progress works to improve the lot of mankind, especially the poor and unfortunate. Conservation wants to preserve friendships made.

Keywords for high development are: benevolence, conservatism, progressive, sincerety, tact, comercial vision. Low development indicates a stay-put person, radical tendencies, lack of sympathy, cynicism. Reform is **against** flattery.

Sociability: This quality makes one likable, genial, kind, considerate, and an agreeable companion. It produces cheerfulness, optimism, good humor, adaptability, and a love of life. It makes one a good listener who is responsive to the wit or good intentions of others. It makes one mindful of others' comfort and pleasure. Sociability is divided into the aspects of courtesy, humor, and hospitality.

High development of this subfaculty manifests as affableness, democratic spirit, variety-loving, courteousness, humor, good mixer, talkativeness, fond of comforts of life, cheerfulness, companionableness, graciousness, tactfulness. Low development indicates despondence, taciturnity, lack of sympathy, vindictiveness.

Vocations: Friendship is a prime factor in many vocations, although no specific vocations arise from its dominance. The employment manager, photographer, dancing teacher, nurse, hotel manager, salesman, insurance agent, and teacher are just a few of the vocations that require high Friendship.

DIGNITY

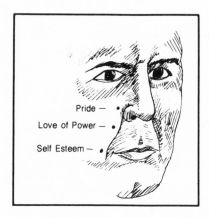

Pride —
Love of Power —
Self Esteem —

Location: This faculty is easy to locate. It occupies the narrow ridge running from the wing of the nose to the outer corner of the mouth and is commonly called the parenthesis of the mouth.

Function: This faculty is the approximate equivalent of the Crown in phrenology. It is the indicator of self-esteem, pride, dignity, aristocratic feelings, and self-confidence.

Development: Keywords for high development are affableness, arrogance, bombast, consistency, intolerance, opinionated, reserve, stoicism, vindictive, ambition, boastfulness, courteousness, dependability, fond of formality, honest tendencies, selfishness, egotism, hard-to-work with, stinginess, talkativeness, boldness.

Keywords for low development are complaining, democratic spirit, humility, lack of confidence, despondency, sensitiveness, stay-put person, timidity, changeableness. When Dignity is low, the parentheses of the mouth are not visible.

Against: Slovenly appearance.

Subfaculties

Pride: Basically, this represents the desire to be able to have self-respect and the respect of others. It seeks to maintain in oneself what is considered to be superior, admirable, worthy, or preeminent and watches over the other faculties so that no act or attitude will tarnish its luster. It tends to be formal socially, adds consistency and care in conduct, stimulates confidence, and makes people careful of their appearance.

Love of Power: This specific induces one to desire an active mastery over people and conditions. It dislikes being dictated to. It is dogmatic, arrogant, and interested in positions of authority. It increases domination tendencies and forcefulness.

Self-Esteem: This subfaculty of Dignity shows itself in various notice-able ways depending on its size. When very large, it is almost certain to show self-conceit, egotism, self-exaltation in conversation and various other idiosyncrasies.

When quite large and not governed by Amity and Sociability, pompousness and egotism run rampant, and the subject is rude and indifferent to the rights of others.

When this region develops downward and merges with Con-tempt and Antipathy, it manifests in a most disagreeable form of egotism. At the least, this area full will give bland self-satisfaction.

Vocations: No specific vocations arise from Dignity. The executive, the superintendent, the professional person, and both cultured and common people all enjoy the impulses of Dignity. Pride in one's work, the egotism of accomplishment, the perfection of a thing well done all spring from Dignity. Dignity also plays a considerable part in ambition.

STABILITY

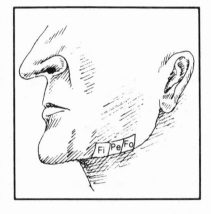

Location: This faculty is located in the middle of the margin of the lower jaw.

Function: This faculty is an as-sociate of Dignity. The two sup-port each other in many direct ways but especially in their con-tribution to the executive incen-tive and power. The chief opera-tion of Stability is to *stand firm*, to persevere, to endure, and to with-stand the tests of life (similar to Firmness in Phrenology).

Development: Keywords for high development are calmness, de-pendability, sunny disposition, patience, harshness, stubbornness, accuracy. See Figure 40a on page 192 for an example of high development. Keywords for low development: complaining, changeableness, lack of confidence, easygoing, wanderlust, time waster. Figure 40b shows us a face with low development of this faculty.

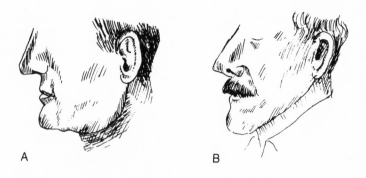

Figure 40. Stability (Merton System). a) A high development of the faculty of Stability indicates stick-to-it-iveness in an individual. b) Low development of this faculty indicates a more changeable, easygoing nature.

Against: Anger, flattery.

Remarks: Perseverance, Integrity, Economy, and Destruction work in harmony. Fortitude, Aspirations, Dignity, and Culture work in harmony. Conservatism, consistency, courage, stoicism, Firmness, Synthesis, and Skillfulness work in harmony.

Subfaculties

Firmness: This element holds its ground, resists influence or on-slaught, and is not turned aside in its purpose. It is a source of resolve or determination, punctuality, and a type of courage that is needed to see things through. It is chiefly resistant in nature and is highly necessary in executive vocations. Stubbornness is indicated unless high Firmness is controlled by other specifics. Small Firmness leads to vacillation in conduct.

Perseverance: Whereas Firmness is resistive, Perseverance is assertive in pushing toward goals that would otherwise be doomed to failure. It hangs on and shuts out evidence of impending disaster. It keeps going, it struggles toward a successful outcome, it is patient. Small Perseverance results in unfinished work and senseless changes in a course of action.

Fortitude: Fortitude endures. Its endurance is more passive than Firmness and Perseverance. It produces the courage that endures hardship, disaster, long convalescent illnesses, mental and physical stress. Small Fortitude generally whines or complains under adverse conditions.

Vocations: Bank president, master mariner, master mariner's mate, chief standard practice engineer, time study engineer, chief of bureau standards, chief planning supervisor, dispatch supervisor, works manager, trust officer, explorer.

LAUDATION

Location: These signs occupy the peak and valley of the narrow strip the runs from the septum of the nose to the upper red lip.

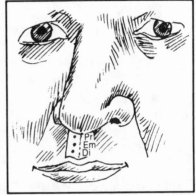

Function: These signs have their use in intersocial relationships, regulating self-conduct, appearance, adherence to convention, and avoidance of offensive behavior.

Development: High development, as shown in Figure 41a, indicates artistic temperament, bombast, democratic spirit, initiative, originality, ostentation, persuasiveness, vanity, variety-loving, ambition, boastfulness, calmness of expression, flattery, talkativeness, tact, exaggeration, fastidiousness, affableness.

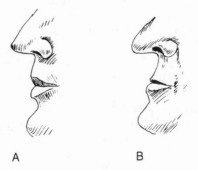

A   B

Figure 41. Laudation (Merton System). a) When the faculty of Laudation is highly developed, a pleasant, personable, and artistic temperament is indicated. b) Low development of this area indicates a person who has difficulty interacting with others.

Low development (Figure 41b) indicates despondency, humility, taciturnity, unsympathetic, slovenly appearance, bad manners, bluntness.

Remarks: Praise is held in line by Stability, Reform, and Caution.

Subfaculties

Praise: This is the source of sincere compliment and the use of flattery. Those with high Praise expect and give praise more easily and accomplish more because of it.

If high Praise is not supported by Friendship, Aspirations, and Reciprocity, then it will seek to gain praise rather than give it. Combined with Emulation it gives the desire to follow and imitate in order to achieve similar results.

Emulation: This specific impells us toward success by following the examples of others. It does not necessarily copy or duplicate but uses a similar direction or approach. It is an aspect of Ambition. It encourages the subject and others onward. It emulates a fine piece of mental or physical work.

Display: The ornamental exhibition of oneself for admiration is the main thrust of Display. Beauty is in the eye of the beholder, and thus this conscious ornamentation takes many forms, from the forehead and belly-button scars of the Mondari tribe to the pierced nose of the punk rocker.

Excessive Display struts and is vain. When developed, it frequently pulls on the upper red lip and closes the distance between the red lip and the bottom of the nose.

High Display is beneficial in the decorative arts and the art parts of the trades and other areas requiring aesthetic sense. This specific is an absolute asset in the theatrical arts.

Vocations: The intersocial expressions of Laudation have uses in such vocations as the ministry, welfare vocations, human and industrial relations work, political and governmental activities.

Although Laudation is not a major requirement in any vocation, its specifics of Praise and Display are called for in unusual amounts in theater, opera, television, and the motion picture industry.

Advertising, window display, decorating, and other art-related fields are assisted by Laudation. Executives, superintendents, supervisors, and managers also will find this faculty beneficial in achieving mutual cooperation through the proper praise and appreciation of others' work.

INTEGRITY

Location: This faculty has its sub-faculties divided in its facial location. Justice and Honor are found in an inverted triangle behind Dignity. The base of the triangle is situated on a line that runs from the bottom of the nose to the center of the ear. The point of the triangle points downward toward Self-Esteem. Equity is found just in back of the chin line.

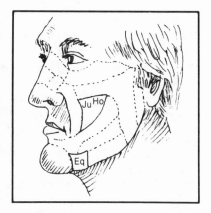

Function: In the affairs of life, business, competition, and responsibility, this faculty urges us to be just, to do what is right and proper as much as possible.

Development: High development (see Figure 42a) indicates integrity, courage, honest tendencies, accuracy. Low development (Figure 42b) indicates low ambition, bluffer, dishonest tendencies, laziness.

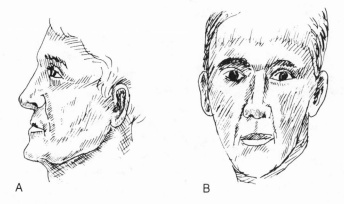

A   B

Figure 42. Integrity (Merton System). a) Both areas of this faculty are highly developed, indicating high standards for conduct and moral principle. b) Integrity is not strongly developed here. This individual will probably not live by higher principles.

Subfaculties

Justice: This specific relates primarily to material things and values. It urges having just compensation, our rightful share, and fair treatment. It urges us to put into practice what our intellect has decided is just, even if it may be against our best interests.

With small Justice and small Aspirations a person may view as just only that which is safe from prosecution or danger of revenge. "Let the buyer beware" is our advice when dealing with such a person.

Honor: This specific relates to matters of conduct and mental relations. Its action may not be controlled by laws or contracts but by ethics and morals of a higher personal standard. It deals with matters that are taken for granted—good conduct, desired friendship, goodwill, and a sense of rectitude that is enjoyed by honorable men and women.

Equity: Equity gives one a sense of value concerning materials, estates, real property, or other things not controlled by price lists or price tags. It adds, in a sense, a value-estimating ability.

Vocation: An asset in all vocations, especially those of high responsibility to firm, customers, or people in general: trust officer, purchasing agent, dealer, salesman, industrialist, manufacturer, legislator, diplomat, weighmaster, doctor, dentist, historian, payroll clerk. One would wish to have this faculty ample in all employees.

INDUSTRY

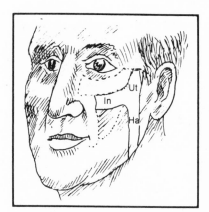

Location: This sign occupies a larger portion of the face than most. It runs below the crest of the cheekbone and gives prominence to that portion of the face. The subfaculty of Hardihood runs down in a strip just in front of the angle of the jaw, allowing room for the faculty of Liberty.

Function: This faculty, like many of the others, has its function suggested in its name. It is the faculty of hard work, steadiness, and intensity in effort and the courage to attempt tasks.

A   B

Figure 43. Industry (Merton System). a) When this faculty is highly developed, we see a person who is driving, intense, and industrious. b) When this faculty has a low development, the individual will lack intensity and force.

Development: Keywords for high development: matter-of-fact, initiative, rashness, systematic, changeableness, driver, efficiency, forcefulness, commercial foresightedness. (See Figure 43a.)

An individual with low development (Figure 43b) will tend to be a drifter, easygoing, lazy, or a procrastinator.

Subfaculties

Intensity: This specific insists on its own accomplishment and keeps up the stress of effort to the point of bearable fatigue. It avoids procrastination and discursive activities. It seeks ways to accomplish its goals directly. It works not only to keep up with others but to surpass them. It moves as fast as methods, tools, and good workmanship will allow.

Utility: The purpose of Utility is to make the best use of time, energy, and materials. It is restless when doing nothing or working without a worthwhile purpose. It will work hard for the practical things in life and gainful ends.

Hardihood: This specific is strong when it is long and hard down by the jaw, or wide, giving a "bull-dog" appearance. Hardihood will commence a task regardless of hardship; it appears fearless, daring, and confident in difficult endeavors. It is interested in adventure.

Vocations: Baggage agent, freight agent, freight/traffic manager, works manager, corporation executives and supervisors on different levels. Of course Industry is an asset throughout the vocational realm.

LIBERTY

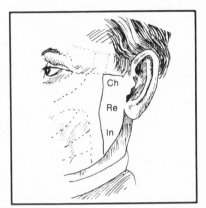

Location: This faculty occupies a narrow perpendicular strip immediately in front of the ear and extends down to the margin of the jaw. Note the relationship of the subfaculties to the ear and jaw.

Function: This is the Will impulse for personal freedom.

Development: Keywords for high development: initiative, opinionated, originality, persuasiveness, radical alertness, changeableness, egotism, lonesome-job person, restlessness, dexterity, fond of travel, visionary, vividness, wanderlust, chance taking. (See Figure 44a.)

A   B

Figure 44. Liberty (Merton System). c) High development of the subfaculties of Choice and Independence is shown. This individual is a free-thinking person who makes his own decisions, right or wrong! b) Low development of the overall faculty of Liberty indicates a person who will submit to convention more easily.

Keywords for low development: humility, submissive, lack of confidence, procrastination, ingratitude. Figure 44b shows us an individual with low overall development of Liberty.

Subfaculties

Choice: This is the impulse toward individual action. It chooses or selects one course of action over another, and generally does so intuitively.

Reciprocity: This specific is the give-and-take aspect of Liberty. It is mutually put to work for the benefit of both sides of an interchange. It works in harmony and general agreement with others.

Independence: This sign is located on the back angle of the jaw. Independence makes its own decisions, travels its own road, acts independently of others, does things its own way. High Independence works best where supervision is at a minimum.

Vocations: Liberty is not a required dominant in any vocation. When high, the subject will work best when he or she has a maximum of freedom and minimum of supervision. Traveling salesman, surveyor, explorer, fisherman, and similar vocations are best for those with high Liberty.

CAUTION

Location: This region extends under the eyes from the base of the nose back toward the ear. Its boundary ends about 1½ inches or less in front of the ear, where it meets the boundary of Choice. It takes in the crest of the cheekbone at is lower border.

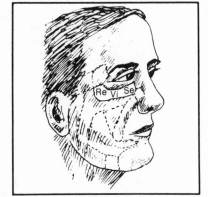

Function: This is a protective faculty. Its main purpose is to ensure the safety and best interests of the subject by being alert to any and every threat. It is the guard or sentinel of the rest of the mentality. It is conservative, protective, and forewarning.

Development: Keywords for high development are: critical, dependable, reserved, loquacity, systematic, alert, calmness, careful worker, conservation, crafty, cruelty, miserliness, accuracy. Figure 45a shows an individual with this faculty highly developed. An individual with low development of this faculty tends to be extravagant, careless, and frank. (See Figure 45b.)

Against: Flattery.

Subfaculties

Secrecy: This specific takes care that what we reveal does not harm us. It guards ideas, takes mental precautions, discretions, concealments.

With large Secrecy there is a cast of the mysterious about the subject. With small Secrecy the subject does not have the discretion needed to keep his or her mouth shut at the proper time.

Vigilance: This gives alertness to danger, whether physical or financial. It is on guard against any threat to its own safety or that of others. It works closely with the senses, through which it receives its information. It helps provide for future security and makes promises only cautiously.

Rest: Basically, this is the energy-saving specific. It conserves strength and vitality for future purposes. It tends to promote relaxation of

A   B

Figure 45. Caution (Merton System). a) Highly developed faculty of Caution, very common in American Indian faces; it indicates alertness, carefulness, reserve, and craftiness. b) Low development of Caution makes one vulnerable to harm through carelessness. This person is open to physical, economic, or emotional harm.

unused muscles and nerves; it works for smooth movement, gracefulnss, lack of excitableness, and an equable temperament.

Vocations: Fatalities and serious injuries in industry are often caused by those who are not observers of dangers on their job. Lack of caution in the vocational world also affects us in other ways: for example, the merchant who overbuys a particular line or does not take enough care in giving credit in sales or purchases. Caution is needed in many vocations but especially should be present in the merchant, mechanic, farmer, miner, fisherman, navigator, trainman, electrician, inspector, foreman, machinist.

ECONOMY

Location: This faculty resembles a foothill at the side of the nose. It is found in the valley above the wing and along the side of the nose.

Function: The faculty of Economy gives an impulse toward proprietary rights, ownership, the conservation of means, and an active interest in the benefit to be derived from any acquisition.

Development: High development indicates sagacity, go-it-alone disposition, commercial tendencies, grouchy disposition, dexterity, stay-put person, stinginess, avariciousness, fastidiousness, miserliness. (See Figure 46a on page 202.) Low development, as shown in Figure 46b, indicates extravagance, frankness, wastefulness.

Subfaculties

Ownership: This specific is equivalent to the phrenological sign of Acquisitiveness. It gives the desire for, and appreciation of, property, possessions, money, and other objects of material value. It is interested more in getting than in holding. If Frugality is small, the subjects may spend as fast at they gather.

Greed is the result of excess Ownership. It loses the reciprocity of a fair deal and regard for the other person. Small ownership is wasteful and has no sense of value.

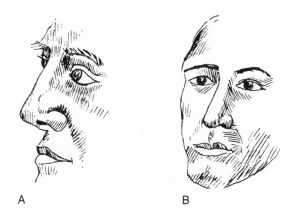

A   B

Figure 46. Economy (Merton System). a) Here we see the faculty of Economy highly developed. This indicates that the acquisitive tendency is extreme. b) Low development of Economy—this man may part with his possessions too easily.

Frugality: This economic impulse urges the conservation of what we already possess. It is the saving disposition. It is thrifty and concerned about that "rainy day."

In business Frugality watches every penny, buys for cash discounts, scrutinizes the wage and salary list, looks for labor-saving devices, tends toward stinginess.

Small or very small Frugality, with Caution and Ownership also small, lets money and possessions slip away from them, makes wasteful expenditures on unaffordable luxuries, and does not take care of what is theirs.

Selfishness: We are concerned here with only one type of Selfishness, that which grows out of economic and material self-interest. Other varieties of Selfishness stem from other parts of the mentality, especially from the Will and Affection specifics.

It is a self-protective attitutde in regard to the use of possessions. It saves its own property for its own use. It does not like its rights imposed on. In moderate amounts Selfishness is equitable and divides evenly what is due others.

Large Selfishness radiates a socially disagreeable disposition. It takes the best for its own without regard for others. It wants the best seat at the table, the window on the train, the first place in line. It takes all the credit when some of it is due elsewhere.

Vocations: Again we have a faculty that is an asset in a great variety of vocations on all levels yet is not necessarily needed in the dominant position. There are endless ways in which large economy can help eliminate wasted material and effort, as with shoe and clothing cutters, woodworkers, printers, construction workers, farmers, and foremen in general. From the lowest person in an organization to the highest, each can be assisted by Economy.

Certain vocations require Economy more or less close to dominant in the mentality; for example, buyer, purchasing agent, treasurer, production manager, and appraiser.

DEFENSE

Location: This faculty is situated on the bridge of the nose and extends downward from the root at Form to the upper boundary of Attention.

Function: This is one of the Wealth faculties (along with Caution and Economy) and is chiefly interested in personal self-protection and personal advantage, both physical and material.

Development: High development of this faculty results in argumentativeness, courage, initiative, progressiveness, sagacity, self-control, alertness, a go-it-alone disposition, avariciousness, self-confidence, commercial tendencies, drivenness, a hard-to-work-with person, radical tendencies, stubbornness, forcefulness, commercial foresightedness, boldness, temper. Figure 47a on page 204 illustrates a face with Defense highly developed.

Low development manifests as submissiveness, calmness, procrastination, a stay-put person, timidity, mildness. (See Figure 47b.)

Against: Secrecy.

Subfaculties

Aggression: This specific is at the upper end of the Defense region. When large, it shows pioneering spirit, self-motivation and a get-out-of-my-way attitude. It works in an individual way and is not good for team work. It will push its way in for its own benefit and will argue with anybody.

Protection: This specific is protective in the sense that it protects our interests by looking out for opportunities, and by hard work to avoid potential danger and bad investments. It is a security factor, but it takes the offensive in financial and working conflicts—unlike Caution, which is a more passive alertness to danger. It shuns irresolution, indecision, and timidity. It also protects one's views, opinions, and beliefs.

Self-Defense: Sometimes this faculty is referred to as courage. It is more personal, more pugnacious than it is commercial. It sometimes springs from resentment, boldness, or excess of courage; in lower-quality individuals it comes out of excessive egotism. Self-Defense provides the mental stimulation for a fighting tendency. It responds to the impulsive and mobile faculties of the Will.

Vocations: Retail (sole proprietor): lumber, grain, hay and feed, dry goods, umbrellas, silk and fur goods, groceries, delicatessen; caterer.

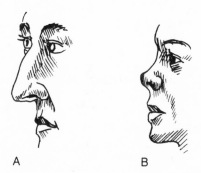

A   B

Figure 47. Defense (Merton System). a) Here we see the faculty of Defense highly developed. This individual might be very difficult to work with, but his strength lies in excellence at breaking through barriers and effecting change. b) The person who has a low development of this faculty is led by the emotions and easily swayed by resistance. This person gives up easily.

AVERSION AND DESTRUCTION

Location: These signs are located on the lower cheek and partly below and back of the corner of the mouth and above the mound of the chin, although its margins are purely tentative. A large development, as shown in Figure 48a on page 206, will extend these margins considerably.

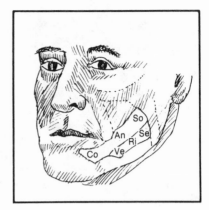

Function: This area locates the Will faculties that are most concerned with commercial activities. They are the organizing elements of the mentality. They make for executive ability, self-control, and the control of others. They resist opposition. They can be insistent. The Will faculties have purposes: for example, to get rich, to execute actions, to drive forward, to oppress others, to impel results.

Development: Keywords for high development are: arrogance, courage, critical, domineering, radical, self-control, vindictive, commercial tendencies, driver, forcefulness, hard-to-work-with person, indifference, irritability, lonesome-job person, reserve, stay-put person, stubbornness, temper, fond of travel. Low development of this area (see figure 48b) results in argumentativeness, idealism, mildness, an easygoing disposition.

Aversion Subfaculties

Contempt: This sign is made manifest by creating various degrees and forms of disgust, from indifference to rancor. It repels by ridicule, sarcasm, and irony. Things or actions that it abhors create a feeling similar to nausea in the appetite. It is negative and resistant rather than insistent. When large, it leans to sarcasm and harsh criticism, even bigotry. With large Self-Esteem, it supports egotism.

Antipathy: This specific can show open hostility. It is harsh and repelling. It does not try to go around provocation but takes the offensive.

Solitude: This feature is without hostility; it is aloof, prefers to be alone. It works better alone and will push others away if it becomes necessary, but in general it is not an aggressive trait. It seeks solitary occupations and pleasures.

A   B

Figure 48. Aversion/Destruction (Merton System). a) High development of these faculties almost invariably results in an individual who is a powerful business executive or some other type of leader or ruler. b) Low development of these faculties indicates a person who is lacking in executive abilities and leadership qualities.

Destruction Subfaculties

Vengeance: This specific produces the desire and intention to "get even," to punish, to retaliate for real or supposed injuries done to us or those we desire to protect. Vengeance looks backward for causes of action and is interested in returning malice for injustice.

Rigor: Acts on present provocation and compels others to accomplish one's own intentions. In this way, it is executive, but it also acts personally as a buffer against the hard tasks of life. It adds the ability to stand against the blows of life and to face either physical or commercial danger.

Severity: This specific affects the personality by giving it the attitude of austerity. It is reserved in manner and acts toward exacting plans and hardness of contracts. It opposes forbearance, forgiveness, or generosity. It gives an unyielding attitude. Rigor usually lets up when an occasion ceases, but Severity keeps on.

Vocations for Aversion and Destruction: No specific vocations are indicated for Aversion and Destruction, although their presence is extremely necessary in the commercial realm.

In the business world, Destruction often precedes Construction. It instigates tearing down old plants in order to build new ones, removing old machinery and replacing it with new, improved machinery. Destruction may also, on occasion, back conservative ideas and fight new opinions and ideas.

In commercial life, Vengeance can act in retaliation by cutting prices and carrying on various trade wars or by breaking up commercial relations. These faculties, as a whole, act as buffers against adversity—as shock absorbers against pressure and competition. They are useful in salesmen, in executive effort, in superintending positions, in laywers, and in master mariners, among others.

MOBILITY

Location: Mobility encompasses the chin. It is the chin itself, which is bordered on the top by the fleshy area just below the lower red lip and bordered approximately on the sides by an imaginary line drawn down from the corners of the mouth.

Function: In a nutshell, Mobility is the faculty that expresses the relative power of coordination, strength, and endurance of the motor muscles, especially to the legs and locomotion. The brain region responsible for locomotion is the cerebellum. Mobility responds to and reacts with the perceptions, especially Form.

Development: A person with high development, as shown in Figure 49a on page 208, will display dexterity, graciousness, courage, recklessness, be fond of outdoor life and fond of travel. When low in development, as in Figure 49b, impulsiveness, lack of endurance, grace, and agility are indicated.

Subfaculties

Strength: This relates to the relative power of the muscles of locomotion and is not concerned with the upper regions of the body. It shows the muscular tonicity in the lower back and legs. It adds response to mental stimulation and elastic ease in movements.

Flexibilty: This is the capacity to bend the body joints more than is normal. It is more observable in action than in repose.

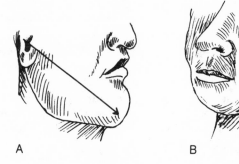

A   B

Figure 49. Mobility (Merton System). a) Here we see this faculty highly developed, indicating athletic abilities, great endurance, and flexibility in the legs. Grace in motion! b) Low development of this faculty indicates an individual who lacks a strong motion impulse—this person may even tend toward clumsiness.

Endurance: Endurance is not necessarily Strength, although Endurance is assisted by Strength. This specific is more obviously a faculty of Will.

Vocations: Athlete, mailman, waitress, dancer, nurse, telephone lineman, coach, referee, meter reader, outdoorsman.

THE ASPIRATIONS

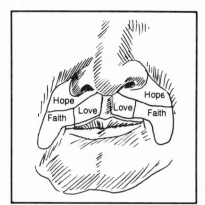

Location: The Aspirations consist of three distinct faculties, all of which are located above the margin of the upper lip and within the parentheses of the mouth (the ridges of Dignity). They extend somewhat around the corners of the mouth and are separated in the middle by the narrow valley of Laudation.

Function: As a group, these faculties create and respond to the highest human emotions. They produce Platonic or moral sentiments of goodwill supported by fraternal or religious sympathy, depending on the background of the subject.

Development: High development of the Aspirations results in affableness, benevolence, changeableness, democratic spirit, good nature, aspirations, initiative, optimism, progressiveness, self-control, bluffer, self-confidence, courage, courteousness, honest tendencies, fluent talker, loyalty. Figure 50a shows an individual with high development of the Aspirations. Keywords for low development are: complaining, cynical, domineering, melancholy, skepticism, taciturnity, unsympathetic, vindictive, gloomy disposition, fond of formality, radical tendencies, sensitivity, temper. (See Figure 50b.)

Faith Subfaculties

This is the faculty that allows us to accept matters that cannot be proved by reason. It exercises belief and holds confidence in things desired or expected in the future.

Belief: This is not solely a religious specific, although it certainly supports religious sentiments. Large Belief will accept unproved ideas, opinions, and ideals much more readily, and will trust others much more readily than small Belief.

Confidence: This specific is more personal and social in nature. It is altruistic and cooperative; it enjoys frankness and directness in social contacts. It has an optimistic influence. When Confidence is small, the subject runs to secrecy, doubtfulness, and lack of frankness.

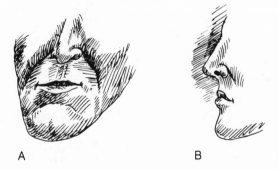

A   B

Figure 50. Aspirations (Merton System). a) High development of all three faculties of Faith, Love, and Hope indicates an individual with humanitarian instincts, higher vision, hope for the future, and a generous nature. b) Low development of this overall area indicates cynicism, selfishness, and a lack of faith.

Serenity: When large, this specific adds a calm, unruffled, undisturbed demeanor. It is sunny in disposition, congenial under reasonable circumstances, and will overlook trouble as much as possible. Small Serenity causes the subject to believe the world owes him enjoyment under all circumstances, and that others are at fault when something is wrong.

Love Subfaculties

This is the faculty that promotes attraction toward others or toward an idealistic philosophy. It is the main origin of Philanthropy, impersonal generosity, and the desire to benefit reciprocally with the world around us.

Goodwill: This specific maintains a common interest in the happiness of others, and an interest in their approval. It wants to be fair and treat others right.

Trust: Trust puts confidence in others, believes that everything will come out right and that others will do their part.

Philanthropy: This is the generosity specific. It wants to aid others in their labors, progress, and personal happiness. It desires to uplift humanity and human progress.

Hope Subfaculties

This faculty anticipates betterment, creates enthusiasm, and adds zest, dynamism, and buoyancy to the character.

Enthusiasm: This specific gives zest and mental ginger to one's attitude and intentions. It stimulates effort and overcomes depression. Small Enthusiasm is negative concerning aims, intentions, goodwill, and efforts of oneself and others.

Zeal: This is a forceful specific. It wants to compel results in what it wants or against what it wants, and it keeps in mind the element of success.

Exaltation: This specific instills effervescence and joyousness. It works against depression and stimulates a healthy attitude.

Small Exaltation gives the mentality a matter-of-fact, routine attitude lacking in enthusiastic demonstration.

Vocations for Aspirations: Minister, welfare worker, missionary, kindergarten supervisor, teacher, physician, counselor. It is necessary in vocations where congeniality and optimism are factors, for example: sales; industrial relations work; club, hotel, restaurant, and store management.

Overlarge or extreme Aspirations not supported by a hard jaw but backed by an excessive Imagination may bite off more than it can chew, overpromise, assume the impossible, and so forth.

Small Aspirations are not favored in any vocation requiring social relations.

SOCIAL AND SEXUAL AFFECTIONS

Location: The function of sexuality is found in the red under lip. Parental and familial functions are just below the red lip in a narrow strip above Contempt.

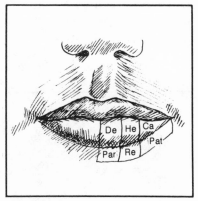

Function: These faculties provide sexual attraction and appreciation of the sexes and the family-oriented motivations. Below we list Merton's tentative analysis of Sexation and Parention. Merton was relatively sparse in his treatment of people's ability to love or raise a family, because his work primarily focused on vocational evaluation.

Sexation Subfaculties

Devotion: Includes desire, winningness, and ardency. Desire manifests as adoration of and yearning for someone, and includes both physical and emotional response. Winningness can be described as charm, persuasion, and sweetness. Keywords for ardency are eagerness, fervency, and passion.

Heredity: Includes the desire to mate, procreate and perpetuate. Keywords to be taken into account here are affinity, transference, polarity, duality, fecundity, spirituality, involution, conservation and catalysis.

Caressing: This subfaculty takes into account luxury (fervor, fondling, petting), amusement (our need for diversion, companionship, romance) and gratification—the need to feel in harmony, concordance, and replete.

Parention Subfaculties

Parentity: Includes parental love, authority (encompassing direction, control, and power), and providence (the ability to provide, solicit, and indulge).

Reverence: This subfaculty takes into account filial love (keywords: piety, veneration, dependence), service, attendance and deference to others, and modesty (meaning gentleness, diffidence and reserve).

Patriotism: Here is included home love, which encompasses domesticity, public spirit, and nationality; also clanship, tribalism, and seclusion; and earth love, which takes into account rurality, abidingness, and pastorality.

VITAL SENSATIONS

Location: In the sidehead, behind and forward from the ear. High development of the Vital Sensations widens the head at these points.

Function: The chief function of the Sensations is to supply information of the external world to the rest of the mental and intellectual functions, and to supply responses for the purpose of self-protection, nourishment, and comfort.

Development: Keywords for high development: appetite indulgences, sensitiveness to stimuli. Low development results in stoicism.

Remarks: The effects of Feeling and Appetite are of great importance in the structure and weight of the body. As a general rule, wider heads in the area of appetite and feeling tend to fleshiness of body, and narrow heads to leanness. Heads that are wide in Destructiveness may be heavy or lean. Again, we offer the Vital Sensations as a group with abbreviated explanations below. Although the Vital Sensations are important, they are translators of direct experience rather than intellectual functions. They are concerned with the nourishment and protection of the physical body and can only indirectly affect us vocationally.

Subfaculties

Impression gives us the subfaculties of *Quality* sense, *Radiance* sense, and *Touch*. These components deal with various sensitivites such as the experience of pain, ingested chemicals from food or drugs, pleasure sensations, and discrimination in the sense of touch.

Feeling gives us components of *Smell*, *Hunger*, and *Motion* and regulate body temperature, odor sense, and our inner sense of balance.

Appetite is composed of *Taste*, *Hunger*, and *Growth*. Its basic function is to supply the spectrum of taste from sweet to sour, stimulate very basic survival drives such as our needs for food and sleep, and to stimulate the intestinal and eliminative functions.

Vocations: Steward, chef, coffee tester, tea tester, gourmet, wine taster, and similar vocations require strong Appetite. Impression and Feeling are required in areas where judgment of cloth, glass, paper, and various other materials is essential. On the whole, the Vital Sensations are more concerned with the maintenance of the body.

THE MENTAL PATH

Experience of the external world follows a pattern in the mentality, with certain faculties supplying material for the other faculties above and beyond it. In the course of the mental path the faculties will support, modify, or counteract each other.

The mental path of experiences begins from the body, through the sensations of Appetite (Alimentiveness, Bibativeness), Feeling, and Impression. Next, the mental path passes Form, Color, and Number, for the brain must have sensations from the body organs before it can remember or arrange its facts. Then, the faculty of Attention arranges these facts, Memory records them, Language names them and also adds the sense of hearing to the senses above noted. Following these, Inspiration foresees their application and gives their future tendency. Reason then analyzes them and arranges rules, laws, and judgments, after which Construction deals with their mechanical relations, if any, and Reform urges or restrains their applications. The faculties of Amity and Sociability make active those impressions that pertain to people, friends, or companions and the communications between them. From there the impulse passes to Faith and Hope, which add encouragement to the executive organs of the Will, but first Dignity molds the organization of power for accomplishing the end, and Stability gives firmness for its execution. From there the path is to the faculty of labor or Co-Action, and from there to the defensive faculties of Wealth, and finally to those of Impulsion (Will) that cause distribution in the commercial faculties of Aversion, Destruction, and Mobility.

PATTERNS OF GROWTH

Holmes Whittier Merton followed the assumptions of his mentor Sivartha that civilization followed the pattern that we witness in the development of children into adults. That development begins at the lower faculties, the Appetites and Sensations and onward to the faculties of Perception and Attention; from there the development of the selfish faculties, the Will, and then to the Intellect. Last to develop are the Spiritual areas of the mentality.

It is generally found that by the age of sixteen most of the predominating mental aspects are shown by the physiognomy. These patterns are seen earlier, in their potential state, in the hand development.

The assumption of Sivartha and Merton was that humans began their development with the Appetites and Vital Sensations pronounced, and as the human race evolved so did the higher faculties.

Although this pattern can be discerned in the growth of an individual, we are still baffled by certain unexplainable and unavoidable facts when we apply this theory to evolution in general. On the surface there is much evidence to support such an idea, but we question it when faced with such mysteries as the pyramids. The precise astronomical, mathematical alignment of the Great Pyramid of Cheops, its ponderous placement of monolithic granite with precise cutting and placement of each stone stands as an eternal epitaph to the wisdom and spiritual development of its architects. We cannot say that modern humanity has evolved to a higher state than that exhibited by the ancient Egyptians, although individual examples of evolvement have appeared throughout history.

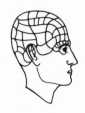

CHAPTER 10

CHARTING AND RATING

Interpreting human nature from the appearance does not require the use of charts, forms, or written data; however, in order to establish a history on your subject and records for future study in the form of case histories, a chart of some type should be kept.

Prior to the time photography was easily available to the public, charts were the only form of maintaining records. It is currently possible to keep slides or snapshots of your clients along with a chart and notes on your interviews. I highly recommend that you do so. In order to overcome the stigma that has been placed on our science, we must endeavor to use the most professional approach possible. Characterology should not be a parlor game but a serious basis for counseling, enlightening, and guiding our fellow men and women.

You may eventually develop a chart that gives you the information you deem important to record. The chart I use is one that I have evolved through trial and error. I think you will find that it allows you to record an accurate profile of your client, but before that I am going to discuss two traditional charting methods. Chart 1 shows the method used in phrenology, and Chart 2 is the Merton Method.

THE SPENCER CHART

With slight modifications Chart 1 on pages 216 and 217 is the one used by Dr. Lloyd Spencer. Using the phrenological chart is quite simple. It requires that you examine the individual faculties or organs and judge their physical size or importance. Check the appropriate

Chart 1. The Spencer Chart

No.	Brain Function	7 Very Large	6 Grade Large	5 Grade Full	4 Aver-age	3 Small
	Age			Weight		
I.	Mental Temperament					
II.	Motive Temperament					
III.	Vital Temperament					
IV.	Organic Quality					
V.	Health					
VI.	Breathing Power					
VII.	Circulatory Power					
VIII.	Digestive Power					
IX.	Activity					
X.	Excitability					
XI.	Size of Brain					
1.	Amativeness					
A.	Conjugality					
2.	Parental Love					
3.	Friendship					
4.	Inhabitiveness					
5.	Continuity					
E.	Vitativeness					
6.	Combativeness					
7.	Destructiveness					
8.	Alimentiveness					
8.	Bibativeness					
9.	Acquisitiveness					
10.	Secretiveness					
11.	Cautiousness					
12.	Approbativeness					
13.	Self-Esteem					
14.	Firmness					

Chart 1 cont.

No.	Brain Function	7 Very Large	6 Grade Large	5 Grade Full	4 Aver- age	3 Small
15.	Conscientiousness					
16.	Hope					
17.	Spirituality					
18.	Veneration					
19.	Benevolence					
20.	Constructiveness					
21.	Ideality					
B.	Sublimity					
22.	Imitation					
23.	Mirthfulness					
24.	Individuality					
25.	Form					
26.	Size					
27.	Weight					
28.	Color					
29.	Order					
30.	Calculation					
31.	Locality					
32.	Eventuality					
33.	Time					
34.	Tune					
35.	Language					
36.	Causality					
37.	Comparison					
C.	Human Nature					
D.	Agreeableness					

strength from very large to small. Those faculties found larger than average will hold sway in the client. Small faculties may need development. Very large faculties will need restraint in some cases. Where Dr. Spencer graded 3 as "moderate," we have changed it to "small." (In my estimation only three grades are important for determining character, and those are large, medium, and small or deficient.) It is important to know in what area your subject excels, but it is equally important for counseling to know where he or she is lacking. The combinations also may modify a large sign considerably. By way of example we had a recent client who showed a very high Defense in the bridge of the nose, usually a fighting or argumentative indication. Also in the face was an extremely high Caution, causing timidity. The high Defense merely made the subject want to do things her own way, whereas the Caution prevented her from doing so when the will of others objected or the fear of failure presented itself. The result was confusion, sensitivity, and a general attitude that the world was against her. Rather than fail, she attempted nothing. Counseling in this case, as in most cases where problems exist, depends on the strongest organs or faculties present. We attempt to build on those focal points while encouraging the client to overcome his or her deficiencies.

The point of charting or rating the individual head or face is based on first being able to discern the various degrees of development in that head or face. One cannot chart unless one can judge the signs. Again, I repeat, this ability will come only through constant observation and comparison.

THE MERTON CHART

Charting as practiced by counselors of the Merton Method is essentially the same as for phrenology, the basic differences being that grading is in relative percentages from 60 to 100, instead of 3 to 7. The result is the same in both cases. We are judging from small or deficient organs to those that are very high or full. The chart itself is graphed for quick scanning. A sample analysis is given so that you may see how the chart is used.

Chart 2 was designed by Merton for use with his system of vocational counseling. Full-strength faculties are at 100, while weak

Chart 2. The Merton Chart *

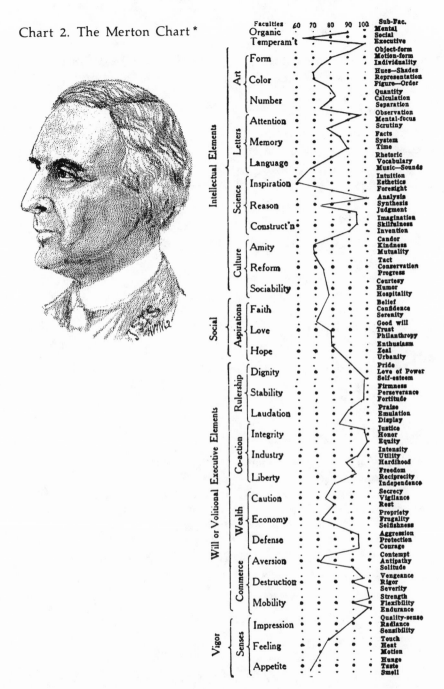

Faculties	60	70	80	90	100	Sub-Fac.
Organic						Mental
						Social
Temperam't						Executive
Form						Object-form / Motion-form / Individuality
Color						Hues—Shades / Representation / Figure—Order
Number						Quantity / Calculation / Separation
Attention						Observation / Mental-focus / Scrutiny
Memory						Facts / System / Time
Language						Rhetoric / Vocabulary / Music—Sounds
Inspiration						Intuition / Esthetics / Foresight
Reason						Analysis / Synthesis / Judgment
Construct'n						Imagination / Skilfulness / Invention
Amity						Candor / Kindness / Mutuality
Reform						Tact / Conservation / Progress
Sociability						Courtesy / Humor / Hospitality
Faith						Belief / Confidence / Serenity
Love						Good will / Trust / Philanthropy
Hope						Enthusiasm / Zeal / Urbanity
Dignity						Pride / Love of Power / Self-esteem
Stability						Firmness / Perseverance / Fortitude
Laudation						Praise / Emulation / Display
Integrity						Justice / Honor / Equity
Industry						Intensity / Utility / Hardihood
Liberty						Freedom / Reciprocity / Independence
Caution						Secrecy / Vigilance / Rest
Economy						Propriety / Frugality / Selfishness
Defense						Aggression / Protection / Courage
Aversion						Contempt / Antipathy / Solitude
Destruction						Vengeance / Rigor / Severity
Mobility						Strength / Flexibility / Endurance
Impression						Quality-sense / Radiance / Sensibility
Feeling						Touch / Heat / Motion
Appetite						Hunge / Taste / Smell

Row groupings (left side labels): Intellectual Elements — Art (Form, Color, Number); Letters (Attention, Memory, Language); Science (Inspiration, Reason, Construct'n). Social — Culture (Amity, Reform, Sociability); Aspirations (Faith, Love, Hope). Will or Volitional Executive Elements — Rulership (Dignity, Stability, Laudation); Co-action (Integrity, Industry, Liberty); Wealth (Caution, Economy, Defense); Commerce (Aversion, Destruction, Mobility). Vigor — Senses (Impression, Feeling, Appetite).

*This chart is from *The Merton Course in Vocational Counseling and Employee Selection;* Lesson twenty-one: The Regional Influence and Products of Integrity. Published by the Merton Institute, New York, 1920. The face in this illustration is not identified, although in all probability it was drawn from life by Merton. The portrait is supplied with the chart for the student to analyze. In this case, the analysis is mine.

faculties are at 60 on this chart. A look at Chart 2 will indicate the subject's strong and weak faculties as listed below:

Strong Faculties

Motive temperament in lead, Mental second
Attention (Observation)
Reason (Analysis)
Construction
Dignity
Stability
Integrity
Industry
Defense
Destruction (Vengeance, Severity)
Mobility

Weak Faculties

Color
Inspiration
Amity
Aversion
Feeling
Appetite

A review of Chapter 9 will show that the realm of activity for such a client would be science, engineering, technical and mechanical crafts, overseer, naturalist. Law and judicial work are also indicated. Weakest are the realms of art and social contact work. He is industrious, severe, stern, reliable, ponderous, analytical, independent, freedom-loving, hard-working, honest, deliberate, slow to act but acts with full force of will when he does act, cynical, critical, imaginative in practical lines, frugal, loves nature and the outdoors.

THE WAGNER CHART

The Wagner Chart for Character Assessment (Chart 3 on page 222) is set up so that visual impressions can be translated directly to the area in question by going from the subject to the chart without searching for words. The biggest disadvantage of the two other systems of charting is that one must read, rather than "see" what is present in the subject.

In the chart I have developed you will find a minimum of words, although they cannot be avoided entirely. With this chart one can record the mental characteristics of the subject easily even if the names of all the faculties have not been memorized. It is a simple matter of marking the diagram as the actual face and head appear to you. A system of numbers from 3 to 10 could be used to indicate relative strength of the various aspects; or a plus (+) for moderate areas, a plus-plus (++) for prominent areas, and a minus (-) for deficient areas could be utilized.

A review of this chart will enable you to visualize your client's face more easily. Also, it is a good idea to review the chart once you have developed the slides or prints you have taken of the client at the initial counseling session. You may suddenly observe something that was missed, overstated, or understated previously. There is less pressure and more objectivity involved when we study a photo than when the subject is in front of us—especially when we are still in the learning process. Errors can be quickly spotted when we review the photo and compare it to the chart we have prepared. With experience, you will not be dependent on slides—your perceptions will have developed accuracy.

In Chart 3 we have attempted to incorporate the most significant aspects of character analysis that are contained in this book. No chart could incorporate them all, nor is it the only method that is possible. We can analyze from the hand, or from the point of view of the chemical constitutions, or by other methods that we are not aware of.

We should observe the client from the moment he or she enters our view. It is good to observe the walk, to mentally measure height, size, and proportion as the client enters the door, to shake hands, to listen to the tone of voice, to observe the method of dress and choice of colors, to watch gestures and expressions, how the client sits, the color tones of the face, the expression in the eyes, the quality of the vibration, and so forth. None of these things is indicated on the chart. Any special features may be added on the back of the chart when they attract your attention or in the space provided below the chart. Highlights of the counseling session and comentary by the client also should be recorded for future reference. Fill out the chart as suggested below.

1. Basic information about the client is recorded in the upper portion of our chart: name, address, phone, height, weight, etc.

Chart 3. The Wagner Chart

Name _____   No _____

Address _____   Date _____

_____   Height _____ Weight _____

Phone _____   Birthdate _____

Present Occupation _____   Present Age _____

	HEAD	BODY
	M	M
	F	F
	N	N

color: wh   pk

TYPE:

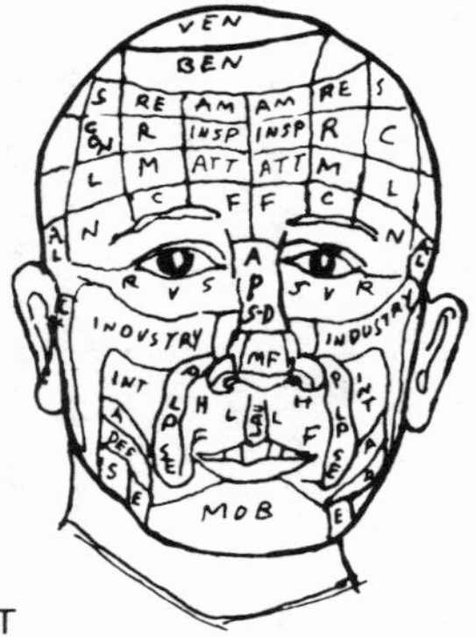

WIDE
NARROW

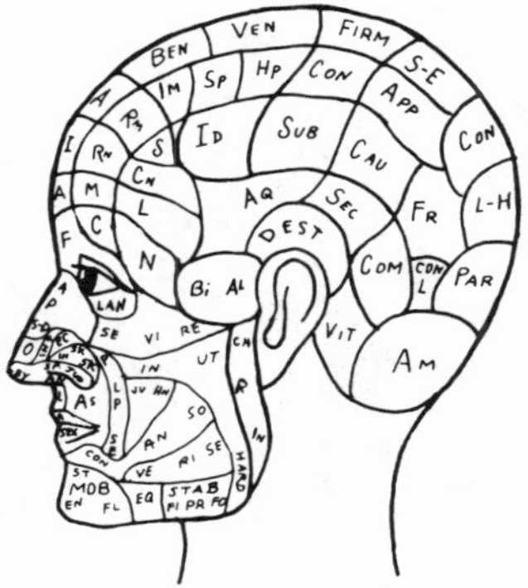

FACT
PLANE
THEORY

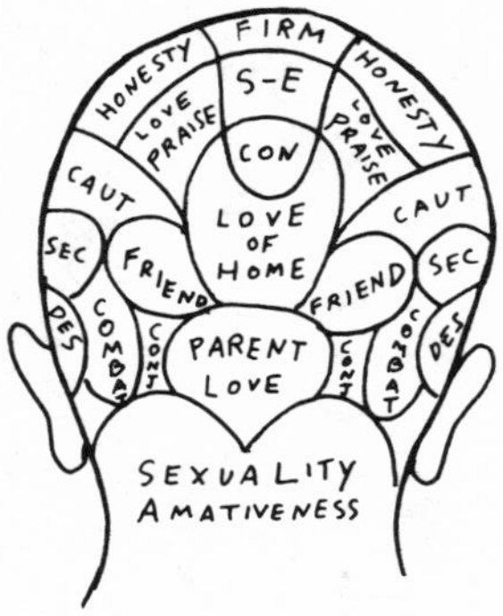

LONG
SHORT

% BLOND

% BRUNETT

2. Beneath the first heavy black line we record information taken directly from observation. On the left are the Temperaments represented by their geometrical symbols.

3. A Vital Temperament subject would be indicated by marking in the circle. A Motive-Mental subject, for example, would be recorded by making a 1 in the rectangle shape and a 2 in the triangular shape. See Chapter 3 for information on the Temperaments.

4. The degree of blond or brunette is recorded next by simply circling blond or brunette. Wide, narrow, fact, plane, or theory, and long, short also are circled where they apply.

5. The color of the skin and especially of the palms of the hands and nails should be examined next. The colors are white, pale pink, mottled pink, pink, blue, yellow, red.

6. The body portions are masculine, feminine, or neutral.

7. By this time you should have a very good grasp of your client's general nature, drives, health patterns, motivations, sphere of expression or repression, and so on. It remains to map the face, indicating the areas that are high, wide, hollow, unusually modeled, and so forth. These will add detail to the basic frame of reference that you have already noted. Some sample analysis will follow in the next chapter.

A method for maintaining records is also important, but again there are many possibilities that may be equally suitable. Records may be kept in file folders that can be stored in files. They may be kept in individual 9 × 12 envelopes, or three-ring-punched and kept in binders. They may be kept in alphabetical order or in numerical sequence. If they are kept in numerical sequence, you will need a cross-reference record that is alphabetical.

Thorough records are an excellent source of comparative study. Learning by comparing similar types or by contrasting types will establish your ability to recognize and understand these types. Through experience you will gain new insight into readings you have already given and can therefore be more helpful to clients who would like an updated session with you. Unlike a psychiatrist, we recommend supplemental readings only after a period of six months to one year or more. There is no need for or benefit from weekly sessions for our clients. In special cases more than one session may be necessary if you feel it will benefit the client.

If you use the information in this text for counseling, please maintain the highest ethical, moral, and professional approach possible. You are pioneers who will help bring this science out of the realm of negative thinking and put it to use in the contemporary world, where it will serve humanity.

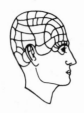

CHAPTER 11

CHARACTEROLOGY STUDIES

By the knowlege of self we may master self, and by the improvement of self we may also improve mankind.

—B. Frank Scholl, Ph.D., M.D.

All the groundwork has been lain in the preceding chapters to enable you to read people on sight. It is really not even necessary for the client or subject to speak. We know him or her from the outside in, so to speak.

In an actual counseling situation, however, clients are there to learn about themselves and about their possibilities and their potentials, and it is our job to get through to them. Each client will come for a different reason. They will come because of personal problems, lack of direction, curiousity, lack of fulfillment, and for countless other reasons. Some of the reasons are really beyond the capacity of characterology to resolve. Many times the characterologist is equated with a psychic advisor or is expected to resolve problems instantly— to give an easy solution, to transform the client miraculously, or to give the client a new occupation.

I have found over the years that you will do your best work if you stick to what characterology does, and that is to recognize the character, potentials, and limitations of the client, to make the client aware of his or her inherent nature, and to work within the framework of that individual.

I also have learned the rather difficult task of counseling. It is one thing to know and understand the person in front of you—the mechanics of characterology will do that quite adequately; it is another thing to make this information useful to the client. There are as many different approaches to counseling as there are reasons for the client to seek you out in the first place. What we all wind up doing is what comes naturally to us as a result of our own training and background. It is imperative then, if you wish to serve your clients, that you be as versatile and broad-minded as possible.

It is extremely important that you make yourself aware of as many different modalities as possible. The so-called New Age modalities offer numerous valid and practical approaches that may be exactly what your client needs. Rebirthing is an excellent cleansing process for emotional garbage. Iridology, herbology, reflexology, and naturopathy are alternatives to the drug solution offered by most of our M.D.'s. Spiritual healing is another alternative. You must become aware of what is available in your area in order to direct clients to what you feel they are in need of. Where can they receive other types of counseling if needed? Where can they find a good chiropractor, doctor, surgeon, employment agency, school, church, social group, club, hypnotherapist, rental agency, health food store, and so on. You will be called on to use every method and insight you have in order to advise and direct those clients who need it.

How you approach each client will differ also. If you detect a timid soul when your client sits in front of you, your words may have to be soothed over and honey-coated, or you may bruise your client and scare him or her away. If your client is obviously hard and rigid, you may have to hit him or her over the head with a verbal baseball bat. Experience and your understanding of human nature will guide you. As your technique develops, you will mold your approach for best results.

The results of your sessions with clients also will vary considerably. Most of the time you may not even see certain clients again, although you may affect them in a way that changes their entire lives. Some clients will leave your office and immediately fall back into the patterns they have set for themselves, content to have had their evening's entertainment. Many need constant support, and the positive results of the session are lost unless you can work with them on a continuing basis or get them into a situation where support is constant. It can be a real drain when you know an individual has tremendous potential, yet you cannot get through to him or her. Occasionally, you will get secondhand information when a new client tells you he was recommended by so-and-so, who was helped tremendously by your reading. Those few who keep in touch, with periodic updates, are the ones who inspire us to continue in what often seems frustrating and fruitless.

I have chosen several subjects as case studies in order to give you an idea of the variety and scope you may encompass in your own career. These may be called typical cases, if such a thing exists. Really great heads and heads of very low caliber seldom present themselves for inspection; thus, I have selected subjects who fall between those two extremes. This remaining group still presents us with a broad spectrum of possibilities. While discussing these subjects I will try to make you aware of how a chart is recorded, what it tells us about the client, and also some of the problems we might face in getting that information to the client.

PREPARATIONS

If your client contacts you by phone, it is always good business sense to get the full name, address, and phone number at home and work. It is also important for you to get the client's height, weight, and birth date or age. The reason for this is to prepre you in advance for what you may expect at the actual session. The height and weight will often quickly identify the Temperament of the subject, which you can reaffirm by visual inspection at the actual session. The birth date will give you an idea of where the subject is in their life cycle at this time. Young subjects present different problems and require different approaches from those of middle-aged and older clients. Their realms of experience will differ, and what they have accomplished in life will vary greatly also. (I have selected subjects from different age groups for the specific reason of dealing with this aspect.) Pay attention to the voice on the phone also; it will tell you much about the person's refinement, communication ability, intensity. It will give you impressions of being warm and inviting, or cold and distant, businesslike, skeptical, and so on.

Now let us assume the client is here. We shake hands to get an impression of energy and to feel if there is any resistance or other factor that can be registered there. You can also note other factors about the client as he or she enters, mainly walk and carriage. Subjects should be seated where the light is good but not direct or glaring, where you will be able to walk around them in order to see and feel the head and face from different angles. It is best to have your chart on a clipboard so it can travel with you.

My personal preference in a session is to complete the entire chart before discussing the findings with the client. This will give you time to assess and balance the different aspects you find and make the reading more accurate and thought-out. At first, the silence may be a little awkward. Your client wants to know what you are doing; they are naturally curious. There are several ways I handle this. You may find your own method or you may prefer to disclose your findings as you observe them. I usually tell clients what I am looking at and how I am going to discuss my findings with them in a few minutes, so they will know the sequence of how things will take place. If the subject asks questions about what I am doing or about characterology or makes small talk in general, it may help to break the tension silence may cause. However, very talkative subjects are distracting and prevent you from doing your mental analysis while you are charting them. My teacher would bluntly tell them to be quiet; it's not time to talk. My method is to place a piece of litmus paper in their mouths until I have finished the chart. That serves the purpose of giving you a few quiet moments and also shows the person's acidity or alkalinity. Acidity is never a good health indicator.

Preparing a chart will condition you to review the entire subject before forming conclusions. These indications of character are all discussed with the client. As mentioned above, I will normally give my conclusions to the client after the chart is complete. Following my "reading," I establish rapport with the subject for feedback and clarification, to touch on points of interest to the client, or to try to help the client solve specific problems based on my understanding of his or her nature, capabilities, and shortcomings. It is here that you will be called on to counsel, teach, instruct, and possibly transform your client.

As mentioned earlier, each of you will approach the actual session in a manner colored by your own background, abilities, and intentions. It is in the area of intentions that the greatest results will be achieved. If your intentions and desires are to help your client, it is more likely that the results of the session will be beneficial to some degree. Sincerity and a desire to help may not be all that is needed, but it will give you a sense of purpose that will guide you always in the client's best interests.

In my own sessions I strive to bring out and work with the client's strongest attributes. My reasons are simply practical. It is far easier to progress and better ourselves when we utilize those qualities that come naturally and are more accessible to us. It is ten times more difficult to develop our weaknesses and they only give a fraction of the results. We get frustrated by lack of progress and mediocre results.

That is not to say that you should not point out weak areas that you detect in your clients, but these should be emphasized only when they are an absolute handicap and detriment to the subject. There will also be times when an overwhelming negative factor is preventing any forward development in the client. It is best to dwell on these factors early in the session and then to bring the client's best strong points out as possible tools for overcoming their barriers. I always try to end a session on a positive note. You may guide your client with such things as positive thinking, goal setting, affirmation therapy, and other techniques. The more you are aware of, the more you can do for your client.

In the studies that follow I will discuss how I determined the strengths and various aspects, what they mean, and how they are recorded on the charts. They are written in the same manner as your mental assessment should take place. When you actually share these thoughts with the client, you may not always reveal what part of the anatomy you derived your information from, because many times it will be a blend of various indicators. In the beginning just simply say what you can remember about the client's Temperament or nose or whatever. Start with what stands out to you or what looks obvious by its absence of development.

For example, if the person is of the Mental Temperament you might say: "Your realm is the world of thoughts and theory. Your tastes are refined and lend themselves to the artistic, literary, and philosophical. You are an idealist and sometimes have difficulty dealing with the strictly practical. You are weak in all of the vital functions of the body and must be very selective about your diet. Coffee, tobacco, condiments, and medication all affect you more intensely than other people. You tend to be nervous and high strung."

You can continue by mentioning as many of the apects of the Mental Temperament as apply and then go on to aspects shown by the client's complexion, features, and so on. If you stick strictly to what you have learned, you will hit many points that strike home for that individual and come up with a very reliable profile. As you advance, you will blend more information because you will begin to feel how different aspects modify each other. I usually start by giving an overall impression that does not come from any one specific aspect but is a general impression of sensitivity, strength, creativity, gentleness, or whatever it may be.

Study the following case histories by reading the description and then try to correlate the photo with the chart. I have used a very simple method of charting. Encircled areas stand out as being strong on the actual face; areas with an X are somewhat weak, sunken, or deficient.

SUBJECT #1

This man's Temperament is Mental-Vital. I have indicated this by putting a 1 in the triangle, and a 2 in the circle on the chart on page 231. If you look at the accompanying photo, you will notice that the head is long-oval, the shoulders definitely rounded. At first glance he

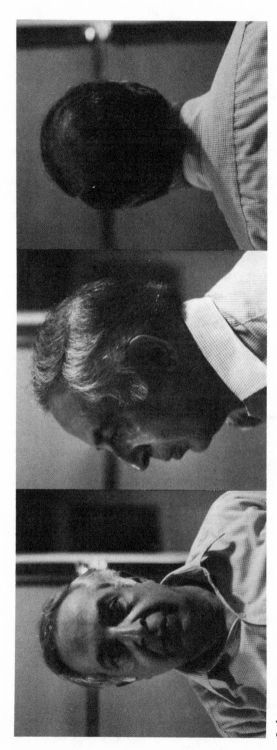

Subject #1

Name _____ SUBJECT #1

No _____ 001

Address _____

Date _____

Phone _____

Height 5'8½" Weight 175#

Birthdate 5-2-1929

Present Occupation OWNS + OPERATES A SMALL GRAPHIC ARTS BUSINESS

Present Age 53

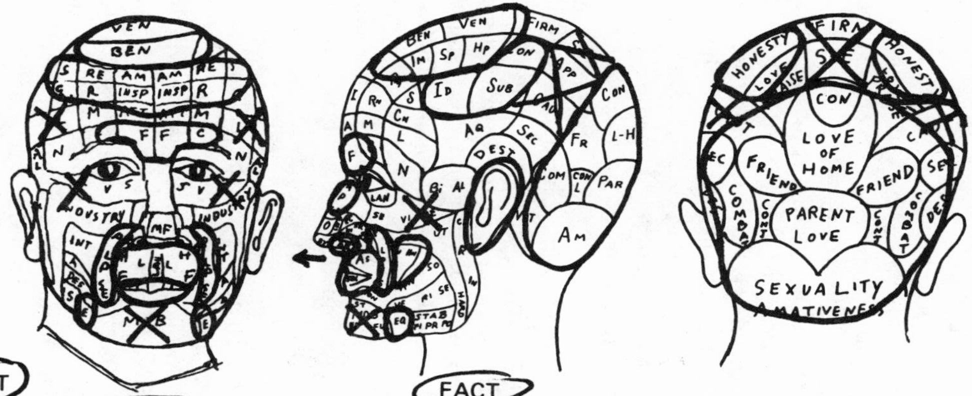

HEAD	BODY
M	M
F	F
N	N

color: wh (pk)

TYPE: MERCURY / VENUS

(LONG +) SHORT

(FACT) PLANE THEORY

(WIDE —) NARROW

BLOND

(BRUNETT)

appears to be of the Vital Temperament, but if you look closely, you will note that the head is fairly large for the frame, with a very strong intellectual development in the forehead. The body does not have the preponderance of flesh of the pure Vital, nor does he have the exceptionally fleshy ear lobes that are usually present in that Temperament.

This is a good marriage of Temperaments. You can tell him that he has the social, economic, and nourishment-conscious qualities of the Vital yet can be overly romantic, too high-strung and idealistic for his own good at times. The intellectual faculties can be put to practical use, prompted by the business instincts of the Vital Temperament and that strong mercantile nose. The nose is circled in our chart to show the strong assertive aspect that it lends to this subject who is otherwise a gentle, romantic, and emotional individual. This emotional aspect should be dealt with in your session, as it is strongly indicated in several areas. First, the entire backhead is encircled because of the fullness you can see there. The strong backhead gives this subject a strong sexual drive and love of home, mate, children, and humanity in general. You know that his home life and marriage are important to him and probably the motivating force behind many of his endeavors.

He has the feminine head and body structure because of the low crown and sloping shoulders. The chart has been marked as such. This body and head type tends to strong emotions, self-sacrifice, and the ability to work with and understand women. It also shows the feminine aspects of a strong intuition, receptivity, and a definite humanitarian impulse. That whole pattern is more gentle and emotional. This aspect of the client's character should definitely be brought out and discussed, or at least presented to him. Since the emotional and family aspects are so strong in development, chances are they will be an area of concern, conflict, or satisfaction to him. When you point out these qualities to your client, he will usually volunteer information on his present concerns in this area. You know from his appearance that he will deal with almost all issues on an emotional level, even in his business and vocation.

The forehead slopes back from the eyebrows when viewed in profile. This is called the "fact" profile and is indicated as such on the chart. The fact profile provides the client with good observational abilities, which are a definite asset in his career in the graphic arts. You will also notice a rise or bump higher on the profile between the brows and the hairline. These are the reasoning faculties. Strong reasoning faculties are also seen in the septum of the nose, the seat of Analysis. On your chart there is a small circle on the septum to indicate this. The arrow you see there means that the nose is projecting forward at the tip. That is the sign for alert attention. It is an asset vocationally for keeping track of many things, and it is a factor in accident prevention.

You will notice a widening of the head around the coronal region—the area where the rim of a hat would seat itself upon the head. The faculties located here are the spiritual, inspirational, and moral impulses. You can confidently tell the subject that he has a well-developed imagination, an appreciation of the sublime and beautiful; he is also honest and generally optimistic. These qualities, which have been circled on the chart, add a visionary quality to him. Also notice the X at Cautiousness, showing a weak development. The combination of high Aspirations with low Caution can indicate a subject who lives on hope and high expectations, even against overwhelming odds. It will keep him going when times are rough.

His high-bridged nose is another factor that will push him onward in spite of difficulties. These visionary and imaginative qualities make it possible for him to project and produce future plans and set future goals. His "long" head is circled in the chart and adds to this ability to plan for the future and anticipate future needs. People without these spiritual and optimistic qualities can become pessimistic; to them the future looks gloomy and dark. The subject here must be warned of opposite tendencies, which are to overlook the presages of doom and to fight against impossible odds.

Another possible area of conflict is the combination of many strong intuitive capabilities shown by the feminine body and high coronal region, and an equally strong set of analytical abilities shown in the nose and forehead. His intuitions should be relied on, especially when dealing with people. Many times his reason will question what his heart feels is right, but he should go with his gut feeling and employ his reason in dealing with problems that are best solved by this method.

He is very oriented toward people because of the many social and humanitarian forces in his anterior top-head, backhead, humanitarian mouth bracket, full lips, and brunette complexion. The mouth bracket itself is full and puffy, showing faith, love, and hope. There is a strong faith in his fellow man and a strong desire to serve and assist those in need. He could be taken advantage of by those evoking his compassion, but he would rather serve than take a chance of turning someone away who is really in need. If it were not for the equally strong physical needs indicated in the lips and backhead, this client could easily become a religious or spiritual leader. Indeed, it would be an excellent choice for him, and he should serve humanity in some capacity. The large ears are encircled also. They are another sign of spiritual evolvement.

The nose presents a good study. The high bridge is indicative of the need for independence, sole proprietorship, or a vocation that requires little restriction or supervision by others. This sign of Defense gives the pioneering spirit and self-motivation. It is not considered a good sign for teamwork; although on this face, with its many other strong social features, you can soften that interpretation somewhat. This nose will "see it through," as mentioned earlier.

The most notable weak aspects in this face are Caution, both in the head below the crown (see the X on the chart), and in the upper cheek below and behind the eye in the subfaculty of Caution we call Rest. Also small is the chin area, which reveals the physical heart. The push of his nose lacks balance in the natural warning to rest and recuperate. You must warn him. Also check the nails, lips, and palms for signs of paleness or blueness. If you look at his eyes and face, you get a sense of tiredness and the impression he is being physically drained. A physical checkup must be recommended as well as the advice to take periods of rest and recuperation. Meditation and other relaxation tools should be employed on a daily basis.

The general quality of this client is medium-fine. The features are smoothly chiseled. There is no coarseness present. Because of the quality and strong nose we can assume the client would prefer to be self-employed as a retail merchant in some line. Good observational faculties, humanitarian patterns, and imagination produce possibilities in the photographic, graphic, grapho-analysis, and manufacturing fields, as well as positions of trust and human services. We could continue this analysis indefinitely; however, enough major areas have been covered for you to sense how it is done.

When I originally saw this client over four years ago, he was valiantly fighting to make a go of his graphics business. I could see the stress registered in his face and attempted to get him involved in meditation and prosperity classes, feeling they would strengthen his hopes as well as serve as a night for him to relax. He had already previously been involved in similar work through Silva Mind Control and other groups. (These types of investigations always go with the Mental Temperament and a strong coronal region of the brain.) Unfortunately, business pressures pulled him away, and subsequently he had a heart attack. He is currently recovering quite well, with a new attitude toward life.

SUBJECT #2

When you have a subject like the one shown on page 236, you will immediately be aware of the Motive Temperament. The rectangular face, square shoulders, height, long arms and legs, bony structure, and strong pronounced chin are signs of the Motive Temperament. The forehead is too large for the pure Motive, so we have classified her on the chart on page 237 as Motive-Mental by putting a 1 in the rectangle and a 2 in the triangle.

We have classified her as white in color because of the paleness in her hands and face. This combination of white color, tall Motive-Mental Temperament, and dark hair are indicative of the Saturnian type. So with this subject we have two very strong indicators to deal with, the Temperament and the Type. Since we did not deal with the Type in our first study, we will review its implications for this client in order that you can see how it is used in delineating character.

The Motive Temperament, of course, is based on the bony framework of the body, and this client is built for action, independence, hard work, and endurance. It is the body structure of our early pioneers. Motive people often overdo. They could easily become workaholics. They make work out of play. They persevere, persist, continue, suffer through. When you describe these qualities to her, she will recognize herself.

She is thin in appearance, but her body weight seems heavy. This is due to the heaviness of the skeleton or bones. The bones of this type are dense; therefore, they weigh heavy on the scale but appear thin. Many of the health problems of the Temperament are related to the bones and joints, spine, ears, and respiratory system. You will notice that one shoulder is higher than the other, so there is some type of imbalance here. The spine, temporomandibular joint dysfunction, or other conditions could be the cause, including various mental states and work habits. Suggest that she see a chiropractor and/or dentist.

This is a strong Saturnian subject, for the reasons we mentioned above. You will remember that Saturnian people are usually serious, somber, and sober. They have studious minds even if they are not formal students in the sense of attending a school. They have introverted moods and often feel the world is one bad experience after another. They are analytical and have an independent spirit. All of these qualities can be applied to this subject, and they will color her outlook on life. In the actual session you can just say: "You are moody, introverted, analytical," simply going over the Saturnian traits, vocations, and health problems. With experience you will use this information more instead of listing it, because you will begin to see how it fits different people in slightly different ways and how it blends with their individual features.

Saturnian subjects can be difficult to reach because they feel they always have bad luck and that they are not good enough or not capable enough. The opposite is true. They have some of the

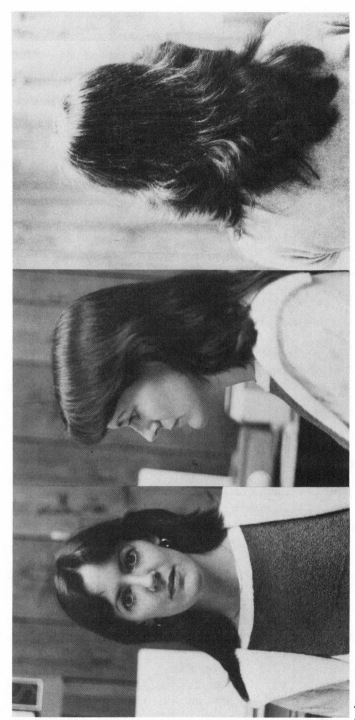

Subject #2

Name _____ SUBJECT #2 _____ No. _____ OO2 _____

Address _____

Date _____

Phone _____ Height 5'9" Weight 137#

Birthdate 2-24-1954

Present Occupation _____ TYPESETTING, LAYOUT, PUBLICATIONS _____ Present Age 28

	HEAD	BODY
FIRMNESS	M	M
	F	F
	N	N

color: wh pk

TYPE: SATURN

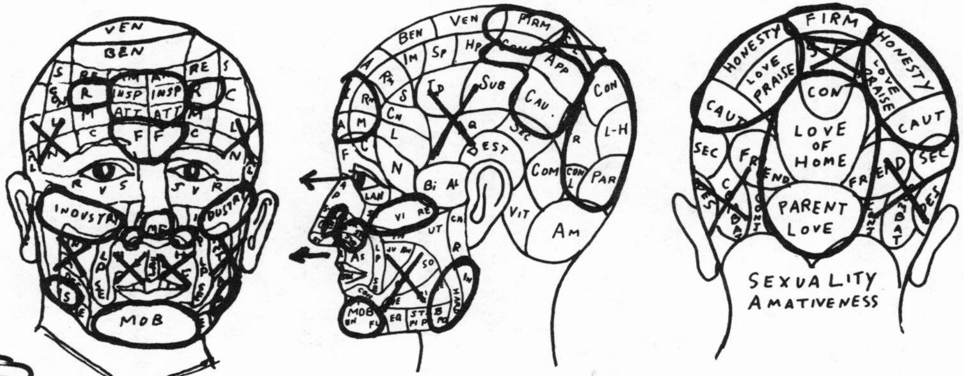

BLOND

BRUNETT

WIDE
NARROW

FACT
PLANE
THEORY

LONG
SHORT

SEXUALITY
AMATIVENESS

HONESTY CAUT CAUT
LOVE
PRAISE
FIRM CON GREED SEC
HONESTY LOVE
OF
HOME GREED SEC
LOVE
PRAISE PARENT
LOVE
CAU SEC FRIEND

strongest attributes and abilities of all the types. It is their negative attitude that holds them back and their perspective on life that sees mostly misery and gloom.

We know this subject will be thoughtful, reflective (see the plane profile circled on the chart), honest, hard-working, serious. She will have spells when it seems the whole world is against her and life is an uphill battle, yet she will endure these periods and see them through. Firmness and Continuity tell us of her consistency. Both areas are strongly indicated and circled on her chart. It is incredible how such people, who seem to lack hope (see the X in the coronal area and mouth bracket), will persevere long after others would give up.

Being a brunette (dark hair and dark eyes; mark brunette on the chart) emphasizes some of the characteristics already identified. She is sentimental and thoughtful, and she has a concentrative mentality. Her work will be thorough, thought-out, precise. She needs time to do a good job, but when the job is done it will be complete and accurate. Too many distractions will interfere with this naturally thorough tendency.

As far as vocations are concerned, you can recommend some phase of the following areas. Prior education, current circumstances, and natural attraction or repulsion will eliminate some and pinpoint others. You can discuss these possibilities with her and weed out the ones that are not viable. Some of the areas may develop as hobbies or part-time interests instead of vocations. Her interests and abilities will be tuned to the technical, the scientific, and the occult; computers, psychology, nature, and things of the earth, such as agriculture, floriculture, archeology, gems. These vocations are Saturnian fields of interest. Her large eyes are marked on the chart with an arrow and add some Apollonian artistic tendencies to her primary technical approach. This opens to her the fields of architecture, photography, design, graphic design, textiles, dentistry, ceramics, horticulture, astrology, and music, especially the keyboards or strings. Remember that no natural tendency or inherent ability can assure us of a job or vocation in any given field. That endowment must be trained, educated, and given experience to prepare us to receive compensation for our ability.

There is a tendency for this type to marry their opposites, and it may be difficult for them to be well mated. However, when they do find proper mates they remain faithful for life. You will probably hit a sore spot when you discuss this topic with this client. She will love and provide for her children (note which backhead faculties are circled on the chart), although she may not be overly demonstrative. She will be a disciplinarian, in a loving way. Harsh Motive and Saturnian characteristics are not shown in her face. Her home will be tastefully decorated with subdued tones. She will be a subtle decorator and fond of muted colors, earth tones, grays, and blacks. Because of her Temperament and Type she will admire that which is useful, practical, and functional. Her tastes will be for simple rather than ornate beauty.

She can be willful, resolute, determined, persistent, consistent, harsh, and even cold under certain circumstances. These qualities are seen in the chin and jaw, Firmness in the top-head, and of course are consistent with her Type endowments. She will not be extravagant, even when financially solvent. Thrift, practicality, and utilitarian methods of approach are her way of dealing with life. She is resigned, patient, and enduring; but when pushed too far she will finally rebel and may strike back with an iron fist or subtler forms of vengeance. You can share all of these thoughts with the subject as they pertain to how she views and handles situations.

Her forehead is high. This is more easily seen in the front view of her face. Her profile shows what we call the plane or straight forehead. This is partially obscured by her hair. (In an actual session you will have to move her hair to see the profile, and actually touch the head to feel the phrenological faculties. Make sure you ask the client first. Occasionally, you will find one who objects. If this is the case, you just work with what you can see.) The high forehead and plane profile are marked on the chart. You will find the intellectual areas circled on the forehead. This shows strong reasoning and analytical approaches. Her thought processes are slow but thorough. Decision making will be slow, and things take a long time to sink in, but once learned they are never forgotten.

Some creative and inspirational impulses are shown in the expressive eyes, the broadening of the crest of the nose by the wing, and the high wing of the nose. These areas should be circled in the chart to indicate importance. They will give you and your client more insights into her capabilities.

The jaw and chin bone are pronounced in her face and circled on the chart. This gives her the leg endurance and strong activity level of the Motive Temperament. It emphasizes the pioneering spirit and gives the potential of a long life if she can avoid excess and an improper diet. Fresh air and affection will do wonders for her health and mental state. The mountains, hills, and forests revive her. She heals better by walking in the fresh air than by lying in bed. All of these things should be shared with her during the session.

Through her type qualities she will be a natural student and teacher, whether it will be teaching her children, co-workers, friends, or in an actual teaching position. She can teach what she knows to receptive minds.

By seeing what is prominent or lacking in her head and face you can counsel her on any number of personal problems. For example, she is low in Acquisitiveness, yet is a thrifty type. This should tell you that she is not the type that accumulates great sums of money easily but is thrifty with what she has.

This client was the sole support of three children because of a broken marriage. When she was married, they lived on a farm and, like the pioneers, she raised vegetables, preserved food, and did similar work. When the marriage failed, she took the three children and made a new life in a new location. The struggle and broken marriage gave her a pessimistic attitude toward life in general and men in particular; however, she always provided and never quit or gave up. She used all kinds of reserve strength and bravery to overcome what life sent her but seemed not to recognize these strong qualities in herself.

It was difficult to encourage her because she could never see the situation as having positive results. You can point out any number of good things to a Saturnian client, and they will say, "Yes, but..." and give you all the negatives.

One consoling factor is that the Motive Temperament people usually do better later in life, after they have paid their dues, so to speak. Because of her hard work, energy and many other strong qualities, she will probably make a gradual upward progress. Loving support is one of the best things a client like this could have; although it is difficult for them to select their own mates properly, you can recommend what she should look for physically in a mate because you know what kinds of qualities those features represent. Also, because this is a type that thrives on competition, awaken her competitive spirit. She will resist any external pressure or force but enjoys competition. Saturnian subjects can be pushed so far and then they rebel. This client eventually moved into a better position after being unhappy with her previous employer for many years.

Slow but steady progress is typical with this type. You will have to help her fight an inferiority attitude, pessimistic attitude, cynicism, and ingrained habits. I use many techniques to do this, including diet and herbs and other modes that are beyond the scope and purpose of this book. You will be able to use tools that I may not have available in my experience.

SUBJECT #3

In dealing with children you have a different situation than you have with adults. Younger children are typically brought to you by interested or concerned parents who want to understand their children better, to give them direction and get them off to a good start in life. You can be of tremendous service in these cases in identifying the child's potentials and handicaps. With children, weaknesses stand a good chance to improve as the child develops. Their potentials are just that. Unless acted on, developed, and given the opportunity to grow and be experienced, they may lose their natural talents to some degree. They may feel unfulfilled and never know why.

Many times the parents have never been exposed to or become interested in the areas in which the child has inherent ability. Therefore, they never even think to expose the child to those areas. For example, a child who has a scientific mind may have a father who owns a delicatessen and a mother who is a saleswoman. Neither parent ever had an interest in science, so they never have magazines on science, visit the Smithsonian, or engage in similar activities. This is quite possible. Many children have talents and capabilities not experienced by the parents, and as a result they are not exposed to those areas young enough. Many times you will counsel older children wanting to know what to study in college, and they will be quite surprised by your findings.

When the characteristics are strong and the parents aware, the child is able to get an early start, as in the case of our subject on page 242. The luxuriant hair, almond eyes, gracious expression, harmonious body structure and pleasant features make this subject easy to identify. We have here a good example of a soul that is expressing itself through the Apollo body and appearance. This stands out so clearly that it is the first thing I entered on our chart on page 243. We know that his direction in life is with people, the arts, fashion, and communication. A review of the Apollonian type will indicate all of his natural talents and propensities. As an Apollonian we know he is brilliant, quick to learn, and quick to adapt. He learns by example or demonstration but is not a book learner or interested in tedious subjects. Apollonians skim the surface of many subjects; however, that does not mean that you will not find a deep and profound Apollonian occasionally.

The Apollonian boy or girl should be exposed to all of the arts as early as possible. Not all Apollonians are artists, but their type abounds in the arts, theater, entertainment, painting, dance, design, television, movies, and radio. At the very least they will have a fond appreciation for art and be tasteful and decorative in the way they dress or do their homes or office.

Active artistic impulses are indicated in this subject by the high and imaginative wings of the nose, the intuitive and aesthetic spread of the sides of the crest of the nose, and by the good development of

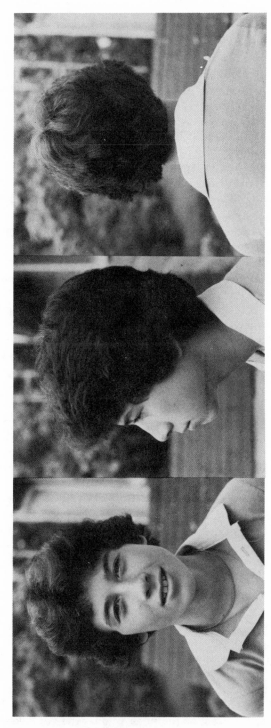

Subject #3

Name _____   No. __003__

Address _____

Date _____

Phone _____   Height _5'8"_ Weight _118#_

Present Occupation _STUDENT-ACTING / ART_   Birthdate _10-26-1968_

Present Age _14_

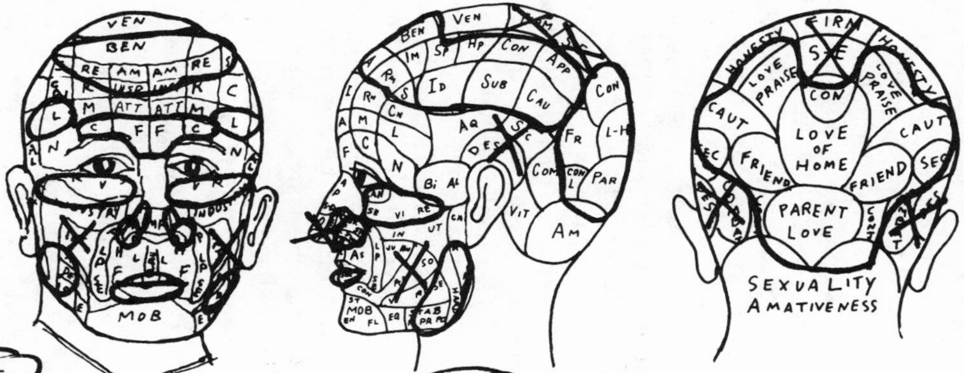

SUBJECT #3

	HEAD	BODY
	M	M
	F	F
	N	N

color: wh (pk)

TYPE: _APOLLONIAN_

BLOND
(BRUNETT)

WIDE
NARROW +

(LONG)
SHORT

FACT
PLANE
THEORY

SEXUALITY
AMATIVENESS

Form and Color sense in the brow area. Look at these various factors in the photo, and you will see why they are circled on the chart.

The nose of our client is slightly upturned and lacks much projection in the bridge. We have indicated this by marking an X on the tip. This is an emotional nose, a social nose, and at times an impulsive nose. As is consistent with his type, he will be creative by mood and inspiration. He will stick to his project while the inspiration is there; when a new idea strikes, he may abandon the old project. Early training in completing and doing thorough work will help him form habits that will bring successful results throughout life. These comments will be given to the parent rather than to the young subject. Early discipline is essential to give them patterns that counter type tendencies that are not positive in nature. We can and should go beyond our type and temperamental limitations.

It is also beautiful and interesting to watch children's features and abilities blossom. The weak bridge of the nose in this client became high and strong as he began to assert his individuality. Although this type is versatile by nature, they should isolate what they do best and perfect it.

He is considered a "pink" type because of his outgoing personality and the color tinting cheeks, lips, palms, and nails. This means he is warm, cordial, friendly, sympathetic, and easy to know and get along with. These qualities make him an excellent salesman and diplomat. He will never have difficulties dealing with people on any level. Apollonians can even make friends out of enemies.

He is of the type that the largest percentage of our models come from. Even if not professional models, they are always interested in clothes and fashion. The high imagination we noted in the wing of his nose will make his tastes inventive and unusual. Not only will he wear clothes well, but he can design them or sell them. He also could work as a model for hair-care products, cosmetics, and other beauty aids.

Caution is high in the upper cheekbones. You will note the circle drawn in that area under the eyes and the corresponding development in the actual face. When Caution is too high, it produces an aversion to anything painful or unpleasant. It is a self-protection device but sometimes prevents a person from doing what may be difficult or needs a breakthrough attitude. It may produce a desire to take the easy way out. Again, this tendency can be overcome through proper parental guidance.

As mentioned, the nose is high in the wings and tends to be wide. This provides imagination, inventiveness, and skill with one's hands. There is some height to the bridge, as mentioned earlier. This is the beginning of the defensive and individualistic tendencies. The nose tip does not project forward from the face far enough and is slightly upturned. What is lacking here is alert attentive ability, and that leaves the subject open more to impression and emotion. We would like to see this develop more, just as the bridge is developing. The chin itself recedes a little, which produces impulsiveness. This is another area we need to develop by making the subject stop and think and plan his actions and activities. These are all areas that can be developed much more easily during youth and will round out his character nicely.

Because of his hair you cannot see the phrenological development easily. Hair can be deceptive. Feel the head with your hands. By noting what I have encircled you will see that I have found high Approbativeness and barely medium Self-Esteem. This need for praise, shown by Approbativeness, is found frequently in entertainers, actors, and those in the arts. It is an impetus for fame and success. It pushes him on for recognition. Once he starts to gain acceptance for his talents, Self-Esteem also may develop.

I have indicated a neutral (harmonious) head and neutral body structure on the chart. The Apollo type tends to harmony in mind and body, and this subject is a good example of that. This combination shows a more versatile subject with a personality that can easily secure friendships and favors, affection and public sympathy. His methods of achieving goals will be more by blending passivity, magnetism, and a winning smile. There is no force, violence, aggression, or head-on approach indicated. His power is in another direction but moves and molds and creates its influence just the same.

Fortunately, this youth has parents who identified his abilities and encouraged involvement in the arts and related fields. You will have to work more with the parents than with the children in such cases. It can be generally assumed that the parent or parents are interested in directing the child's development or they wouldn't be there in the first place. In dealing with children we are always dealing with potential. You can expect more rapid results and observable development with youths. You can actually watch your science at work.

• • •

Each client will present a new problem and test your skills. As with anything in life, practice and study will increase your skill and quicken your judgment. You will develop your own approach or blend characterology with what you already know. I have given you a firm foundation in the principles of human analysis. I pray that you will be guided by your higher self in their use.

BIBLIOGRAPHY

The literature listed below represents most of the sources I have used to gather the information found in this book. A great deal of my information comes directly from the teachings of Ann Koernig, or from those two great teachers known as Experience and Observation. If any other sources exist that I have failed to enumerate, I offer those authors my sincere apologies.

Atkinson, William Walker. *How to Read Human Nature*. Holyoke, MA: L.N. Fowler & Company, 1916.

Balkin, Harry H. *The New Science of Analyzing Character*. Philadelphia: David McKay, 1922.

Baugham, Rasa. *Papers on Physiognomy*. London: George Redway, 1885.

Benham, William G. *The Laws of Scientific Hand Reading*. New York: Hawthorne Books, 1900.

Brandt, Anthony. "Face Reading." *Psychology Today*, December, 1980, pp. 90-96.

Donovan, H. C. *The Brain Book*. London: Rider & Son, 1914.

Fowler, Orson S. and Lorenzo N. *Phrenology*. Reprint. New York: Chelsea House, 1980.

Hall, Dorothy. *Iridology*. New Canaan, CT: Keats Publishing, 1980.

Hargrave, Gordon J. A. *Secrets of Selling*. New York: Hargrave Service Systems, 1931.

Jensen, Bernard. *Science & Practice of Iridology*. Los Angeles: Bernard Jensen Enterprises, 1952.

Kolata, Gina. "Weight Regulation May Start in Our Cells, Not Psyches." *Smithsonian*, January, 1986, pp. 91-97.

Kushi, Michio. *Oriental Diagnosis*. London: Sunwheel, 1978.

Mainwaring, Marion. "Phys/Phren." *Smithsonian*, November, 1980, pp. 193 ff.

Merton, Holmes W. *Descriptive Mentality from the Head, Face and Hand.* Philadelphia: David McKay, 1899.

_____. *Merton Course in Vocational Counseling and Employee Selection.* New York: Merton Institute, 1928.

Rocine, Victor G. *Eating for Beauty.* Everett, WA: Rocine Institute, 1929.

_____. *Types of People from Chemical Standpoint.* Chicago: Rocine School of Human Nature Studies, 1927.

Sivartha, Alesha. *The Book of Life.* New York: Holmes W. Merton, 1884.

Sheldon, William. *The Varieties of Temperament.* New York: Hafner Publishing, 1970.

Spencer, Lloyd G. *Heads and Faces.* New York: L.N. Fowler & Company, 1890.

Wells, Samuel. *How to Read Character.* New York: Fowler & Wells, 1896.

_____. *New Physiognomy.* New York: Fowler & Wells, 1894.